Industrial Internet Application Development

Simplify IIoT development using the elasticity of Public Cloud and Native Cloud Services

Alena Traukina
Jayant Thomas
Prashant Tyagi
Kishore Reddipalli

BIRMINGHAM - MUMBAI

Industrial Internet Application Development

Commissioning Editor: Merint Mathew
Acquisition Editor: Alok Dhuri
Content Development Editor: Anugraha Arunagiri
Technical Editor: Ruvika Rao
Copy Editor: Safis Editing
Project Coordinator: Ulhas Kambali
Proofreader: Safis Editing
Indexer: Priyanka Dhadke
Graphics: Tom Scaria
Production Coordinator: Aparna Bhagat

First published: September 2018

Production reference: 1290918

Published by Packt Publishing Ltd.
Livery Place
35 Livery Street
Birmingham
B3 2PB, UK.

ISBN 978-1-78829-859-9

www.packtpub.com

`mapt.io`

Mapt is an online digital library that gives you full access to over 5,000 books and videos, as well as industry leading tools to help you plan your personal development and advance your career. For more information, please visit our website.

Why subscribe?

- Spend less time learning and more time coding with practical eBooks and Videos from over 4,000 industry professionals

- Improve your learning with Skill Plans built especially for you

- Get a free eBook or video every month

- Mapt is fully searchable

- Copy and paste, print, and bookmark content

Packt.com

Did you know that Packt offers eBook versions of every book published, with PDF and ePub files available? You can upgrade to the eBook version at `www.packt.com` and as a print book customer, you are entitled to a discount on the eBook copy. Get in touch with us at `customercare@packtpub.com` for more details.

At `www.packt.com`, you can also read a collection of free technical articles, sign up for a range of free newsletters, and receive exclusive discounts and offers on Packt books and eBooks.

Contributors

About the authors

Alena Traukina is the IoT practice lead at Altoros. She has over 12 year experience in the delivery and support of business-critical software applications, working closely with business owners and providing strategic and organizational leadership for software development. Over the years, Alena has served in different capacities, ranging from software engineer, to software engineering manager, to head of Altoros's Ruby department. She was also one of the first GE Predix Influencers.

Jayant Thomas (JT) has a passion for IoT, machine learning, and cloud-native architectures at scale. His passion has led him to many successful adventures at Veritas, GE, Oracle, AT&T, Nuance, and other start-ups, building platforms at scale. JT is an MBA graduate from UC Davis, and has an M.Tech from NIIT, as well as more than 15 patents in IoT, NLP processing, and cloud architectures. JT is also an enthusiastic speaker/writer, and has contributed to many conferences and meetups. In addition, JT is an active fitness and health freak, dabbling in various diets and health fads.

> *I would like to thank the co-authors of this book; it's been a joy working with them on it. I would also like to thank GE Digital and GE Digital Colleges for providing us with this great opportunity to learn and build IIoT platforms at scale. Finally, I would like to thank my family and friends for all their sacrifices in supporting me during the course of writing this book.*

Prashant Tyagi is responsible for enabling the big data strategy at GE Digital for IIoT, leveraging IT and operational data for predictive analytics. He works with P&L verticals to enable their IoT use cases on the data and analytics platform.

He is on the board of ISSIP, focused on service innovation. He leads a cross-industry special interest group on IoT and analytics, and is an adviser to the open source fog computing initiative, ioFog, which is an Eclipse foundation initiative. He holds a B.Tech from IIT Delhi, an MBA from IIM Bangalore, and an MS in computer science from Clemson University. He has publications in leading journals and magazines and is a renowned public speaker and panelist, having featured at several conferences.

Kishore Reddipalli is a software technical director and expert in building IIoT big data and cloud computing platforms and products at ultra scale. He is passionate about building software for analytics and machine learning to make the authoring of algorithms at scale, from inception to production, a simpler process. He has been a speaker at global conferences on big data technologies. Over the years, he has provided leadership in various capacities. Throughout his career, his roles have ranged from software engineer to director of engineering and architecture for the development of platforms and products in domains such as clinical decision support systems, electronic medical records, Predix Platform, Predix Operations Optimization for IIoT, and etch-process control at nanometer level using big data and machine learning technologies in the semiconductor industry. He holds an MS in computer science from Texas A&M University Corpus Christi.

I would like to thank my family, who supported me in the course of writing this book.

About the reviewer

Shyam Varan Nath is an industry expert in IoT and cloud computing. His professional experience has involved roles at Oracle, GE Digital, IBM, Deloitte, and Halliburton. His area of focus is IIoT and enterprise cloud architecture. He is a regular speaker at global conferences on IoT and analytics. He is the author of *Architecting the Industrial Internet*, published by Packt Publishing in 2017. He also wrote the chapter on IoT architecture in the *Internet of Things and Data Analytics Handbook*. Shyam is the founding president of the Oracle BIWA User Community, which started in 2006 as a global professional special interest group for BI, data warehousing, advanced analytics, IoT, and big data. Shyam is very active on Twitter (@ShyamVaran). He also leads two task groups under the IIC.

> *I would like to thank all my professional colleagues over the last five years at Oracle and GE, who have helped me learn about all aspects of IIoT. Additionally, I would like to thank the IIC for facilitating the development of the various architecture frameworks and testbeds for prototyping IIoT solutions. Finally, I would like to thank my family and friends, who support me all the time.*

Packt is searching for authors like you

If you're interested in becoming an author for Packt, please visit authors.packtpub.com and apply today. We have worked with thousands of developers and tech professionals, just like you, to help them share their insight with the global tech community. You can make a general application, apply for a specific hot topic that we are recruiting an author for, or submit your own idea.

Table of Contents

Preface

The Industrial Internet refers to the integration of complex physical machines with networked sensors and software. Growth in the number of sensors deployed in heavy machinery and industrial equipment over the next five years is going to lead to an exponential increase in data being captured, which needs to be analyzed and leveraged for predictive analytics. This opens up a new avenue for developers who would like to build exciting industrial applications.

This book will serve as a one-stop guide for software professionals to design, build, manage, and operate IIoT applications.

The book begins by providing the business context to ensure that you are aware of the actual use cases that are being enabled by these IIoT applications and that you understand its fundamental concepts. Once the business objectives are outlined, it will familiarize you with the different layers of the IIoT platform and their key components. You will learn about Edge Development, along with the analytics portions of the IIoT stack. After this, the key elements of the development framework will be identified and the importance of these elements will be highlighted in light of the overall architecture and design considerations for IIoT applications. You will develop your first application for IIoT and learn about its deployment and security considerations. Finally, the software development details for the implementation of these applications will be outlined and the use of platforms such as GE Predix will be highlighted, along with the best practices for development.

Who this book is for

This book is intended for software developers, architects, product managers, and executives who would like to gain deeper insights into the development of IIoT.

What this book covers

Chapter 1, *IIoT Fundamentals and Components*, will explain different use cases in industrial verticals such as aviation, healthcare, transportation and power. The three layers of the IoT platform will be outlined and described, namely: edge, connectivity, and the cloud

Chapter 2, *IIoT Application Architecture and Design*, will cover IIoT application architecture, go in depth into the various tiers of IIoT applications, as well as providing a simple implementation of an end-to-end IIoT application.

Chapter 3, *IIoT Edge Development*, will help you with the most common tasks in the development of IIoT applications: communication, storing data, and prototyping the devices themselves.

Chapter 4, *Data for IIoT*, will make you aware of all the different tools, technologies, and methodologies of handling data in IIoT applications. This will cover data ingestion, storage, search, security, and governance for both batch and streaming data.

Chapter 5, *Advanced Analytics for IIoT*, will cover all the different tools, technologies, and methodologies you need to do analytics in IIoT applications.

Chapter 6, *Developing Your First Application for IIOT*, will help you develop a simple monitoring and diagnosis application that brings together your assets and time series sensor data. You will develop your first analytics and visualize the outcome.

Chapter 7, *Deployment, Scale, and Security Considerations*, will address the most common tasks in the security, deployment, and scalability of IoT cloud applications: scaling your microservices, CI/CD, security considerations while interfacing with devices, and securing your cloud applications using UAA/Oauth.

Chapter 8, *Reliability, Fault Tolerance, and Monitoring Your IIoT Application*, will address concerns such as building reliability, fault tolerance, and monitoring your IoT.

Chapter 9, *Implementing IIoT Applications with Predix*, will cover modeling your asset and explains how it will help normalize the assets for analytics, along with storing time series sensor data for assets and developing your first analytics in GE's Predix.

Chapter 10, *Best Practices of IIoT Applications*, will cover the things you need to consider when choosing the language to build your microservices. Discovery of your microservices using Hystrix, Zookeeper, and so on as well as integration with enterprise systems and other cloud providers.

Chapter 11, *Future Direction of IIoT*, will explain the competitive landscape, emerging use cases and technology, and research.

To get the most out of this book

The book assumes familiarity with programming languages such as Java, JavaScript, Node.js, Go, or Python. It also assumes familiarity with data and analytics technologies.

Download the example code files

You can download the example code files for this book from your account at `www.packt.com`. If you purchased this book elsewhere, you can visit `www.packt.com/support` and register to have the files emailed directly to you.

You can download the code files by following these steps:

1. Log in or register at `www.packt.com`.
2. Select the **SUPPORT** tab.
3. Click on **Code Downloads & Errata**.
4. Enter the name of the book in the **Search** box and follow the onscreen instructions.

Once the file is downloaded, please make sure that you unzip or extract the folder using the latest version of:

- WinRAR/7-Zip for Windows
- Zipeg/iZip/UnRarX for Mac
- 7-Zip/PeaZip for Linux

The code bundle for the book is also hosted on GitHub at `https://github.com/PacktPublishing/Industrial-Internet-Application-Development`. In case there's an update to the code, it will be updated on the existing GitHub repository.

We also have other code bundles from our rich catalog of books and videos available at `https://github.com/PacktPublishing/`. Check them out!

Download the color images

We also provide a PDF file that has color images of the screenshots/diagrams used in this book. You can download it here: `https://www.packtpub.com/sites/default/files/downloads/9781788298599_ColorImages.pdf`.

Conventions used

There are a number of text conventions used throughout this book.

`CodeInText`: Indicates code words in text, database table names, folder names, filenames, file extensions, pathnames, dummy URLs, user input, and Twitter handles. Here is an example: "To enable Wi-Fi, create the `wpa_supplicant.conf` file with the following content."

A block of code is set as follows:

```
network={
 ssid="YOUR_SSID"
 psk="YOUR_WIFI_PASSWORD"
 }
```

Any command-line input or output is written as follows:

```
cd /Volumes/boot
touch ssh
```

Bold: Indicates a new term, an important word, or words that you see on screen. For example, words in menus or dialog boxes appear in the text like this. Here is an example: "You can select an **Asset service** instance from the **Authorized Services** list."

Warnings or important notes appear like this.

Tips and tricks appear like this.

Get in touch

Feedback from our readers is always welcome.

General feedback: If you have questions about any aspect of this book, mention the book title in the subject of your message and email us at customercare@packtpub.com.

Errata: Although we have taken every care to ensure the accuracy of our content, mistakes do happen. If you have found a mistake in this book, we would be grateful if you would report this to us. Please visit www.packt.com/submit-errata, selecting your book, clicking on the Errata Submission Form link, and entering the details.

Piracy: If you come across any illegal copies of our works in any form on the internet, we would be grateful if you would provide us with the location address or website name. Please contact us at copyright@packt.com with a link to the material.

If you are interested in becoming an author: If there is a topic that you have expertise in and you are interested in either writing or contributing to a book, please visit authors.packtpub.com.

Reviews

Please leave a review. Once you have read and used this book, why not leave a review on the site that you purchased it from? Potential readers can then see and use your unbiased opinion to make purchase decisions, we at Packt can understand what you think about our products, and our authors can see your feedback on their book. Thank you!

For more information about Packt, please visit packt.com.

1
IIoT Fundamentals and Components

This introductory chapter provides an overview of the **Industrial Internet of Things (IIoT)**, its impact on businesses, and the various components that make up the IIoT technology stack. It will introduce several key concepts relevant to this domain that are required in order to go deeper in these areas later in this book.

The following topics are covered in this chapter:

- The impact of The IoT on businesses
- An overview of four layers of the IoT technology stack
- Emerging IoT business models

IIoT fundamentals and components

The IoT has gone from a promise for the future to being part of the mainstream set of technologies in both consumer and business market segments. The internet has gone through its evolution over the past several years. It started with connecting computers so they can communicate with each other, which was quickly followed by the phase of connecting people (online social media). Now that all things around us generate data, have some sort of sensors associated with them, and can be connected to the internet, it becomes significant that this third phase of the internet, where all things the generate data can talk to each other is set to grow exponentially in the coming years. This book is targeted toward architects and engineers who intend to build applications for the IoT domain; as connectivity between devices grows, it's applications that will harness the power of interconnectivity and generate useful knowledge to drive productivity for businesses and provide the next level of services for consumers.

We will start by looking at the different parts of the technology stack that make up the IoT, what are the specific parameters required to satisfy the technology solutions, and how they interact and communicate with each other. The intent is to go deeper into these technologies and provide an end-to-end framework for developers to design and build IoT applications for any industrial vertical. We will also provide sample source code for developers to build upon for each component such as the edge, data, analytics, communication, and cloud portions. We will be covering use cases in various verticals as examples to provide some real-world scenarios for readers.

Impact of the IoT

The IoT has already started to change the way large companies operate. A large majority of these companies are currently using the IoT to track their customers, products, and supply chains. Investment in the IoT is therefore going up significantly year after year for such businesses. Some trends in this spending can be forecast based on returns. For example, predicting the operating efficiency or preventing a major outage of a high-priced service offering will result in higher returns, so it's natural that corporations providing such high-priced offerings will invest more in this area. This is evident from the fact that industrial manufacturers that have very high priced large asset product and service offerings are the ones that have reaped the maximum benefits of the IoT when compared to other major industry segments. Mobile and sensor-based tracking of goods through the supply chain and tracking their usage by customers will continue to increase over the next several years.

Today, companies in the United States and Europe are leading the investment in this area but Asia-Pacific has already caught up fast. So far, the largest impact has been in the area of better customer service and faster product improvements for customized offerings. Adoption of these technologies will require the businesses to overcome challenges such as identifying new business models, product offerings, and revenue sources as they adopt these technologies; overcoming cultural shifts that are needed to enable the full adoption of these technologies; identifying what data to collect and analyze and how to secure this huge data stream; and integrating that with existing legacy systems and data.

We think the greatest impact will be mostly felt in the following areas:

- Enhanced servicing and availability of information for products and service offerings
- Increased uptime in services to customers; this will be attributed to reduction in downtime by predictive monitoring and pre-emptive fixes and replacements

- Emergence of new business models in the industrial sector due to better insights and leveraging of data
- New industrial products and service offerings that are more autonomous

Overview of the IoT technology components

We will define three broad areas in which all of the technology pieces required for enabling the IoT can be classified. The first one is **edge-related technologies**, which enable all of the activities that can be performed close to the source of the data. This includes sensors and sensor hubs that interface with the actual machines and devices. These perform data acquisition, basic data filtering, and data transfer to the cloud or gateway. Data from the sensor hubs flows to controllers or mobile devices that are used for storage and perform advanced data cleaning and filtering. The analytics on the edge happen on the gateways where data aggregation and analytics take place. Edge applications can also be deployed on the gateways, which can perform the real-time analytics to be done close to the source the of data. Apart from these, there are management applications that are required to manage devices and edge analytics applications. A platform to support the runtime environment for these also needs to be provided on this layer. Now, let's check the following diagram:

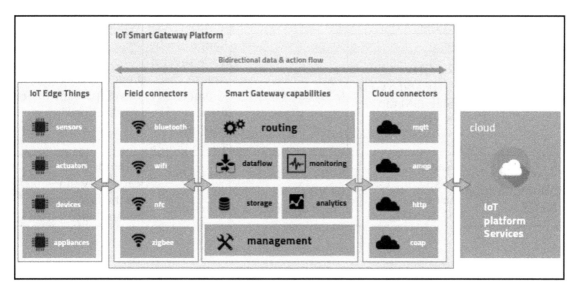

A key component of the IoT architecture is the gateway, which acts as the interface or proxy between the edge devices and the cloud/enterprise data center (see smart gateway in the preceding diagram). Apart from handling the connectivity between the edge and the cloud, the gateway acts as the interpreter/translator between field and cloud protocols. These gateways are increasingly becoming smart as they are embedded with logic to direct traffic based on rules, such as should data be transmitted as is or does it need to be aggregated or filtered prior to being transmitted? The following table describes the commonly used protocols on the edge layer:

Field Protocol	Specifications	Standards	Key Features	Typical Use Case
Bluetooth Low Energy (BLE)	ISM band from 2.4 to 2.485 GHz (short wave lengths)	Bluetooth SIG standards	Low energy, small distances (couple of meters)	Inter-device communications on the edge
Zigbee	2.4 GHz	IEEE 802.15.4 protocol	Distances of up to 100 m in a given area	Applications that require relatively infrequent data exchanges at low data-rates over a restricted area
Wi-Fi	2.4 GHz UHF and 5 GHz SHF ISM radio bands	IEEE 802.11	Range can be up to several square kilometers using multiple access points	Leveraged by developers for their applications
Near Field Communication (NFC)	Radio frequency ISM band of 13.56 MHz	RFID standards ISO/IEC 14443 and FeliCa	For distances that are less than 4 cm	Extends the capability of contactless card technology

Common protocols utilized at the edge

Similarly, we have prepared a table for the common cloud protocols that are used as part of the IoT stack, which is presented as follows:

Cloud Protocol	Specifications	Standards	Key Features	Typical Use Case
Message Queue Telemetry Transport (MQTT)	Protocols availability depends on context	ISO/IEC PRF 20922	Publish/Subscribe architecture with broker for pub/sub	Connections with remote locations where a *small code footprint* is required or the network bandwidth is limited
Advanced Message Queuing Protocol (AMQP)	AMQP 1.0 a binary application layer protocol to support messaging and communication patterns	SO/IEC 19464	Pub/sub with broker with broker being either exchange or queue type	Mostly used for financial industry applications
Constrained Application Protocol (CoAP)	Built on UDP and easy translation to HTTP and multicast	RFC 7252/7228	Functionalities specific for IoT and M2M applications	Intended for use in resource-constrained internet devices, such as wireless sensor network (`https://en.wikipedia.org/wiki/Wireless_sensor_network`) nodes
HTTP	HTTP/1.1 HTTP/2.0 application protocol	RFC 2616	Utilizes TCP but can be modified to use UDP	Standard request response for WWW

Common cloud protocols

The second important piece is the **Connectivity layer**, which connects all edge-related technologies to each other and further to the cloud. Often times, the IoT device network is geographically dispersed and edges require multiple carrier relationships for secure **Quality of Service (QoS)** enabled networks. This requires policy driven connectivity, security, and QoS for the edge components and additionally policy authoring, management, and deployment on the cloud. Mobile sites require selection of networks based on cost, availability, and bandwidth in a dynamically changing environment.

In order to achieve this, we need a connectivity layer that is aware of IIOT applications and data semantics; a layer that is a **Software Defined Network (SDN)** and based on **Machine to Machine** (M2M) and **Machine to Client** (M2C) communications. Variable network characteristics of M2M and M2C require adaptable traffic shaping based on the nature of applications. Carrier-agnostic, QoS-enabled secure tunnels for M2M and M2C connectivity are required.

The third type of technologies is the **cloud analytics platform** capabilities that will process and analyze the data coming from the edge devices. The analytical platform provides capabilities to ingest, store, search, analyze, and finally visualize or consume data. The different types of technologies that enable each of these capabilities are required as part of this analytics stack. The requirements for each part of the stack are varied as well. For example, different types of ingestion capabilities, such as real-time ingestion, batch ingestion, and change data capture ingestion are required to be part of the complete stack. Similarly, the storage requirements for different types of data are different. For example, time series data requires NoSQL databases and image data requires Blob storage. A partial list of these capabilities is shown in the *Common protocols utilized at the edge* table, which gives an idea of the variety of technologies that are required to complete the stack.

IoT business models

As the penetration of the IoT continues in various industry verticals, we will see new business models evolve and new and creative ways of generating value for the end customers and therefore generating revenue. Before we look at possible emerging business models, it's important to take a deeper look at how these technologies are being used today. We can divide the use of IoT technologies into the following broad categories:

- **Smart monitoring of the existing product or service install base**: The products and services that businesses sell today have monitoring, alerting, and reporting solutions. However, these are siloed and not interconnected with each other or to the internet. That limits their utility and usage; the IoT will enable these monitoring solutions to be smart in the true sense of the word.
- **Smart remote diagnostics**: It is another area where businesses have started using IoT technologies. This is especially useful for verticals where the operating conditions are harsh and not suitable for human intervention and involvement at all times. The ability to seamlessly integrate edge solutions with the internet has enabled companies to take remote operations to the next level.

- **Cross vertical domain data integration**: This allows businesses to generate new insights by integrating data and correlating parameters to identify new trends. An example would be the integration of weather data with operational maintenance data for an asset that is deployed in the field and exposed to weather conditions. The integration of these data points will help discover new models for remote monitoring and diagnostics for the asset.

- **Product/service promotion**: It can be augmented by IoT devices as they can help transmit messages to a customer's smart phone and other devices, which will help them be aware of new promotions and products available in their vicinity. They can also help with targeted ads to be delivered on billboards, and so on.

- **Creating open and scalable interfaces for products and services that were earlier closed systems**: For example, the automobile industry, which produces engines and power trains for vehicles, are now exposing these assets through interfaces such as software APIs that help with the tracking and maintenance of these systems.

How the IoT changes business models

The continuation of these trends will lead to new business models. We predict some of the following and this is by no means the entire list. There are models that will emerge that we cannot comprehend today:

- **Revenue sharing models**: It is based on the efficiencies created by using IoT and advanced analytics. As an example, **General Electric (GE)** produces smarter wind turbines for its renewables business. These wind turbines have several sensors and IoT applications that can gather and harness data, combine with weather data, and predict service operations and maintenance opportunities. GE upgrades the existing install base at the customer site for no cost and the costs saved and additional revenue generated by the customers are shared with GE.

- **Service ownership models**: Existing product companies will package their offerings as services and take ownership of the end to end delivery for the service. So essentially, they are not selling them outright but rather leasing them and moving to a product as a service model.

- **Data-driven business models**: It will become prevalent as businesses deploying IoT solutions will gather a variety of customer data. So, they essentially become custodians of their customer data and, in partnership with the customer, they can use this data to generate additional revenue by packaging and selling it.

- **Efficiencies in the supply chain**: It will result in eliminating unnecessary middle layers and hence, generate additional cost optimizations.

IIoT use cases

Here we describe use cases for three industry verticals that have deployed and started using IoT solutions. The healthcare industry benefits through enhanced patient monitoring capabilities as well as monitoring and management of medical devices, while manufacturing and aviation are trying to address their high availability and quality challenges through IoT solutions. We will provide some details about these in this section to give you a good understanding of these existing use cases.

Healthcare

With the growth in the medical device and equipment market, there is an increased need to manage the growing install base and harness it through analytics for generating new insights for cost reduction, identify new sales opportunities, and respond to customer needs. Optimizations around the supply chain can be accomplished by having a real-time view of the install base.

The use cases for improved install base visibility fall under four categories. The first one is the use case of upgrades, which allow for accurate upgrade offerings enabled by more granular install base visibility aligned to upgrades. Automation of top upgrade campaigns has led to several million dollars in operational productivity.

The second use case is about parts pricing. Parts price getting and price setting algorithms drive margins as well as additional benefits from setting better parts pricing strategies. This requires automation of price getting reports and engagements of SMEs for price setting.

The third use case is about product quality and reliability. The focus in this use case is on system analytics to identify parts and systems that fail more. Early identification can lead to up-selling opportunities as well as troubleshooting to reduce cost to serve. Implementation of a parts recommendation engine helps identify what parts fail more often and why.

Lastly, inventory optimization can lead to significant cost reductions. This is accomplished by driving customer segmentation to fulfill parts to customers based on their entitlement and also managing inventory through better visibility to systems and system failures.

Manufacturing

The reduced margins in manufacturing have led companies, such as GE, which are based on heavy industries, to rethink their strategy beyond just automation. The idea expands automation to creating intelligent factories that are not only automated but also continuously learning and improving. This use case will change the way the main personas in this space work and interact—plant managers, manufacturing engineers, plant and business team leads, and quality professionals.

In simple terms, the business use case that will enable manufacturing to become brilliant is centered on the effective use of business intelligence, data science, and self-service models. A proper **Business Intelligence** (**BI**) strategy should help identify *What happened?* and *When did it happen?* The strategy should incorporate utilization of reports, dashboards, trending KPIs, and related genealogy (traceability) for it to be effective. Proper application of data science advanced statistical analysis, modeling, and machine learning will lead to answers to *Why it happened?* and *What could happen?* Finally, data preparation and blending for root cause and data quality analysis is a requirement that should be automated as self-service for effective use.

Aviation (quality control)

The production of aviation turbine blades requires data science models to be built in order to identify and optimize the decisions to scrap parts instead of shipping with some impacting defects. This requires applying advanced analytics techniques to help realize the ROI through this improved quality control. Typical blade operations consists of the following steps:

1. Create router and drill EDM holes
2. Grind dovetail and CMM inspect
3. Heat treat (transfer data has run number in it FYI)
4. FPI inspect
5. Visual inspect
6. Farm out transaction to OV
7. Coat at OV
8. Visual inspect
9. Farm in transaction from OV
10. Shotpeen
11. Waterflow

12. Airflow inspect
13. X-ray inspect
14. Final visual inspect and package for shipment
15. Ship transaction
16. Closes router

In a case study, the data engineering team created *flattened* data by serial number for these steps, which was the framework for all data analysis. This included data such as percent of pieces above and below control limits, by **Coordinated Measuring Machine (CMM)** dimension. It was identified that the top defects were due to EDM and grind. It was also identified how grind defects correlated to CMM dimensions. This was accomplished by grouping all serial numbers into two groups—those that had grind defects (red) and those that don't have any grind defects (green). The **frequency distribution (d)** of four key dimensions was plotted to see if there was a perceptible difference in the two groups. See the first figure of the chapter.

The data science effort involved predicting each KPI based on diverse data sources. Analytics models were developed for two KPIs—**Part Defect Rate** and **Machine Uptime**. It was identified that mostly EDM and casting issues lead to scrap and some grind defects can be recovered. Plots were generated for the count of serial # with at least one defect, the count of scrapped and shipped, as well as the defect count by type (EDM, cast, and grind). CMM data shows statistical differences in individual measurements for parts shipped healthy with no defects, shipped with grind defects and scrapped with grind defects. See the *Common cloud protocols* table.

Summary

In this chapter, we provided an overview of the entire IoT landscape. We covered the business impact and the technology stack components and described use cases for major verticals. This should have given you a good idea of this entire space, made you familiar with the different pieces of the IoT puzzle, and prepared you for going deeper into some of these topics.

In the next chapter, we will introduce you to how you should consider the overall architecture and design when building out IoT applications. We will take you through the details that are required for you to start visualizing and building your applications.

IIoT Application Architecture and Design

2

In the previous chapter, we covered the core components and many of the business cases, of IIoT. We will continue the journey and dive deep into IoT application architecture and develop our first end-to-end IoT application utilizing the knowledge we have gained.

In this chapter, we will cover some of the key aspects of IIoT application development:

- The challenges of developing IIoT applications
- IIoT system architecture
- Deep diving into edge and cloud application development
- The core concepts of using a sample end-to-end IIoT application

IIoT applications – an introduction

The **Industrial Internet of Things (IIoT)** is designed to harness the power of IIoT and cloud in health care, manufacturing, and industrial environments to monitor performance, optimize operations, and solve problems remotely, all using IIoT applications. The focus of IIoT applications is on connecting equipment such as turbines, jet engines, and locomotives, to the cloud and to each other, in meaningful ways. As such, IIoT application design has many similarities with typical IoT application design in addressing concerns such as edge connectivity, massive data, high-speed data ingestion, and security. But there are some unique challenges, such as knowledge of asset models, industrial analytics, and industrial operations, when you create applications for industrial customers.

The challenges of building an IIoT application

There are many challenges to building IIoT applications, such as a lack of network connectivity due to the remote location of industrial plants. Using a proper Edge Gateway design is essential in mitigating this challenge. Getting access to data from equipment sensors is a challenge, due to the disparate equipment types from many different manufactures. Using protocols such as **Modbus** and **OPCUA** will help mitigate some of these connectivity challenges.

Industrial equipment, such as jet engines and power turbines, produces very large volumes of data in a short amount of time. For example, on landing, a jet engine alone generates up to 1 TB of data. This data needs to be processed and insights gathered from it. To provide data security at all levels, from edge to cloud, is a challenge, therefore careful design decisions should be made regarding security.

Modeling industrial assets, such as jet engines and power turbines, are the foundation of a successful IIoT application. Asset models typically classify complex assets along with their various characteristics. Once this has been properly done, various algorithms can be applied to get insights from the assets. Challenges include the following:

- How to store huge numbers of assets and related objects
- How to define huge numbers of relationships between assets and other objects
- How to organize and make sense of them
- How to discover and query relationships among them
- Modeling requires a deep level of industrial equipment and domain knowledge and collaboration with industry experts

Developing analytics targeted for a specific asset is another challenge, and this requires deep domain knowledge as well as knowledge of the equipment. New general-purpose predictive algorithms such as **anomaly detection** and **K-Cluster** analysis are available for their application.

IIoT system architecture

IIoT system architecture, in its simplistic view, consists of three tiers (as the following diagram illustrates):

- **Tier 1**: Devices
- **Tier 2**: The Edge Gateway
- **Tier 3**: The cloud

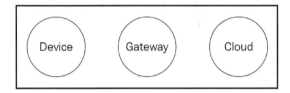

Three-tier architecture of a typical IIoT end-to-end application

Tier 1 of the IIoT architecture consists of networked components, typically sensors and actuators, from the IIoT equipment, which use protocols such as Modbus, Zigbee, or proprietary protocols, to connect to an Edge Gateway. Tier 2 includes sensor data aggregation systems called Edge Gateways that provide functionality, such as preprocessing of the data, securing connectivity to cloud, and using systems such as WebSockets, the event hub, and, even in some cases, edge analytics or fog computing. Tier 3 includes the cloud application built for IIoT using the microservices architecture, which is usually polyglot and inherently secure in nature using HTTPS/OAuth. Tier 3 also includes storage of sensor data using various database systems, such as time series databases or asset stores using backend data storage systems such as Cassandra or Postgres. In addition to data storage, we analyze the data using various analytics, predictive, or threshold-based, or regression-based, to get more insights on the IIoT equipment. In the following sections, we will explore these tiers in more detail so that you have a good idea of the underlying concepts.

Tier 1 – IIoT machines and sensors

In a typical industrial setting, data has to be collected from industrial equipment from many different vendors, such as GE or Siemens. It is very common to see many different equipment types and protocols, such as Modbus, OPCUA, and Zigbee. A typical IIoT machine will have some inbuilt controller and processing logic that can handle the immediate processing of sensor data. In many cases, the sensor data is usually collected and processed by SCADA systems in real time and monitored by a technician, as can be seen in the following diagram:

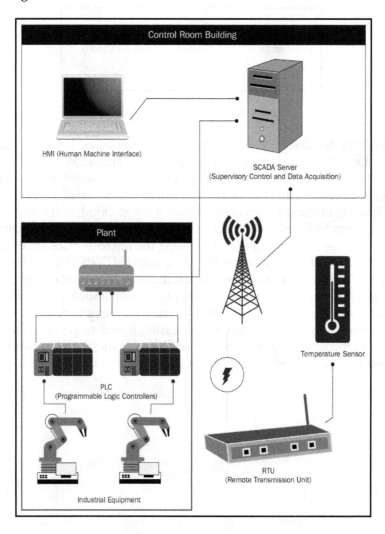

Data gathered from this equipment is very valuable and it is sent to cloud for further upstream processing. Successful implementation of the IIoT application will require digital modeling of the equipment and its chain. This is done by asset modeling, which is essentially the creation of a digital model of the equipment along with its sensors and the sensor's data types, the unit of measures and so on. Usually this effort requires close coordination between IIoT application developers, equipment manufactures and customers to get the required appropriate information.

As a guideline, in an IIoT architecture, some data processing can occur in each of the three tiers. However, processing capabilities will be limited by the footprint to each of the IIoT tiers, for example, the processing capabilities of the devices are much smaller than the gateway. Similarly, the gateway's processing capabilities are smaller than the cloud. Hence, only basic computation can happen at the device level and, progressively, massive computation and predictive algorithms can be applied at the cloud. Data is at the heart of an IIoT architecture and, at the device level, data can be processed immediately but it lacks the depth of processing. However, at the cloud, we get the depth of insight through processing of data by applying machine learning and deep learning algorithms to gain insights. As an example for the data processing at the Edge, industrial machines use SCADA to process data in real time and provide controls to the machines. Similarly, autonomous vehicle processing happens on board the vehicle using LIDAR technology, which in turn uses AI and machine learning to help navigate the vehicle.

Further data processing at cloud is useful to gain much deeper insights and require more extensive processing. Cloud data processing involves bringing several sources of data together from many different machines/systems to predict a problem or gain insights. As an example, we can collect data from sensors from various machines in an industrial plant and do processing across these machines to gain insights to optimize the plant operations. Another example is to use historical data from sensors, and the outcomes from analytics, to provide recommendations. In this case, we would store the historical data, both the input and output action, in a cloud datastore and then use this data as a training model for supervised and unsupervised machine learning algorithms to provide recommendations for case management systems.

Tier 2 – Edge Gateway and cloud connectivity

Sensor data from various sensors, such as temperature or pressure sensors, starts as analog data and then gets converted into digital streams. It is then aggregated and sent downstream to systems for in-depth processing. **Data Acquisition Systems** (**DAS**) typically do these conversation and aggregation functions on-board the Edge Gateways. The DAS connects to the sensor network using various industrial protocols such as ModBus and OPCUA, aggregates data, converts the data from analog into digital streams and then forwards it to data processing systems. The Edge Gateway receives the data from the DAS and then, using a cloud connector, sends the data to Tier 3 cloud systems for further processing.

Edge Gateway

The Edge Gateway is in close proximity to the sensors and actuators and it is usually located on a customer site or on the equipment itself. For example, a wind turbine might contain a hundreds sensors and actuators that feed data into an Edge Gateway. The Edge Gateway then collects, digitizes, and forwards the data to the cloud and, sometimes, may also have edge analytics which can take detect patterns and anomalies at the edge itself. Edge Gateways usually support various types of protocols, such as Modbus and OPCUA to connect with the various types of industrial sensors, as can be seen in the following diagram:

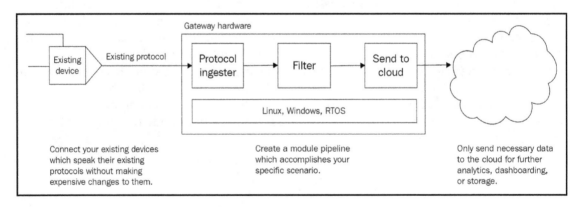

Edge Gateway that connects to the device and does some basic pressing before forwarding data to the cloud

Edge Gateway can also pre-process data by applying functions for filtering and resampling of data. The data generated by sensors creates large volumes of data rapidly and, by pre-possessing the data, the gateway can only send relevant data to cloud. Analog sensors, such as temperature, voltage, pressure, and vibration can generate huge volumes of continuous streams of data that are changing rapidly. As an example, a jet engine can have thousands of sensors, and these sensors can generate ~40 TB of data during aircraft takeoff or landing alone. Pre-processing data on the Edge is therefore beneficial in many cases.

Edge Gateways can build basic gateway functionality by adding such capabilities as security, analytics, malware protection, and data management services, which are collectively known as **fog computing**. Fog computing enables the analysis of data streams in near realtime by running machine learning algorithms directly onto the Edge Gateway. The Edge Gateway is the perfect junction where there are enough compute, storage and networking resources to mimic cloud capabilities at the edge, and hence support the local ingestion of data and the quick turnaround of results:

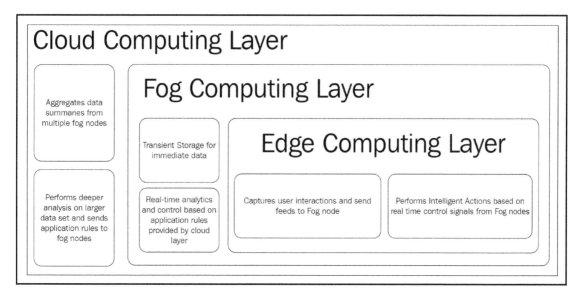

Fog computing versus edge computing versus cloud computing aspects

Edge Gateways are edge devices that are deployed on customer premises or customer data centers. In the wind turbine example, if you have a wind farm with many hundreds of turbines and you want to process data on-premises, you might have instant data at each turbine. You would then aggregate the information to create a wind farm wide view and pass the data on to the cloud for a company-wide view. Edge Gateway device hardware footprints are very diverse and supported in various form factors to support specific deployment needs. Most of the manufacturers will support many different specifications, all the way from onboard gateways to specialized servers called **Edge Nodes**. All of them have typically common characteristics, such as ease of deployment, being rugged, and the ability to support remote management of the devices using edge managers.

Because IIoT data is voluminous, it can easily consume large amounts of network bandwidth, it needs huge storage space and can swamp the resources in Cloud. It's optimal to intelligent Edge Gateways which are capable of performing analytics as a way to get immediate insights. Alternatively, we can apply different time-based filtering such as a Bloom filter. Adding this type of filtering can reduce the resource needs and hence it can be much more efficient. By adding an intelligent Edge Gateway, or Edge Node, we can pre-process the data, run appropriate Edge Analytics to gain immediate insights, and then pass data to the cloud for further processing and correlations across multiple sites, and so on. For example, a power company may have multiple wind farms, and processing in each of these individual farms can happen at the site using the Edge Gateway or Nodes. In addition, these Nodes can send relevant data to the cloud for further processing to gain insights and comparisons between farms.

Edge Analytics is an up-and-coming field, whereby instead of sending the data to the cloud for processing and gaining insights, data is processed near the source on the Edge Gateway or Node. For example, machine learning algorithms, such as anomaly detection, can be applied to sensor data to scan for anomalies that can identify many different maintenance problems of the machines, thereby preventing any downtime, as long appropriate action is taken. In the next section, we will cover different ways to connect to the cloud to send data to the cloud.

Cloud Connectivity

Connectivity from the edge to the cloud is essential and there are many ways to securely connect to the cloud. Typical infrastructure includes mutual authentication, which is essentially two-way authentication between the Edge Gateway and the cloud, at the same time using a certificate. Once the secure connection is established, the communication typically happens using one of the asynchronous protocols such as WebSockets, binary protocols using Event Hub, MQTT, STOMP, and HTTP 2. In addition to the connectivity, typically an Edge Manager manages all the connected Edge devices to provide dashboards for operations capability.

MQTT Communication

MQTT stands for **Message Queuing Telemetry Transport**. It is a lightweight messaging and bi-directional protocol that works well in resource constrained network scenarios, such as low network reliability or low-bandwidth, or high-latent clients. It provides a simple way to send telemetry information between devices, or from devices to cloud. The protocol uses a publish/subscribe communication paradigm, and is used for **Machine-to-Machine** (**M2M**) communication and is widely adopted in the IoT.

MQTT was originally developed by IBM to do M2M communication and is currently widely adopted in many different applications, such as messaging services and IoT applications. MQTT is very lightweight and requires only a 2 byte header and supports a payload of up to 256 MB of data. The format of the data is application specific. MQTT defines three levels of **Quality of Service** (**QoS**). QoS defines how the messages are delivered between the publisher and subscriber by the message broker. Publishers and subscribers can choose the type of QoS they would like and the broker will make sure that level of QoS is adhered. The first QoS is *fire and forget,* whereby the publisher sends the message to the broker and the broker sends it to the subscribers. However, there is no guarantee that the subscribers receive the messages correctly. The second QoS is *at least once*. In this case, the broker retries delivering the messages. They then get an acknowledgement from the subscriber that they have received the messages. The third QoS is *exactly once,* whereby the subscriber is guaranteed to get the message only once. MQTT is ideally suited for IoT applications due to its characteristics, such as very light overheads, flexible payloads, and various levels of QoS.

In considering MQTT for cloud connectivity, it is good to know some of the limitations as well. MQTT is primarily designed for use within an enterprise behind the firewall and mainly for communication between the devices. Hence, using it for connecting to the cloud will add security overheads, such as adding authentication headers and SSL/TLS encryption using client certificates. Even after adding these security measures, it is difficult to prevent unauthorized publishers from publishing to an MQTT topic (that is, anyone with the authentication credentials can publish messages to the topic and we need additional mechanisms to enforce authorization). Another limitation is a lack of interoperability in the message structure since it is open-ended and hence specific to a given application. It is also difficult to scale MQTT to many devices, and MQTT does not lend itself well for transfer of a large amount of data, as, for example, in a sensor data bulk ingestion.

WebSocket communication

WebSocket cloud connectivity is another option to consider for IoT applications and solves some of the issues with MQTT. WebSockets is designed to be complementary to HTTP, yet it is closer to TCP and lean—it only uses 2-6 bytes of headers for data transmission. WebSocket leverages the existing HTTP infrastructures such as servers, proxies, and security headers for authentications/authorizations. WebSocket is a bi-directional, full duplex, and low-level communication protocol that runs on top of TCP. A WebSocket starts off as a standard HTTP connection but then gets upgraded to a WebSocket connection to create a persistent TCP connection with the server using a single socket. WebSocket is part of the HTML5 standard. Many of the modern browsers support WebSocket protocols natively and web applications can use the JavaScript library to use WebSocket communications. WebSocket outshines HTTP in the development of real-time, event-driven, and low latency applications and will be a great fit for IoT use cases.

Although WebSocket enables us to use the HTTP security infrastructure for the IoT devices, it does not eliminate interoperability issues since the messaging format is not defined by WebSockets, and it is up to the application to utilize standards such as JSON. WebSocket also requires a full web client to run on the device, which may not be possible in all situations due to device hardware footprints limitations. WebSocket is also less reliable than a messaging protocol such as MQTT and it is difficult to scale WebSockets servers as the load increases. Scaling WebSockets using a load balancer is a complex task.

MQTT over WebSockets

Another possibility is to use MQTT over WebSocket. This scenario is frequently used in IoT web application to display sensor data outputs in a time-series graphs, and so on. Also, this combination provides us the best of both worlds, such as utilizing the HTTP infrastructure for ports, security, and so on, in addition we can bring the Publish/Subscribe mechanism which is lacking in WebSockets but is the basis of MQTT. Also, MQTT provides a variety of quality services as well.

This combination lends itself well to a larger footprint device or gateway and still lacks the messaging interoperability, but can scale well to support many devices. Another possibility is to use WebSocket with other messaging infrastructures such as Kafka, which is a common pattern in large scale deployment and can scale well to support a large volume of data ingestion and large numbers of subscribers.

Event/Message hub-based connectivity

The Event/Message hub Publish-Subscribe connectivity is another option for IoT application, specifically if the volume of data ingestion is huge and the number of clients is also large. Event Hub uses Kafka messaging infrastructure and can operate on top of many different connectors, such as WebSocket, HTTP, gRPC, MQTT, and so on. The best case architecture is to use WebSocket with message format in JSON to connect to the Kafka service, or you can use gRPC (HTTP/2 Streaming protocol) with protobuf messaging protocol. Event hub is built to be secure, massively scalable, fault tolerant, and language-agnostic. As can be seen in the following example, the Event Hub acts as a cloud connector and queuing system, which provides durability for many producers (such as devices that can produce time-series information) and forwards it to many subscribers.

The following example shows that, with this model, we can stream data from the devices to the cloud and various types of applications can act on the data:

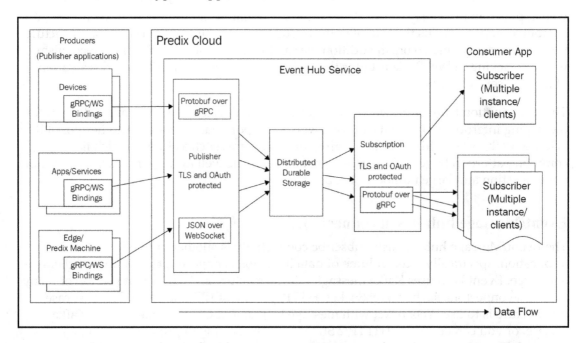

Event Hub, with many publishers from remote locations, connecting to the cloud to transmit data for subscribers to consume the data and act on it

The publish-subscribe model supports binary JSON over WebSocket and protobuf over gRPC streams for publishing, and binary (protobuf over gRPC) for subscribing. Devices communicate with the Event Hub service by publishing messages to topics. Applications, devices, and services can use Event Hub as a one-stop solution for their communication needs. You can use Event Hub to ingest streaming data from anywhere to the cloud for processing.

Event Hub uses gRPC for publishing and subscribing. A full-duplex streaming RPC framework, gRPC uses protocol buffers for wire protocol. gRPC is implemented over HTTP/2 and uses header compression, multiplexing TCP connections, and flow control. Protocol buffer is a binary protocol, suited for IIoT devices that publish high-velocity data over networks with low bandwidth.

The Event Hub also provides the following:

- Streaming high volumes of data to the cloud for processing, from anywhere
- Payload-agnostic publishing of any type of data for subscriber consumption
- Handling message distribution for subscribers scaling from single to multiple instances
- Handling of large-scale asynchronous message processing applications
- Using OAuth provider for authentication and authorization

Tier 3 - Cloud (IIoT application, data, and analytics)

IIoT data that has been digitized and aggregated is sent to the Cloud for storage and further processing using analytics. Finally, IIoT cloud apps enable the user to visualize insights about the IIoT devices and enable the user to apply specific workflows. Once the data is sent to Cloud, the primary concerns are as follows:

- Securely ingesting and storing the data. Typical IIoT storage includes a time-series data store and storage of asset models and alerts output of analytics.
- Processing data using various different types of analytics such as predictive, physics-based, threshold-based, streaming or deep learning analytics to determine the health and insights about the IIoT device.
- Building IIoT applications that can enable the end user to do the following:
    - Visualize the health of the IIoT device using dashboards and charts
    - Interact and process events such as, alerts, alarms, and so on, from analytics using specific workflows

In the following sections, we will go over IIoT cloud application design using microservices, storage options of data in the Cloud, and finally go over different types of analytics.

Microservice-based application design for IIoT cloud applications

"Microservices are loosely coupled service oriented architecture with bounded contexts."

- Adrian Cockcroft

A few key characteristics of IIoT applications are diversity in data, security, IIoT scale-machines generating tons of data, visualization of data and finally, high availability and reliability. Microservices architecture is a perfect fit for these types of IIoT application demands. Microservices architecture is all about developing applications using small but well defined, decomposed, modular services that can be deployed independently. Each of these services can model a business function and expose a set of APIs. Microservices architecture enables development of services that are loosely coupled and uses technology choices appropriate for that service.

In a microservice architecture, applications are built using smaller services aligned with business functions which interact with each other using RESTful APIs. These services are secure by design using HTTPS protocols and OAuth for authentication, and can use a variety of programming languages appropriate for their implementation; for example, a service which needs high parallelization may use the Go language, and, if the application has lots of business logic, a good choice will be to use Java and so on. This model of using different languages is called **polyglot programming**. In addition, these services have a choice of various different messaging services and datastores such as relational DBs, or NoSQL stores, or in-memory stores, to implement a robust service. Typical in an IIoT application architecture, as an example, is the time series service which can use a NoSQL DB along with Java as its data store/programming language. And also, perhaps, the events service can use a relational datastore as its database, which includes the Events table. Visualization can be built using an Angular/React application, such as using the Node.js application, as given in the following example. There are many advantages to this design. Because the services are isolated from each other, a developer can change their service's schema without having to coordinate with developers working on other services and can independently deploy the software to production:

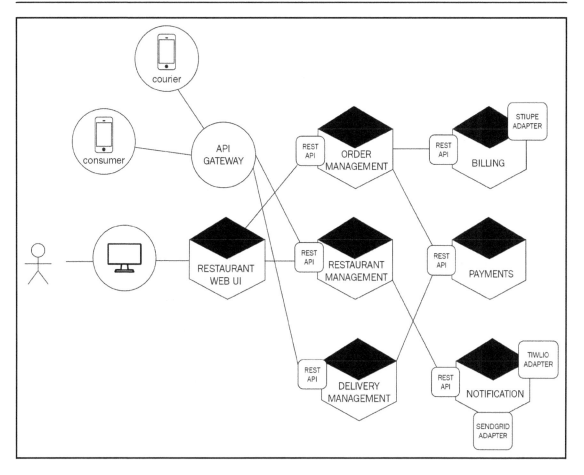

Describing the microservices ecosystem of an application and its interactions

This type of decoupling in-turn enables development of highly salable services that can scale independently from each other, for example, the time series store can be scaled to multiple VMs (virtual machines) versus a user management service which can use two to three VMs.

Our preceding example shows that we have broken the IIoT application into various smaller services, such as:

- Time series service, which was typically developed using either Java or Scala with an NoSQL data store such as Cassandra
- An Events service, developed using Java with a data store of relational db, such as Postgres

- A User Management service using a relation data store
- IIoT, UI, and visualization applications using Node.js and Web UI frameworks, such as Angular or React
- Notification services using SendGrid/Twillo
- Asset services using PostgreSQL
- An analytics service using Python, or real time systems such as Spark with its own data storage systems

For developing a robust microservices architecture **The 12-factor app** (`https://12factor.net/`) methodology is highly recommended to be adopted. The 12-factor app methodology covers best practices, based on a few specific parameters for deployment of cloud-native applications:

- It uses declarative formats such as YAML—yet another markup language—files to store environment specific configuration regarding dependent services, log levels, API keys, services, and database credentials for greater portability between environments.
- It limits differences between development and production, for continuous deployment.
- It aims for stateless applications that are designed to degrade gracefully. That means that, if a dependency fails, the app itself does not become a failure.
- It allows for scaling up and down without major changes.

The 12-factor methodology is programming language agnostic and works with any combination of backing microservices.

Platform as a Service (PaaS)

Developing applications using microservices is very complex since microservices are numerous, polyglot (having many different technologies) and distributed in nature. To successfully develop, deploy and run at scale a choice of good **Platform-as-a-service (PaaS)** is essential.

PaaS provides core application infrastructures, such as application runtimes, persistent stores and messaging services in such a way that microservices developers can focus on the core application aspects rather than worrying about the infrastructure operational burdens. A robust PaaS also eliminates all manual actions and increases the quality of service (reliability, availability, scalability, and performance). The key characteristics of a typical PaaS environment are automatic deployment, provisioning, and support for full-stack microservices. PaaS, in its core, provides many tools to support various aspects of application infrastructure, such as service registries, metadata services, discovery services, logging services, monitoring services, service gateways, and routers for load balancing. In addition, PaaS also provides a robust security infrastructure to support authentication and authorization for microservices to connect with each other. The following example shows a typical PaaS infrastructure, along with an ecosystem of microservices interaction to form an IoT application:

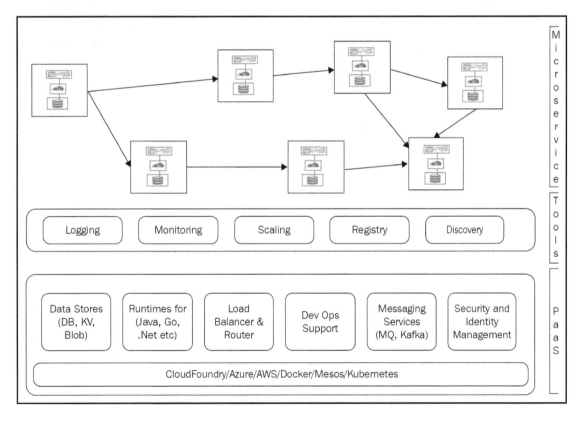

PaaS infrastructure along with an ecosystem of microservices' interaction to form an IoT application

PaaS fits perfect with any microservices applications in which a typical application is made up of many small microservices, and uses service composition to connect different microservices' endpoints, and realize a fully functional application. Microservices leverages PaaS infrastructure in various ways, such as registering service endpoints for seamless discovery, adding security to the endpoints, handling failures using circuit breakers, and offloading the scaling and load balance to the PaaS infrastructure.

Overview of Cloud Foundry

Cloud Foundry (**CF**) is an industry-standard PaaS, a platform for developing cloud-native applications. It is an open source platform (`https://github.com/cloudfoundry`), originally developed by VMware and now owned by Pivotal Software, a joint venture by EMC, VMware and General Electric (GE). You can deploy it and run your apps on your own computing infrastructure, or deploy it on an IaaS, such as AWS, vSphere, or OpenStack. The Cloud Foundry PaaS is available from a commercial CF cloud provider (`https://www.cloudfoundry.org/learn/certified-providers/`), such as GE Predix, or Pivotal Cloud Foundry, or IBM Bluemix, or you can deploy the platform at scale on top of a cloud provider. A broad community (`https://www.cloudfoundry.org/community/`) contributes to and supports Cloud Foundry. GE's Predix leverages Cloud Foundry and so does IBM's Bluemix. The platform's openness and infrastructure agnostic support prevent its users from being locked into a single cloud provider or framework, or set of app services. An overview of the key architecture and components of Cloud Foundry is given in the following diagram:

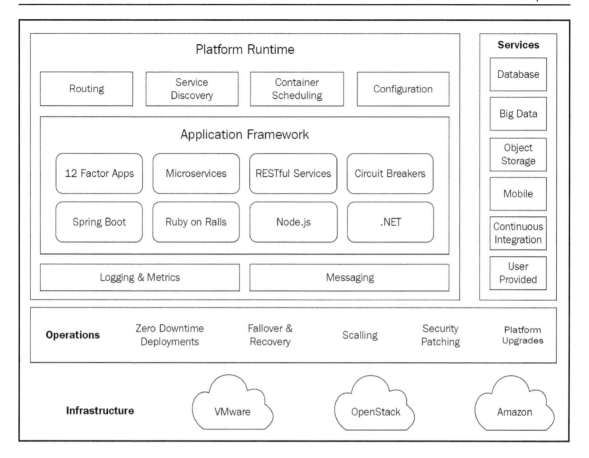

Cloud Foundry high-level architecture showing the cloud agnostic nature of the platform

Cloud Foundry was primarily written in the Go language. The platform's openness and extensibility prevent its users from being locked into a single framework, set of application services, or cloud. Cloud Foundry is ideal for IoT application development because developers can deploy their applications to Cloud Foundry using their existing tools and with zero modification to their code.

The Hello world application using Cloud Foundry

In this section, we will develop a very basic Cloud Foundry application to illustrate the nature of the cloud-native application using PaaS. The application itself is a basic HTML page `index.html` as given in the following example.

 Optional step: A prerequisite for executing this application is to have access to a PaaS provider, such as the Pivotal CF platform `https://pivotal.io/platform/`, the command-line tools for connecting to the cloud provider, and so on. This is optional seeing as the focus is to highlight some of advantages of running in a PaaS environment.

Download the source code from GitHub:

```
git clone https://github.com/tjayant/Predix-HelloWorld-WebApp # replace
with the final git
cd HelloWorld-WebApp
```

The content of `Index.html` is given in the following example:

```
// Index.html
<html>
<head>
<title>Hello World</title>
</head>
<body>
Hello World
</body>
</html>
```

The `Manifest.yml` file given in the next example describes the runtimes needed using build packs, memory requirements, dependent services such as logservice, in-memory key-value store Redis, and Security using UAA:

```
#  Manifest.yml for a basic hello world index.html file


applications:
  - name: HelloWorld-WebApp #  your application name
    buildpack: staticfile_buildpack # built pack
    memory: 256M
    stack: cflinuxfs2
  services:
    - log-stash # inject dependency such as log service
    - redis
    - my-uaa
```

Deploy the application using the `cf` command line and one simple command:

```
cf push
```

List the applications using the following:

```
cf apps
```

And scale the applications using the following:

```
cf scale HelloWorld-WebApp -i 5
```

Data design for IIoT applications

Data generally covers an overall strategy on how to ingest data, store data, process data, and retrieve data. In addition, data can be of various different types such as OLTP data, telemetry data, analytical data, in-memory data, and special purpose data such as documents, images and, waveforms. Robust data architecture should handle all of these scenarios. The diverse nature of the data stores is captured in the following diagram:

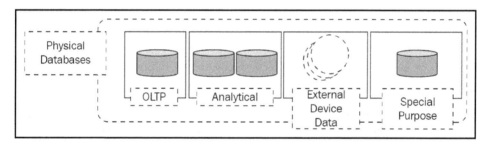

The diagram captures the diverse nature of the data support needed for an IIoT application

Data ingestion

Data from the IIoT devices typically gets ingested to the Data APIs, such as the time series store, the asset store, or the event store. Ingestion typically happens using a well defined end point such as the REST API End Point, or using a Pub/Sub model using one of the cloud connector protocol options we discussed before, such as MQTT, HTTPs or WebSockets. A typical Publisher/Subscribe model is implemented using event hub/HTTP REST proxy, or custom clients for Kafka. Data can then be processed using real-time processing engines such as Storm or Spark runtime, and then kept for longer time storage in the HDFS, NoSQL, or OLTP data store, depending on the types of data. This can be seen in the following diagram:

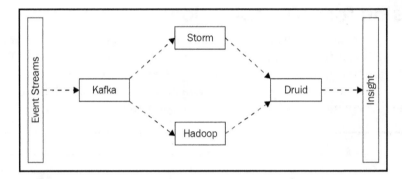

Timeseries/telemetry data

Data collected by the device is called *telemetry*. This is data that IIoT devices provide to applications which is collected from the sensors on the devices. Timeseries data is a sequence of data points collected at set time intervals over a continuous period of time. Sensor data is an example of a common way to generate time series data. A time series data store requires a measurement with a corresponding timestamp. The time series service provides an attributes field to include additional relevant details about that specific data point, such as units or site, for example, *"Site":"SanFrancisco"*.

Each source of telemetry results in a *tag in the asset model*. Telemetry data can be processed at the Edge Gateway, and it is usually sent to the cloud for further processing using various different types of algorithms. Frequency of the data sent varies on the sensor type. Usually it is a data point per second, but this data can add up quickly when we consider the need to store historical data at cloud. We may have to use NoSQL data stores to store a large volume of TimeSeries data.

Time Series data can consist of regular data (data sampled at regular time intervals), or irregular data, for example, data that is recorded only when a certain event occurs (so always at random times).

The Time Series service should provide the following benefits:

- Efficient storage of time series data
- Indexing the data for quick retrieval
- High availability so you can access and query your data from anywhere via HTTP
- Horizontal scalability
- Millisecond data point precision

Typical Timeseries data stores are implemented using the NoSQL DB or using Elasticsearch servers.

The in-memory, Blob, and OLTP data stores

The in-memory data store stores data in RAM and is usually mostly used to store key-value types of data for quick lookup. Redis is one of the popular in-memory data stores. Blob stores such as **Riak** are specialty data stores used to store data such as documents, wave forms, images, and so on. Data can also be stored in HDFS and accessed during batch processing of data using map-reduce as part of the analytics. Finally, some data, such as events, is stored in a relational DB for faster access and processing.

Analytics for IIoT

Analytics is at the heart of a robust IIoT application, and understanding different types of analytics and utilizing the appropriate technology is essential for the success of developing an IIoT application. There are different types of analytics that can be developed for IoT applications, all the way from a simple threshold analytic to streaming analytics using Kafka, Spark and NoSQL stores, as given as following. We will go into details of these different types of analytics.

Descriptive analytics – insight into device health

Descriptive analytics, or threshold analytics, does basic computation based on past data to generate some meaningful insights. These analytics consist of very simple computation logic, applied typically over a time range of data from the device's sensors. Parameters for the thresholds are typically given by the device manufacturers, hence identifying any deviation from the threshold can provide valuable insights into the health of the device. Descriptive analytics is useful because it allows us to learn from past data, and understand the health of the machine. In a typical real life scenario some of this data could come from sensors and others could be collected over time from manual readings. Analytics could be triggered based on firing of an event, or scheduled at the given time frame.

The vast majority of the IIoT analytics fall into this category. These analytics can also be used to detect any maintenance events, such as when to power wash a turbine or when to replace a part. We can use basic technology such as scheduler to execute these programs, and various programming languages to implement these types of analytics.

Predictive analytics - understanding the future failure modes of the device

Predictive analytics has its roots in the ability to predict what might happen based on analysis of the sensor data, typically using machine learning algorithms, given a training dataset. These analytics are about understanding the future based on past data models. Predictive analytics typically provides the user with actionable insights based on past data. In IoT applications, these types of analytics can generate actionable alerts or advisories or KPI.

Predictive analytics, using machine learning, is, at its root, the basic practice of using algorithms to parse data, learn from it, and then make a determination or prediction about something in the future. So, rather than hand-coding software routines with a specific set of instructions to accomplish a particular task, the machine is "trained" using large amounts of data and algorithms which give it the ability to learn how to perform the task and provide estimates about the likelihood of a future outcome. Spark ML provides a nice infrastructure to develop/deploy predictive analytics. One of the successful analytics that has been in the market for IIoT is the SmartSignal analytics which is offered by GE Digital for many different industrial use cases.

Prescriptive analytics: advice on possible outcomes

We can take the machine learning one step further and, if we can also track the outcomes that happen after an alert/anomaly is generated and use that as a training set to the machine learning algorithm, then we gain the ability to prescribe a number of different possible actions or recommendations as guidance for the solution. In a nut-shell, we are training these analytics to provide us with recommendations on possible courses of action. Prescriptive analytics attempts to use the past outcomes or actions of the users to provide recommendations to help with the actual decisions.

Prescriptive analytics uses many of familiar tools such as data aggregation, machine learning, and business rules and operationalizes these process for daily consumption to help users. Prescriptive analytics works by using historical outcome data as training dataset and, once the algorithm is tuned, it combines it with real-time data feeds at runtime to provide the needed recommendations.

Prescriptive analytics is relatively complex to administer since it requires a certain level of understanding of the domain data, but some general purpose deep learning algorithms such as anomaly detection and K-Means clustering have been used in production settings. Prescriptive analytics is mostly custom in nature, that is, built by a data scientist for a specific problem domain. Few general purpose algorithms such as anomaly detection and K-Means Clustering have evolved to be successful in the IIoT space.

The anatomy of our first IIoT application

We will design our first IIoT application end-to-end architecture using a very lightweight Edge Gateway that checks for any deviation in the temperature data using basic threshold analytics. When the threshold is breached, an alert is sent to the alert service in the cloud for storage and further processing of the alerts:

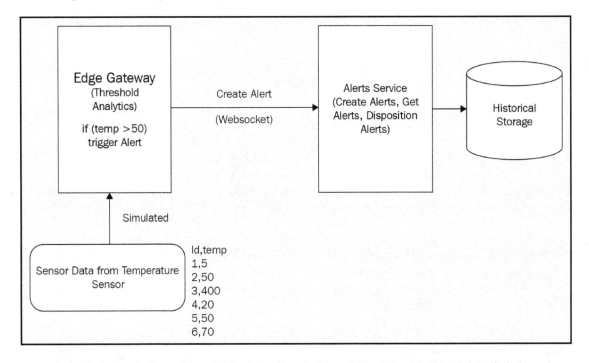

High level end-to-end architecture of the sample IIoT application with an Edge Gateway which has a basic analytic which sends alerts to the cloud

We will use a node server to design the analytics and use WebSocket as the cloud connectivity. We will connect to the cloud application using Spring Boot with PostgreSQL as the data store. Analytics will be a very simple descriptive analytics deployed in the Edge Gateway that is threshold-based which generates the alerts in the Cloud. The architecture of the sample application is as following:

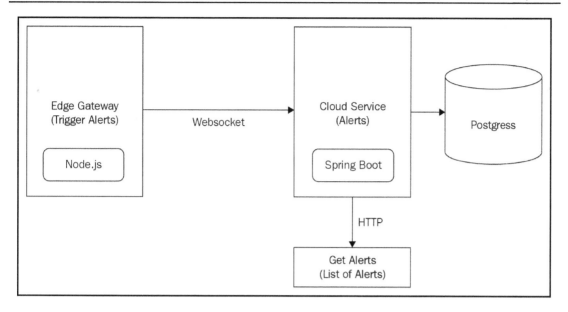

Details of the technologies used in implementing the sample IIoT application

Edge Gateway triggering alerts

To run the Edge Gateway code, the prerequisites are given as follows:

- Download the code from GitHub. Samples are in the chapter 2 Iiot-Sample 1 project.
- The Edge Gateway code is in the folder iiot-edge-gateway.
- NPM and Node should be installed.
- To install the application, issue the following command:

```
npm install
```

- For this example, we are using socksjs as the client library for WebSocket. SocksJS provides the fallback between WebSockets and HTTP/HTTPS.
- Stomp protocol to send the data between the cloud and gateway.

 WebSocket itself does not provide any message transfer protocol, hence using stomp over WebSocket solves that issue. Stomp is a generic protocol to send messages. In our example, we are using JSON to transfer the data.

- Details of the sample Edge Gateway is given in the following example. The code essentially reads data from a simulated sensor, in this case a .csv file, and then establishes connection to the server using the WebSocket protocol:

```
//include the stomp package and socks js

var Stomp = require('webstomp-client');
var SockJS = require('sockjs-client');

// reading CSV files using
var csv=require('fast-csv'),
    fs = require("fs");



// open the connection to the WebSocket end point.
var socket = new
SockJS('http://localhost:5074/iiot-sample-WebSocket');
//create a stomp session
var stompClient = Stomp.over(socket);
```

- Read from the CSV file and check for any deviation. Check for any reading above 50.
- If so, trigger an alert to the cloud service API.
- We will add security in the later chapters. This sample does not add authentication:

```
function readFromSensorDataAndCheckforAnomalies(){

  var stream = fs.createReadStream("sensordata.csv");

  csv
    .fromStream(stream, {headers : true})
    .validate(function(data){
        return data.temp <= 50; //all reading under  50 are valid
    })
    .on("data-invalid", function(data){

        var alertData = JSON.stringify({'alertsUuid':'alertsid'+
new Date(),
                    'severity':1,
                    'alertName':'HighTemprateAlert',
                    'alertInfo':'Temperature Value:' + data.temp
});
        stompClient.send("/app/createAlert",alertData,{});
    })
    .on("data", function(data){
        console.log(data);
```

```
    })
    .on("end", function(){
        console.log("done");
```

- Sample temperature data given in the following example should trigger two alerts to the cloud and it is contained in the `sensordata.csv`:

```
id,temp
1,5
2,50
3,400
4,20
5,50
6,70
```

- The JSON structure of the alerts that gets generated is given in the following example:

```
{
"alertsUuid": "alertsId",
"severity": 1,
"alertName": "HighTemperature Alert",
"alertInfo": "Temperature Value"
}
```

- Establish connection to the cloud service for generating alerts by subscribing to the `alertCreated` topic.
- Sending the alerts to the alerts service in the cloud is given as following (essentially we publish any WebSocket message to the cloud):

```
function createAlertInCloud() {

  // Connect to cloud using WebSocket and create alerts
    stompClient.connect({}, function (frame) {
        //setConnected(true);
        console.log('Connected: ' + frame);
        stompClient.subscribe('/topic/alertCreated', function
(alert) {
            console.log('gotResponse from CloudService: ' +
alert);
        });
        readFromSensorDataAndCheckforAnomalies();
    });
};


createAlertInCloud();
```

- Run the node `idiot-edge.js` to see the result. It should send two alerts to the server:

```
node iiot-edge.js
```

Cloud connectivity using WebSockets

We've already covered how the WebSockets along with STOMP can be used to send data to and from the Edge to the Cloud. In this section, we will cover how to build a WebSocket server using Spring Boot:

- Before you run the server-side code you will need to install `postgresql`.
- Start `postgresql` using the following command line:

```
./pgc start
pg96 starting on port 5432
```

- The code for this application is in `iiot-sample-alert-server`.
- This application uses Maven, you will need to have maven installed on your machine.
- *Step 1* is to add the Spring Boot WebSocket support and `mvn` dependency to the `pom.xml` under `iiot-sample-alert-server` as follows:

```
<dependency>
    <groupId>org.springframework.boot</groupId>
    <artifactId>spring-boot-starter-WebSocket</artifactId>
</dependency>
<dependency>
    <groupId>org.webjars</groupId>
    <artifactId>stomp-WebSocket</artifactId>
    <version>2.3.3</version>
</dependency>
```

- Add the WebSocket configuration for the Spring Boot application as given in the following code snippet. This enables us to configure a simple Spring Boot application to listen to WebSocket connections for incoming traffic:

```
@Configuration
@EnableWebSocketMessageBroker
public class WebSocketConfig extends
AbstractWebSocketMessageBrokerConfigurer {

    @Override
    public void configureMessageBroker(MessageBrokerRegistry
```

```
config) {
        config.enableSimpleBroker("/topic");
        config.setApplicationDestinationPrefixes("/app");
    }

    @Override
    public void registerStompEndpoints(StompEndpointRegistry
registry) {

        RequestUpgradeStrategy upgradeStrategy = new
TomcatRequestUpgradeStrategy();
        registry.addEndpoint("/iiot-sample-WebSocket")
                .withSockJS();
        registry.addEndpoint("/iiot-sample-
WebSocket").setHandshakeHandler(new
DefaultHandshakeHandler(upgradeStrategy))
                .setAllowedOrigins("*");

    }

}
```

- Add the REST controller to handle the WebSocket messages. Essentially, as the messages arrive in the WebSocket they calls this REST endpoint to create alerts.
- IIotWebSocketController listens to messages at /app/createAlert and sends the response to any subscribers listening at /topic/alertCreated.
- The format of the message is the same Alert JSON and it's response is also of the Alert type:

```
@RestController
public class IiotWebSocketController {
    private static final Logger logger =
LoggerFactory.getLogger(IiotWebSocketController.class);
    private final IiotService iiotService;

    @Autowired
    private TenantUtil tenantUtil;


    @Autowired
    public IiotWebSocketController(IiotService iiotService) {
        this.iiotService = iiotService;
    }



    @MessageMapping("/createAlert")
```

```
      @SendTo("/topic/alertCreated")
      public Alert createAlert(Alert alertMessage) throws Exception {
            StopWatch stopWatch = new StopWatch("create WebSocket using
Alerts");
            logger.info("{Message Received}", new
StopWatchUtil(stopWatch));

            //pass empty credentials since security and tenancy are not
enabled
            Credentials credentials = new Credentials(null,
tenantUtil.getTenantUuid());

            Alert createdAlert =
iiotService.createAlerts(alertMessage,credentials,stopWatch);


            return createdAlert;
      }

}
```

- Add a `case-IIotSampleTest.java` test, to test our new `IIotWebSocketController`.
- This test case simulates the WebSocket client using the Stomp protocol, but connects to the server to test the end-to-end functionality.
- For the next step, we will go into details of the database connection, data model, and service details, as can be seen in the following example:

```
@Before
public void setup() {
    List<Transport> socketTransports = new ArrayList<>();
    socketTransports.add(new WebSocketTransport(new
StandardWebSocketClient()));
    this.sockJsClient = new SockJsClient(socketTransport);

    this.stompClient = new WebSocketstompClient(sockJsClient);
    this.stompClient.setMessageConverter(new
MappingJackson2MessageConverter());
    headers.add(HttpHeaders.CONTENT_TYPE,"application/json");
}

@Test
public void createAlert() throws Exception {

  final AtomicReference<Throwable> alertCreationfailure = new
AtomicReference<>();
  final CountDownLatch alertlatch = new CountDownLatch(1);
```

```
StompSessionHandler alertHandler = new
TestSessionHandler(alertCreationfailure) {

@Override
public void afterConnected(final StompSession session,
StompHeaders connectedHeaders) {
session.subscribe("/topic/alertCreated", new StompFrameHandler() {
@Override
public Type getPayloadType(StompHeaders headers) {
return Alert.class;
}

@Override
public void handleFrame(StompHeaders headers, Object payload) {
Alert alert = (Alert) payload;

try {
assertEquals("Tempreture Alert", alert.getAlertName());
} catch (Throwable throw) {
failure.set(throw);
} finally {
session.disconnect();
alertlatch.countDown();
}
}
});

try {
Alert alert = new Alert();
alert.setAlertsUuid(String.format("AlertUUid" + new
SimpleDateFormat("yyyy-MM-dd HH:mm:ss").format(new Date())));
alert.setSeverity(1);
alert.setAlertName("Tempreture Alert");
alert.setAlertInfo("Tempreture Value:50");
session.send("/app/createAlert",alert);

} catch (Throwable throw) {
failure.set(throw);
alertlatch.countDown();
}
}
};

this.stompClient.connect("ws://localhost:{port}/iiot-sample-
WebSocket", this.headers, alertHandler, this.port);

if (alertlatch.await(3, TimeUnit.SECONDS)) {
if (failure.get() != null) {
```

```
  throw new AssertionError("Failed to create Alerts",
failure.get());
  }
  }
  else {
  fail("Alerts Response not received");
  }


  }
```

- Run the test to make sure the unit tests passes, as follows:

```
./build.sh

[INFO] ----------------------------------------------------------
--------------
[INFO] Test Summary:
[INFO]
[INFO] IIOT Sample Management Modules .....................
SUCCESS [ 1.091 s]
[INFO] IIOT Sample Domain Entities ........................
SUCCESS [ 3.158 s]
[INFO] IIOT Sample Management ...........................
SUCCESS [ 19.893 s]
[INFO] ----------------------------------------------------------
--------------
[INFO] BUILD SUCCESS
[INFO]
```

Cloud microservices aggregating the alerts

The primary goal of the Cloud Service is to store the Alerts data that is generated in the Edge Gateway, and the ability to retrieve the data for future access. In the previous sections have covered the Edge Gateway, and the Cloud connectivity with WebSockets on both the Edge Gateway and the Cloud Server. In this section, we will implement the alerts Cloud service and APIs. To implement the Alerts Service we used the following:

- Spring Boot to build out the REST API: Spring Boot applications are typically run in a cloud system such as Cloud Foundry or AWS/Azure and hence all the configurations have to be externalized
- REST end points to transfer JSON messages
- Used Liquibase to manage the DB connection
- Eclipse link to manage the DB access and as a **Java Persistence Access** (**JPA**)

We will start by adding out the dependencies, as can be seen in the following example:

```
<dependency>
    <groupId>org.springframework.boot</groupId>
    <artifactId>spring-boot-starter-web</artifactId>
</dependency>

<dependency>
    <groupId>org.springframework</groupId>
    <artifactId>spring-core</artifactId>
    <version>4.3.7.RELEASE</version>
</dependency>

<dependency>
    <groupId>org.eclipse.persistence</groupId>
    <artifactId>eclipselink</artifactId>
    <version>2.5.0</version>
</dependency>

<dependency>
    <groupId>org.liquibase</groupId>
    <artifactId>liquibase-core</artifactId>
    <version>3.4.0</version>
</dependency>
```

- The `Domain` model is in the directory `iiot-sample-domain` folder.
- The `Alerts` model is given in the following example. It is wired to the `Alerts` table using JPA annotation. `@Table` points to the `Alerts` table and `@column` identifies the mapping of the Java Bean field to the table field.
- We are also using `lombok` `@slf4j` to add getters and setters boilerplate code to the bean, as follows:

```
@Entity
@EntityListeners({AuditContext.class})
@Data
@Table(name = "Alerts")
@Cacheable(value=false)
@Slf4j
public class Alert implements Serializable {
    @Id
    @Column(name = "ID", nullable=false)
    @GeneratedValue(strategy = GenerationType.IDENTITY)
    @JsonProperty(access = JsonProperty.Access.WRITE_ONLY)
    private Long id;
```

```java
@JsonProperty
@Column(name = "alerts_uuid")
private String alertsUuid;

@Column(name = "severity")
private int severity;

@Column(name = "alert_name")
private String alertName;

@Column(name = "alert_info")
private String alertInfo;

@JsonProperty(access = JsonProperty.Access.WRITE_ONLY)
@Column(name = "created_by")
private String createdBy;

@JsonProperty(access = JsonProperty.Access.WRITE_ONLY)
@Column(name = "updated_by")
private String updatedBy;

@JsonProperty(access = JsonProperty.Access.WRITE_ONLY)
@Column(name = "tenant_uuid")
private String tenantUuid;
```

- Persistence configuration provides the details of the persistence storage. The types of persistence engine we are using, such as Eclipselink, and detailed in the following example:

```xml
<persistence xmlns="http://java.sun.com/xml/ns/persistence"
        xmlns:xsi="http://www.w3.org/2001/XMLSchema-instance"
version="2.0"
xsi:schemaLocation="http://java.sun.com/xml/ns/persistence
http://java.sun.com/xml/ns/persistence/persistence_2_0.xsd">
    <persistence-unit name="iiotSamplePersistentUnit"
                transaction-type="RESOURCE_LOCAL">

        <description>Persistence Unit</description>
<provider>org.eclipse.persistence.jpa.PersistenceProvider</provider
>
        <mapping-file>META-INF/custom-orm.xml</mapping-file>

        <exclude-unlisted-classes>false</exclude-unlisted-classes>

        <properties>
            <property name="eclipselink.logging.level" value="FINE"/>
            <property name="eclipselink.logging.level.sql"
value="INFO"/>
```

```
        <property name="eclipselink.weaving" value="static"/>
        <property name="eclipselink.profiler"
value="QueryMonitor"/> <!-- probably disable this in prod -->
        <property name="eclipselink.jdbc.native-sql"
value="true"/>
        <property name="javax.persistence.query.timeout"
value="10000"/>
      </properties>
  </persistence-unit>
</persistence>
```

- We will use the env property only when running locally. In a cloud deployment, we will use the manifest.yml to bind to appropriate PostgreSQL instances at cloud, but the code does not need to change to support various environments.
- Liquibase configuration and DDL scripts are given in the following example. We are reading from an env property file and Spring automatically binds such configurations as the driver and credentials without hardcoding one of the 12-factor concepts we discussed previously:

```
@Configuration
public class LiquibaseConfiguration {
    private final DataSource dataSource;
    @Value("${spring.datasource.driver-class-
name:org.postgresql.Driver}")
    private String dataSourceDriverClassName;

    @Value("${vcap.services.${iiot_sample_postgres_name:iiot-
sample-postgres}.credentials.uri}")
    private String dataSourceUrl;

    @Value("${vcap.services.${iiot_sample_postgres_name:iiot-
sample-postgres}.credentials.username}")
    private String dataSourceUsername;

    @Value("${vcap.services.${iiot_sample_postgres_name:iiot-
sample-postgres}.credentials.password}")
    private String dataSourcePassword;
    @Autowired
    public LiquibaseConfiguration(DataSource dataSource){
        this.dataSource = dataSource;

    }

    @Bean
    public SpringLiquibase liquibase(TenantDataSourceConfig
tenantDataSourceConfig) {
        SmarterSpringLiquibase liquibase = new
```

```
SmarterSpringLiquibase(tenantDataSourceConfig);
        liquibase.setChangeLog("classpath:db/changelog.xml");
        liquibase.setDataSource(dataSource);
        liquibase.setDefaultSchema("iiot-sample");
        liquibase.setDropFirst(false);
        liquibase.setShouldRun(true);
        return liquibase;
    }
}
```

- DDL scripts are for Liquibase. All of the DB scripts are saved in the resources/db directory as follows:

```
CREATE TABLE alerts
(
  id bigserial NOT NULL,
  alerts_uuid text NOT NULL,
  severity integer,
  alert_name text,
  alert_info text,
  created_by text NOT NULL,
  created_date timestamp with time zone NOT NULL DEFAULT now(),
  updated_by text,
  updated_date timestamp with time zone,
  tenant_uuid text NOT NULL,
  CONSTRAINT alerts_pkey PRIMARY KEY (id)
);


CREATE UNIQUE INDEX ALERTS_TENANT_IDX ON Alerts(alerts_uuid,
tenant_uuid);
```

- Cloud applications should be multi-tenant and hence we added a tenant_uuid column. For now, we will use the default tenant but we can change it at any time by sending the tenant identifier as part of the header.
- We saw the DB layer, domain objects now we will move on to the repository layer, which we will leverage JPA heavily; AlertsRepository.java is given. It has two calls to get the list of alerts given a tenant and find an alert given a UUID. I have also used pageable to get the paginated list of alerts, as can be seen in the following example:

```
public interface AlertsRepository extends CrudRepository<Alert,
Long> {
    Alert findByAlertsUuidAndTenantUuid(String alertsUuid, String
tenantUuid);
    Page<Alert> findByTenantUuid(String tenantUuid,Pageable
```

```
pageable);
    }
```

- We will now look at IioTController which exposes the REST APIs to the outside world. This has two APIs, CreateAlert and GetAlertList. Creating the alert is done though the WebSocket controller, but we can leverage the same code here to add a RestEnd point for other clients who are not using the WebSockets:

```
@RestController
@RequestMapping("/v1/iiotsample")
@Slf4j
public class IiotController {
    private static final Logger logger =
LoggerFactory.getLogger(IiotController.class);
    private final IiotService iiotService;

    @Autowired
    private TenantUtil tenantUtil;

    @Autowired
    public IiotController(IiotService iiotService) {
        this.iiotService = iiotService;
    }


    @RequestMapping(value = "/alerts", method = RequestMethod.POST,
produces = "application/json", consumes = "application/json")
    public  ResponseEntity<Page<Alert>> getListofAlerts(
            @RequestHeader(value="Authorization",required=false)
String authorization,
            @RequestHeader(value="referer", required = false)
String referer, HttpServletRequest request) {

        logger.error("referer {}", referer);
        StopWatch stopWatch = new StopWatch("getList of Alerts");
        Credentials credentials = new Credentials(authorization,
tenantUtil.getTenantUuid());
        credentials.setReferer(referer);
        Page<Alert> listofAlerts =
iiotService.getAlerts(tenantUtil.getTenantUuid(),stopWatch);
        logger.info("{}", new StopWatchUtil(stopWatch));
        return new ResponseEntity<>(listofAlerts, HttpStatus.OK);
    }
```

```
        @RequestMapping(value = "/alert", method = RequestMethod.POST,
produces = "application/json", consumes = "application/json")
    public  ResponseEntity<Alert> getAlert(
            @RequestBody Alert alert,
            @RequestHeader(value="Authorization",required=false)
String authorization,
            @RequestHeader(value="referer", required = false)
String referer, HttpServletRequest request) {

        logger.error("referer {}", referer);
        StopWatch stopWatch = new StopWatch("Create Alert");
        Credentials credentials = new Credentials(authorization,
tenantUtil.getTenantUuid());
        credentials.setReferer(referer);
        Alert createdAlert =
iiotService.createAlerts(alert,credentials,stopWatch);
        logger.info("{}", new StopWatchUtil(stopWatch));
        return new ResponseEntity<>(createdAlert,
HttpStatus.CREATED);
    }
}
```

- To test this application, I have created a simple Postman collection. Please do install Postman which is a chrome plugin and import the `iiot-postman` collection
- Run the application in server mode. This should launch the server application as follows:

  `./run_app_dev.sh`

- Create alert and then get the list of alerts to see if the alert is created using the Postman collections.

 Import the file `iiot-cloud-alert-service.postman_collection` (`https://github.com/tjayant/iiot-book-samples/blob/master/iiot-cloud-service/iiot-cloud-alert-service.postman_collection`) file to the Postman tool.

- Issue the `createAlert` operation.
- Issue the `List` alert operation. You should see the list of alerts in the Postman window.
- Now let us run the system end to end.

- Run the `IIot-Edge-Gateway` in a new terminal, as can be seen in the following example:

```
node iiot-edge.js
```

- Issue the `List` alert operation. You should see the list of alerts in the Postman window.

- You should see four alerts created (as given in the following example) once you run the applications, which show that the application is running successfully.

- This wraps up our sample IIoT application and all of the code as follows:

```
{
    "content": [ {
        "alertsUuid": "AlertUUid2017-09-25 08:44:07",
        "severity": 1,
        "alertName": "Trempreture Alert",
        "alertInfo": "Trempreture Value:50"
    }, {
        "alertsUuid": "AlertUUid2017-09-25 09:33:55",
        "severity": 1,
        "alertName": "Trempreture Alert",
        "alertInfo": "Trempreture Value:150"
    }],
    "totalPages": 1,
    "totalElements": 3,
    "last": false,
    "size": 10,
    "number": 0,
    "numberOfElements": 10,
    "sort": null,
    "first": true
}
```

IIoT/IoT platforms overview

Now that we have seen the basic components of IIoT application architecture let us look at a few options to choose before building our IIoT solutions. Building a IIoT application from the ground up is possible and requires a large amount of setup, computer power and storage. For a typical IIoT application we need to set up various different programming language environments, database options, analytics frameworks, such as Spark or Storm, data ingestion pipelines and so on. It is possible to build the entire setup from the ground up, but we can also potentially use a robust IIoT platform if it meets our needs.

Utilizing a good IIoT platform will provide you with the needed infrastructure and guidelines to successfully build and launch your IIoT applications, and also it will shorten your go to market timeline. IIoT platforms free up the developer's time building infrastructure so that they can focus on the problem domain and solutions rather than on the infrastructure. In the following sections, I will go over a few of the interesting IIoT platforms that I find very promising.

Predix IIoT architecture

Predix is an IIoT platform which is targeted for industrial use cases. The primary components is Predix Machine. The Predix Machine is the Edge Gateway tier responsible for communicating with the industrial asset and the IoT Cloud tier, as well as acting as a Fog computing node running edge analytics. Predix cloud provides the cloud tier and provides a comprehensive set of services for building a robust cloud application. Predix services include security services for authentication, asset management, time series management, UI widgets, and many pre-built analytics:

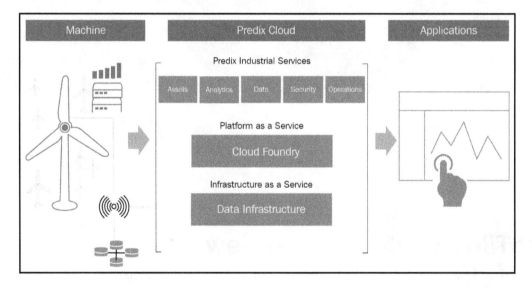

AWS IoT application architecture

AWS IoT solution architecture is given in the following diagram. I find this well integrated with other AWS services, I especially like the integration with Lambda, Kinesis, and S3. We will go into details of how to build an IoT solution on AWS in the best practices section:

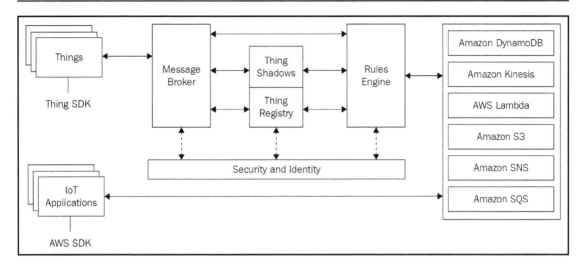

Google IoT application architecture

The Google Cloud IIoT PaaS platform provides an impressive array of features which are fully managed on Google Cloud. I find the platform interesting with its integration to the Google analytics platform. We will go into depth on how to build an IIoT solution on a Google platform in our best practices section:

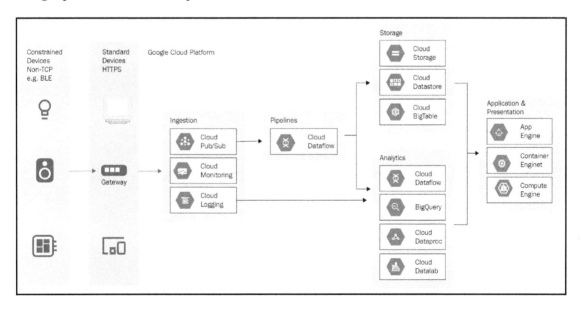

Summary

In this chapter the high-level architecture of IIoT applications. Furthermore, we developed our own sample application to illustrate the richness and depth of the IIoT application ecosystem. To summarize: IIoT consists of three key components namely device, the gateway, and the cloud. Devices, with their sensor, gets connected to gateway, which aggregates the data from sensors and typically applies some basic analytics. Gateways, using secure protocols such as MQTT or HTTPS/WebSockets, connect to the Cloud, which stores the data for further processing.

In addition, we covered in depth the details of each of the tiers, including a good overview of PaaS and a sample PaaS platform, Cloud Foundry, and the development model using microservices in cloud. We also covered a sample application covering all of the three tiers. Finally, we ended this chapter with an overview of a few of the top IoT platforms as a reference.

In the ensuing chapters, we will go in depth into each of these core components such as IoT Edge, data, and analytics.

IIoT Edge Development 3

This chapter describes the process of prototyping a device for beginners. We provide detailed instructions on how to assemble four different prototypes, and how to build and run simple IoT apps for the prototypes, together with sample source code. Finally, we explore the Predix services that can be used to store, analyze, and merge the sensor data from the prototypes.

In this chapter, you will learn about the following topics:

- Choosing hardware for prototyping
- The Open Systems Interconnection model and its layers
- Application-layer protocols—HTTP and WebSocket
- Industrial M2M protocols—Modbus and OPC UA
- Assembling a device for a prototype
- Preparing an SD card for a prototype
- Building and running simple IoT apps using the HTTP, WebSocket, Modbus, and OPC UA protocols
- Data management services in Predix

Hardware for prototypes

This section overviews the available variety of hardware that can be used for prototyping, and gives some tips on choosing the hardware and a data exchange protocol to ensure communication between the components of a prototype.

Variety and cost

One can find a variety of open source hardware for prototyping—**Arduino**, **Raspberry Pi**, **Orange Pi**, **LinkIt**, **BeagleBone**, and **Tessel**. Most of them are really cheap; you can buy an Orange Pi for just $33. The price usually depends on how powerful the board is and what interfaces it supports.

In addition to a board, it is possible to purchase a starter kit that usually costs about $70. It includes a few sensors, a small display, lamps, cables, and a breadboard for connecting it all without soldering. The price of a single sensor starts from $1.

Modifications

The most popular boards are Arduino and Raspberry Pi. Each of them has different modifications. If additional features are required, such as Wi-Fi, Bluetooth, USB, HDMI, or more powerful hardware, it is recommended to compare the modifications to find a board that fits one's exact needs.

Comparing options

All boards are quite small—about 8 cm wide, 5 cm high, and 2 cm thick (without a box). More powerful hardware will have bigger dimensions (for example, Intel NUC is 35 x 25 x 4 cm).

The most significant parameter is connectivity options, as not all the boards support Wi-Fi or Bluetooth. GSM, GPS, a camera, an FM module, and other features common for mobile phones are usually not available either, and one needs to buy them separately.

Another important parameter is the number of connectors for sensors. One needs to understand what sensors are required and whether they are compatible with a chosen board. The number of pins can be extended by connecting special additional boards to the existing ones.

Supported sensors

Some connectors on a board may support only analog sensors, while others are only digital.

Digital sensors output a discrete signal, meaning that there is a limited set of possible values for that signal. For example, temperature sensor DHT11 outputs an integer in a range between 0 and 50.

On the other hand, analog sensors output a continuous signal, meaning that there is an infinite number of possible values for that signal. For example, temperature sensor TMP36 can measure temperature from -50°C to 125°C including floating point values such as 11.9°C.

While converting one type of the signal to another is possible, it requires additional components and complicates the design.

Choosing hardware

When choosing hardware, one has to take into consideration its intended purpose, its size, the connectivity options, the architecture, and whether it can work with analog and digital sensors, as well as software requirements.

For prototyping, the best choice is Arduino or Raspberry Pi. However, for industrial IoT tasks, it would be better to use (mini) Field Agents by GE or Siemens solution.

In our case, we chose Raspberry Pi because it is an open source solution featuring versatile usage options. With support from a huge community, users get access to a wide variety of compatible extensions and software solutions that can help to speed up the development process.

Community

Strong communities have been formed around the most popular boards. They offer a range of software with drivers for the most widely used sensors. There are also some hardware initiatives that sell extensions for boards, enabling one to easily scale a device. Some of the major communities include the following:

- The Raspberry Pi Community (https://www.raspberrypi.org/community/)
- Arduino Forum (https://forum.arduino.cc/)

Following the links, you can find a lot of examples for different experience levels.

You can try to reproduce an existing project, following the provided detailed instructions. Another option is to create something unique. If all you have is an idea and you do not know how to implement it, consider discussing it at a specialized forum.

Choosing a data exchange protocol

You need to choose a proper data exchange protocol to establish efficient communication between the prototype components. The choice is largely dependent on the communication function for which you intend to use the protocol. The functions are described by the **Open Systems Interconnection** (**OSI**) model. Note that some protocols can cover multiple functions.

The OSI model divides a communication system into a number of abstraction layers (originally seven, as shown in the following table). Each layer is responsible for its specific jobs (functions), servicing the instances from an above layer and requesting services from an underlying one.

The following table shows seven layers of the OSI model:

Layer	Protocol data unit	Function
1. Physical	Bit	Transmitting and receiving of raw bit streams through a physical medium
2. Data link	Frame	Dependable transmission of data frames bounded by two nodes connected by a physical layer
3. Network	Packet	Configuring and managing a multi-node network, involving addressing, routing, and traffic control
4. Transport	Segment (TCP)/Datagram (UDP)	Dependable transmission of data segments bounded by points on a network, inclusive of parting, acknowledgement, and multiplexing
5. Session	Data	Governing communication period, that is, consecutive change of data in the form of multiple back-and-forth conveyance between two nodes
6. Presentation	Data	Transcription of data among a networking benefit and an exercise, including character encoding, data confining, and encryption/decryption
7. Application	Data	High-level APIs, together with resource sharing, remote file access

Unlike web applications, IoT devices send really small amounts of data, but frequently. This means that transfer of IoT data can be optimized on the application (P2P, AMQP), transport (Modbus, OPC UA), network (Zigbee), or even physical (NB-IoT) layers (see the preceding table).

Devices may be connected directly to a cloud, through a hub, or in a mesh network where they can communicate with each other.

The subsequent chapters cover the following four protocols in more detail—HTTP, WebSocket, Modbus, and OPC UA.

Application-level protocols – HTTP

In this section, we will try to build a simple IoT application for sending data from a DHT-12 temperature and humidity sensor to a receiver device, using a Raspberry Pi hub and the HTTP protocol:

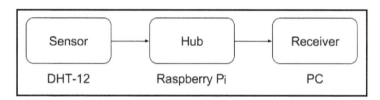

Data flow from a DHT-12 sensor to a receiver

Offering a variety of usage options, HTTP is one of most popular protocols on the web. Every time you open a website or run a mobile application, it is most likely the HTTP protocol you are using.

In the following table, you can find a more detailed description of the protocol to understand whether it is suitable for your needs:

Key	Value
Open source	Yes
OSI layer	Application
Data types	Text, HTML, script, style, font, JSON, XML, stream, binary
Limitations	Not suitable for large amounts of binary data
Possible operations	Send/receive data
Latency	Low
Usage	On-demand requests
Security	Yes
Compression	Yes

For building the application, we will need the following.

Required software:

- Node.js 6+ (`https://nodejs.org/en/download/`)
- The `request` package (`https://www.npmjs.com/package/request`)
- The `rpi-dht-sensor` package (`https://www.npmjs.com/package/rpi-dht-sensor`)
- Docker (`https://docs.docker.com/engine/installation/`)

Required hardware:

- Raspberry Pi 3 (model B)
- A power adapter (2A/5V)
- A microSD card (8 GB+) and an SD adapter
- A DHT-12 temperature and humidity sensor module
- A breadboard and a set of dupont cables
- An Ethernet cable for a wired network connection

Assembling a device

Before building an application, you need to connect a DHT-12 sensor to a Raspberry Pi via a breadboard.

Preparing an SD card

To prepare an SD card, follow the sequence of actions as described:

1. Download the latest Raspbian LITE image (available at `https://www.raspberrypi.org/downloads/raspbian/`).
2. Connect your SD card to a computer and use **Etcher** (`https://etcher.io/`) to flash the Raspbian `.img` file to the SD card.
3. Enable SSH:

```
cd /Volumes/boot
touch ssh
```

4. To enable Wi-Fi, create the `wpa_supplicant.conf` file with the following content:

```
network={
 ssid="YOUR_SSID"
 psk="YOUR_WIFI_PASSWORD"
}
```

To create a file in a Linux console, you can use the GNU nano editor. It is pre-installed in most Linux distributives. All you need is to run the `nano FILE_NAME` command and follow the displayed instructions.

5. Create the `/home/pi/sensor` folder.

6. Create the `/home/pi/sensor/package.json` file with the following content:

```
{
  "name": "sensor",
  "version": "1.0.0",
  "description": "",
  "main": "index.js",
  "scripts": {
    "start": "node index.js",
    "test": "echo \"Error: no test specified\" && exit 1"
  },
  "author": "",
  "license": "ISC",
  "dependencies": {
    "request": "^2.81.0",
    "rpi-dht-sensor": "^0.1.1"
  }
}
```

7. Create the `/home/pi/sensor/index.js` file, replacing REMOTE-SERVER-ADDRESS.com with a real value. The file should contain the following:

```
var rpiDhtSensor = require('rpi-dht-sensor');
var request = require('request');
var receiver = 'http://REMOTE-SERVER-ADDRESS.com:8080';
var dht = new rpiDhtSensor.DHT11(2);
function read () {
  var readout = dht.read();
  var data = {
    temperature: readout.temperature.toFixed(2),
    humidity: readout.humidity.toFixed(2)
  };
  console.log(data);
```

```
    data.device = 'raspberry';
    request.post({url: receiver, form: data}, function(err) {
      if(err) console.log('Failed to send to ' + receiver);
    });
    setTimeout(read, 1000);
  }
  read();
```

8. Create the `/home/pi/sensor/Dockerfile` file with the following content:

```
FROM hypriot/rpi-node:boron-onbuild
```

Running a sensor application on an RPi

To run a sensor application on an RPi, proceed as the following steps stipulate:

1. Insert an SD card into the RPi.
2. Connect an Ethernet cable and open an SSH connection.
3. Navigate to `/home/pi/sensor`.
4. Build an image and run a Docker container:

```
# Build an image from a Dockerfile
docker build -t http-sensor .
#
# Run container in foreground
docker run --privileged -it --rm --name http-sensor-container
http-sensor
#
# Run container in background
# docker run --privileged -d  --rm --name http-sensor-container
http-sensor
#
# Fetch the logs of a container
# docker logs -f http-sensor-container
#
# Stop running container
# docker stop http-sensor-container
```

```
●  ●  ●                    receiver — -bash --login — 83×19
  pi@raspberrypi: ~/sensor/dht_12 — ssh pi@...    ×  ...ects/iot-book/http/receiver — -bash --login    +
em:receiver melnikaite$ npm start

> receiver@1.0.0 start /Users/melnikaite/projects/iot-book/http/receiver
> node index.js

{ temperature: '26.00', humidity: '31.00', device: 'raspberry' }
{ temperature: '26.00', humidity: '31.00', device: 'raspberry' }
{ temperature: '26.00', humidity: '31.00', device: 'raspberry' }
{ temperature: '26.00', humidity: '31.00', device: 'raspberry' }
{ temperature: '26.00', humidity: '31.00', device: 'raspberry' }
{ temperature: '26.00', humidity: '32.00', device: 'raspberry' }
{ temperature: '26.00', humidity: '32.00', device: 'raspberry' }
{ temperature: '26.00', humidity: '35.00', device: 'raspberry' }
{ temperature: '26.00', humidity: '35.00', device: 'raspberry' }
{ temperature: '26.00', humidity: '38.00', device: 'raspberry' }
{ temperature: '26.00', humidity: '38.00', device: 'raspberry' }
{ temperature: '27.00', humidity: '38.00', device: 'raspberry' }
{ temperature: '27.00', humidity: '38.00', device: 'raspberry' }
{ temperature: '26.00', humidity: '42.00', device: 'raspberry' }
```

Console output when a sensor app is running

Running a receiver application on a PC

To run a receiver app on a PC, follow this sequence:

1. Create the `receiver` folder.
2. Create the `./receiver/package.json` file with the following content:

```
{
  "name": "receiver",
  "version": "1.0.0",
  "description": "",
  "main": "index.js",
  "scripts": {
    "start": "node index.js",
    "test": "echo \"Error: no test specified\" && exit 1"
  },
  "author": "",
  "license": "ISC"
}
```

3. Create the `./receiver/index.js` file with the following content:

```
var http = require('http');
 var querystring = require('querystring');

 http.createServer(function (req, res) {
   req.on('data', function (chunk) {
     var data = querystring.parse(chunk.toString());
     console.log(data);
   });
   req.on('end', function () {
     res.writeHead(200, 'OK', {'Content-Type': 'text/html'});
     res.end('Data received.')
   });
 }).listen(8080);
```

4. Create the `./receiver/Dockerfile` file with the following content:

```
FROM node:boron-onbuild
 EXPOSE 8080
```

5. Navigate to `./receiver`.

6. Build an image and run a Docker container:

```
# Build an image from a Dockerfile
docker build -t http-receiver .

# Run container in foreground
docker run -p 8080:8080 -it --rm --name http-receiver-container
http-receiver

# Run container in background
# docker run -p 8080:8080 -d  --rm --name http-receiver-container
http-receiver

# Fetch the logs of a container
# docker logs -f http-sensor-container

# Stop running container
# docker stop http-receiver-container
```

```
● ● ●  ⌂ melnikaite — pi@raspberrypi: ~/sensor/dht_12 — ssh pi@raspberrypi.altoros.corp...
 pi@raspberrypi: ~/sensor/dht_12 — ssh pi@...      ...ects/iot-book/http/receiver — -bash --login   +
[pi@raspberrypi:~/sensor/dht_12 $ sudo node index.js
{ temperature: '0.00', humidity: '0.00', device: 'raspberry' }
Failed to send to http://172.16.32.193:8080
{ temperature: '0.00', humidity: '0.00', device: 'raspberry' }
Failed to send to http://172.16.32.193:8080
{ temperature: '26.00', humidity: '31.00', device: 'raspberry' }
Failed to send to http://172.16.32.193:8080
{ temperature: '26.00', humidity: '31.00', device: 'raspberry' }
{ temperature: '26.00', humidity: '31.00', device: 'raspberry' }
{ temperature: '26.00', humidity: '31.00', device: 'raspberry' }
{ temperature: '26.00', humidity: '31.00', device: 'raspberry' }
{ temperature: '26.00', humidity: '31.00', device: 'raspberry' }
{ temperature: '26.00', humidity: '32.00', device: 'raspberry' }
{ temperature: '26.00', humidity: '32.00', device: 'raspberry' }
{ temperature: '26.00', humidity: '35.00', device: 'raspberry' }
{ temperature: '26.00', humidity: '35.00', device: 'raspberry' }
{ temperature: '26.00', humidity: '38.00', device: 'raspberry' }
{ temperature: '26.00', humidity: '38.00', device: 'raspberry' }
{ temperature: '27.00', humidity: '38.00', device: 'raspberry' }
```

Console output when a receiver application is running

Application-level protocols – WebSocket

In this section, we will try to build a simple IoT app for sending data from an XD-80 light sensor module to a receiver device, using a Raspberry Pi hub and the WebSocket protocol:

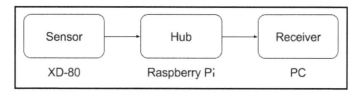

Data flow from an XD-80 sensor to a receiver device

WebSocket is most widely used in the case that one needs to enable fast transfer of real-time data. The protocol allows for two-way interaction between a client and a server, and for streaming multiple messages using the same TCP connection, which lowers the communications overhead.

In the following table, you can find a more detailed description of the protocol to understand whether it is suitable for your needs:

Key	Value
Open source	Yes
The OSI layer	Application
Data types	String
Limitations	Not suitable for large amounts of binary data
Possible operations	Send/receive data
Latency	Very low
Usage	Real-time communication
Security	Yes
Compression	Yes

Table 3: WebSocket protocol specifications

For building the application, we will need the following.

Required software:

- Node.js 6+ (https://nodejs.org/en/download/)
- RPIO (https://www.npmjs.com/package/rpio)
- WebSocket (https://www.npmjs.com/package/ws)
- Docker (https://docs.docker.com/engine/installation/)

Required hardware:

- Raspberry Pi 3 (model B)
- A power adapter (2A/5V)
- A microSD card (8 GB+) and an SD adapter
- A XD-80 light sensor module
- A breadboard and a set of dupont cables
- An Ethernet cable for a wired network connection

Assembling a device

Before building an application, you need to connect an XD-80 sensor to a Raspberry Pi via a breadboard.

Preparing an SD card

To prepare an SD card, follow the sequence of actions as described:

1. Download the latest Raspbian LITE image (available at `https://www.raspberrypi.org/downloads/raspbian/`).
2. Connect your SD card to a computer and use Etcher (`https://etcher.io/`) to flash the Raspbian `.img` file to the SD card.
3. Enable SSH using the following command:

```
cd /Volumes/boot
touch ssh
```

4. To enable Wi-Fi, create `wpa_supplicant.conf` with the following content:

```
network={
 ssid="YOUR_SSID"
 psk="YOUR_WIFI_PASSWORD"
}
```

 To create a file in a Linux console, you can use the GNU nano editor. It is pre-installed in most Linux distributives. All you need is to run the `nano FILE_NAME` command and follow the displayed instructions.

5. Create the `/home/pi/sensor` folder.
6. Create the `/home/pi/sensor/package.json` file with the following content:

```
{
  "name": "sensor",
  "version": "1.0.0",
  "description": "",
  "main": "index.js",
  "scripts": {
    "start": "node index.js",
    "test": "echo \"Error: no test specified\" && exit 1"
  },
  "author": "",
  "license": "ISC",
```

```
        "dependencies": {
          "rpio": "^0.9.16",
          "ws": "^2.3.1"
        }
      }
```

7. Create the `/home/pi/sensor/index.js` file with the following content, replacing REMOTE-SERVER-ADDRESS.com with a real value:

```
var WebSocket = require('ws');
var rpio = require('rpio');

var ws;
var receiver = 'ws://REMOTE-SERVER-ADDRESS.com:8080';
rpio.open(11, rpio.INPUT);

var establishConnection = function () {
  ws = new WebSocket(receiver);
  ws.on('close', establishConnection);
  ws.on('error', establishConnection);
};
establishConnection();

var sendStatus = function () {
  var status = rpio.read(11) === 0;
  console.log('light status: ' + status);

  var data = JSON.stringify({
    device: 'raspberry',
    timestamp: Date.now(),
    light: status
  });

  try { ws.send(data); }
  catch (e) { console.log('failed to send data to ' + receiver); }

  setTimeout(sendStatus, 1000);
};
sendStatus();
```

8. Create the `/home/pi/sensor/Dockerfile` file with the following content:

```
FROM hypriot/rpi-node:boron-onbuild
```

Running a sensor application on an RPi

To run a sensor application on an RPi, proceed as the following steps suggest:

1. Insert an SD card into the RPi.
2. Connect an Ethernet cable and open an SSH connection.
3. Navigate to /home/pi/sensor.
4. Build an image and run a Docker container:

```
# Build an image from a Dockerfile
docker build -t websocket-sensor .
#
# Run container in foreground
docker run --privileged -it --rm --name websocket-sensor-container
websocket-sensor
#
# Run container in background
# docker run --privileged -d  --rm --name websocket-sensor-
container websocket-sensor
#
# Fetch the logs of a container
# docker logs -f websocket-sensor-container
#
# Stop running container
# docker stop websocket-sensor-container
```

```
pi@raspberrypi:~ $ sudo node device4.1.js
light status: true
failed to send data to ws://172.16.32.193:8080
light status: true
failed to send data to ws://172.16.32.193:8080
light status: true
failed to send data to ws://172.16.32.193:8080
light status: true
light status: false
light status: false
light status: false
light status: true
light status: true
light status: true
light status: true
light status: true
light status: true
light status: true
light status: true
```

Console output when a sensor app is running

Running a receiver application on a PC

To run a receiver app on a PC, follow this sequence:

1. Create the `receiver` folder.
2. Create the `./receiver/package.json` file with the following content:

```
{
"name": "receiver",
"version": "1.0.0",
"description": "",
"main": "index.js",
"scripts": {
  "start": "node index.js",
  "test": "echo \"Error: no test specified\" && exit 1"
},
"author": "",
"license": "ISC",
"dependencies": {
  "ws": "^2.3.1"
}
}
```

3. Create the `./receiver/index.js` file with the following content:

```
const WebSocket = require('ws');

const wss = new WebSocket.Server({port: 8080}, function () {
 console.log('Websocket server started');
});

wss.on('connection', function connection(ws) {
 ws.on('message', function incoming(message) {
   console.log('received: ', message);
 });

 // Send message to connected client
 ws.send('hello, client');
});
```

4. Create the `./receiver/Dockerfile` file with the following content:

```
FROM node:boron-onbuild
EXPOSE 8080
```

5. Navigate to `./receiver`.

6. Build an image and run a Docker container:

```
# Build an image from a Dockerfile
docker build -t websocket-receiver

# Run container in foreground
docker run -p 8080:8080 -it --rm --name websocket-receiver-
container websocket-receiver

# Run container in background
# docker run -p 8080:8080 -d  --rm --name websocket-receiver-
container websocket-receiver

# Fetch the logs of a container
# docker logs -f websocket-sensor-container

# Stop running container
# docker stop websocket-receiver-container
```

The console output displays that the application is running:

```
● ● ●                    receiver — -bash --login — 80×20
pi@raspberrypi: ~ — ssh pi@raspberrypi...   ...book/websocket/receiver — -bash --login    +

> iot-book@1.0.0 start /Users/melnikaite/projects/iot-book/websocket/receiver
> node index.js

Websocket server started
received:   {"device":"raspberry","timestamp":1495626336926,"light":true}
received:   {"device":"raspberry","timestamp":1495626337936,"light":false}
received:   {"device":"raspberry","timestamp":1495626338940,"light":false}
received:   {"device":"raspberry","timestamp":1495626339941,"light":false}
received:   {"device":"raspberry","timestamp":1495626340944,"light":true}
received:   {"device":"raspberry","timestamp":1495626341946,"light":true}
received:   {"device":"raspberry","timestamp":1495626342948,"light":true}
received:   {"device":"raspberry","timestamp":1495626343950,"light":true}
received:   {"device":"raspberry","timestamp":1495626344953,"light":true}
received:   {"device":"raspberry","timestamp":1495626345955,"light":true}
received:   {"device":"raspberry","timestamp":1495626346957,"light":true}
received:   {"device":"raspberry","timestamp":1495626347959,"light":true}
received:   {"device":"raspberry","timestamp":1495626348961,"light":true}
^C
em:receiver melnikaite$ █
```

Console output when a receiver app is running

For the source code as shown in this example, go to `https://github.com/Altoros/iot-book/`.

Industrial M2M protocols – Modbus

In this section, we will try to build a simple IoT application for sending data from a sensor simulator module to a receiver device (a PC or a cloud), using a Raspberry Pi hub and the Modbus protocol:

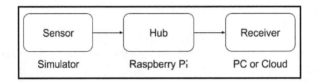

Data flow from a sensor simulator to a receiver device

For devices with limited hardware resources, it makes sense to use the Modbus protocol for serial communication. While simple, it has several open and proprietary implementations that vary in functionality.

Note that this protocol can be used on the transport layer, but, in our example, we are going to use Modbus TCP, working on the application level.

In the following table, you can find a more detailed description of the protocol to understand whether it is suitable for your needs:

Key	Value
Open source	Yes*
The OSI layer	Transport or an application
Data types	Integer, float, string, Boolean
Limitations	• No support for large binary objects • The master node regularly polls each device for data modifications* • Maximum 254 devices addressed on a single data link* • Only contiguous transmissions are allowed
Possible operations	Read and write registers and coils, diagnostics
Latency	High
Usage	SMS, GPRS, wireline, wireless, mesh communication
Security	No
Compression	No

Table 4: The Modbus protocol specifications

The values marked with * are not applicable to all implementations of the Modbus protocol.

For building the application, we will need the following:

- Required software:
    - Node.js 6+ (https://nodejs.org/en/download/)
    - PostgreSQL (https://www.postgresql.org/download/)
    - The Cloud Foundry CLI (https://github.com/cloudfoundry/cli#downloads)
    - Request (https://www.npmjs.com/package/request)
    - Modbus (https://www.npmjs.com/package/modbus)
    - Docker (https://docs.docker.com/engine/installation/)
- Required hardware:
    - Raspberry Pi 3 (model B)
    - A power adapter (2A/5V)
    - A microSD card (8 GB+) and an SD adapter
    - An Ethernet cable for a wired network connection

Preparing an SD card

To prepare an SD card, follow the sequence of actions as described:

1. Download the latest Raspbian LITE image (available at https://www.raspberrypi.org/downloads/raspbian/).
2. Connect your SD card to a computer and use **Etcher** (https://etcher.io/) to flash the Raspbian .img file to the SD card.
3. Enable SSH:

```
cd /Volumes/boot
touch ssh
```

4. To enable Wi-Fi, create `wpa_supplicant.conf` with the following content:

```
network={
 ssid="YOUR_SSID"
 psk="YOUR_WIFI_PASSWORD"
}
```

To create a file in a Linux console, you can use the GNU nano editor. It is pre-installed in most Linux distributives. All you need is to run the `nano FILE_NAME` command and follow the displayed instructions.

5. Create the `/home/pi/hub` folder.

6. Create the `/home/pi/hub/package.json` file with the following content:

```
{
  "name": "hub",
  "version": "1.0.0",
  "description": "",
  "main": "index.js",
  "scripts": {
    "start": "node index.js",
    "test": "echo \"Error: no test specified\" && exit 1"
  },
  "author": "",
  "license": "ISC",
  "dependencies": {
    "modbus": "0.0.16",
    "request": "^2.81.0"
  }
}
```

7. Create the `/home/pi/hub/index.js` file with the following content, replacing `REMOTE-SERVER-ADDRESS.com` and `REMOTE-SENSOR-ADDRESS` with real values:

```
var request = require('request');

var log = console.log;
//var mb = require('modbus').create(true); // enable debug output
var mb = require('modbus').create();

var sensor = 'REMOTE-SENSOR-ADDRESS';
var receiver = 'http://REMOTE-SERVER-ADDRESS.com:8080';

mb.onError(function (msg) {
  log('ERROR', msg);
});
```

```
// create master device
var ctx = mb.createMaster({

  // connection type and params
  con: mb.createConTcp(sensor, 1502),
  //con: mb.createConRtu(1, '/dev/ttyS1', 9600),

  // callback functions
  onConnect: function () {
    log('onConnect');
    log(ctx.getReg(2));
    ctx.setBit(1, false);

    //send to receiver
    var data = {
      device: 'sensor1',
      timestamp: Date.now(),
      reg2: ctx.getReg(2)
    };
    request.post({url: receiver, form: data}, function (err) {
      if (err) console.log('Failed to send to ' + receiver);
    });

    ctx.destroy();
  },
  onDestroy: function () {
    log('onDestroy');
  }
});
```

8. Create a `/home/pi/hub/Dockerfile` file with the following content:

```
FROM hypriot/rpi-node:boron-onbuild
RUN apt-get update && apt-get install -y libmodbus5
```

9. Create the `/home/pi/sensor` folder.

10. Create the `/home/pi/sensor/package.json` file with the following content:

```json
{
"name": "sensor",
"version": "1.0.0",
"description": "",
"main": "index.js",
"scripts": {
  "start": "node index.js",
  "test": "echo \"Error: no test specified\" && exit 1"
},
"author": "",
"license": "ISC",
"dependencies": {
  "modbus": "0.0.16"
}
}
```

11. Create the `/home/pi/sensor/index.js` file with the following content, replacing REMOTE-HUB-ADDRESS.com with a real value:

```js
var log = console.log;
var mb = require('modbus').create();

mb.onError(function (msg) {
 log('ERROR', msg);
});

// create device memory map
var data = mb.createData({ countReg: 5, countBit: 2 });
data.setReg(2, 321);
data.setBit(1, true);
data.dumpData(); // show memory map

// create slave device
var ctx = mb.createSlave({

 // connection type and params
 con: mb.createConTcp('REMOTE-HUB-ADDRESS.com', 1502),
 //con: mb.createConRtu(1, '/dev/ttyS0', 9600),

 // data map
 data: data,

 // callback functions
 onQuery: function () {
   log('onQuery');
   //ctx.dumpData();
```

```
      log(ctx.getBits(0, 2));
    },
   onDestroy: function () {
      log('onDestroy');
    }
  });

  // destroy device
  //setTimeout(function () {
  //
  ctx.destroy();
  //}, 5000);
```

12. Create the `/home/pi/sensor/Dockerfile` file with the following content:

```
FROM hypriot/rpi-node:boron-onbuild
RUN apt-get update && apt-get install -y libmodbus5
```

Running a hub application on an RPi

To run a hub application on an RPi, proceed as the following steps suggest:

1. Insert an SD card into the RPi.
2. Connect an Ethernet cable and open an SSH connection.
3. Navigate to `/home/pi/hub`.
4. Build an image and run a Docker container:

```
# Build an image from a Dockerfile
docker build -t modbus-hub .
#
# Run container in foreground
docker run --privileged -it --rm --name modbus-hub-container
modbus-hub
#
# Run container in background
# docker run --privileged -d  --rm --name modbus-hub-container
modbus-hub
#
# Fetch the logs of a container
# docker logs -f modbus-hub-container
#
# Stop running container
# docker stop modbus-hub-container
```

Console output when a hub app is running

Running a simulator application on an RPi

To run a simulator application, follow the sequence of actions as described here:

1. Open an SSH connection.
2. Navigate to `/home/pi/sensor`.
3. Build an image and run a Docker container:

```
# Build an image from a Dockerfile
docker build -t modbus-sensor .
#
# Run container in foreground
docker run -p 1502:1502 --privileged -it --rm --name modbus-sensor-container modbus-sensor
#
# Run container in background
# docker run -p 1502:1502 --privileged -d  --rm --name modbus-sensor-container modbus-sensor
#
# Fetch the logs of a container
# docker logs -f modbus-sensor-container
#
# Stop running container
# docker stop modbus-sensor-container
```

```
sensor — node • npm MANPATH=/Users/melnikaite/.nvm/versions/node/v6.9.4...

node • npm...ite/.rvm/bin        ...us/hub — -bash --login        node • npm...aite/.rvm/bin  ...  +

em:sensor melnikaite$ npm start

> sensor@1.0.0 start /Users/melnikaite/projects/iot-book/modbus/sensor
> node index.js

{ nb_bits: 2,
  nb_input_bits: 0,
  nb_input_registers: 0,
  nb_registers: 5,
  tab_bits: [ 0, 1 ],
  tab_input_bits: [],
  tab_input_registers: [],
  tab_registers: [ 0, 0, 321, 0, 0 ] }
onQuery
[ false, true ]
onQuery
[ false, false ]
onQuery
[ false, false ]
```

Console output when a simulator app is running

Running a receiver application on a PC

To run a receiver application on your PC, proceed as follows:

1. Install and launch a PostgreSQL container:

    ```
    docker run --rm --name postgres-container -e
    POSTGRES_PASSWORD=password -it -p 5433:5432 postgres
    docker exec -it postgres-container createdb -U postgres iot-book
    ```

2. Create the `receiver` folder.

3. Create the `./receiver/package.json` file with the following content:

    ```
    {
    "name": "receiver",
    "version": "1.0.0",
    "description": "",
    "main": "index.js",
    "scripts": {
      "start": "node index.js",
      "test": "echo \"Error: no test specified\" && exit 1"
    },
    "author": "",
    ```

```
      "license": "ISC",
      "dependencies": {
        "pg": "^6.2.3"
      }
    }
```

4. Create the `./receiver/index.js` file with the following content, replacing the database credentials with the correct values:

```
var http = require('http');
var querystring = require('querystring');
var Pool = require('pg').Pool;
var pool = new Pool({
 user: 'user',
 database: 'database',
 password: 'password',
 host: 'host',
 port: 5432
});

//ensure table exists in db
pool.query('CREATE TABLE IF NOT EXISTS "sensor-logs" (id serial NOT
NULL PRIMARY KEY, data json NOT NULL)', function (err, result) {
 if (err) console.log(err);
});

http.createServer(function (req, res) {
 req.on('data', function (chunk) {
   var data = querystring.parse(chunk.toString());
   console.log(data);

   //save in db
   pool.query('INSERT INTO "sensor-logs" (data) VALUES ($1)',
[data], function (err, result) {
     if (err) console.log(err);
   });
 });
 req.on('end', function () {
   res.writeHead(200, 'OK', {'Content-Type': 'text/html'});
   res.end('ok')
 });
}).listen(process.env.PORT || 8080);
```

5. Create the `./receiver/Dockerfile` file with the following content:

```
FROM node:boron-onbuild
EXPOSE 8080
```

6. Navigate to `./receiver`.

7. Build an image and run a Docker container:

```
# Build an image from a Dockerfile
docker build -t modbus-receiver .

# Run container in foreground
docker run -p 8080:8080 -it --rm --name modbus-receiver-container
modbus-receiver

# Run container in background
# docker run -p 8080:8080 -d  --rm --name modbus-receiver-container
modbus-receiver

# Fetch the logs of a container
# docker logs -f modbus-sensor-container

# Stop running container
# docker stop modbus-receiver-container
```

```
receiver — node · npm MANPATH=/Users/melnikaite/.nvm/versions/node/v6.9....

   node · npm...ite/.rvm/bin        ...us/hub — -bash --login      ● node · npm...aite/.rvm/bin      +
em:receiver melnikaite$ npm start

> receiver@1.0.0 start /Users/melnikaite/projects/iot-book/modbus/receiver
> node index.js

{ device: 'sensor1', timestamp: '1495713113784', reg2: '321' }
```

Console output when a receiver app is running

Running a receiver application in Predix

To run a receiver app in Predix, follow the sequence shown here:

1. Install and connect the Cloud Foundry CLI to your Predix account.
2. Create a PostgreSQL service and obtain the credentials.
3. Create the `./receiver/manifest.yml` file with the following content:

   ```
   applications:
   -
   name: receiver
   memory: 128M
   random-route: true
   ```

4. Replace the database credentials in `./receiver/index.js`.
5. Deploy to the cloud:

   ```
   cf push
   ```

6. Change the REMOTE-SERVER-ADDRESS in the hub application on the RPi to the newly deployed receiver.

 For the source code as shown in this example, go to `https://github.com/Altoros/iot-book/`.

Industrial M2M protocols – OPC UA

In this section, we will try to build a simple IoT app for sending data from a sensor simulator module to a receiver device (a PC or a cloud), using a Raspberry Pi hub and the OPC UA protocol:

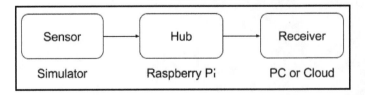

Data flow from a sensor simulator to a receiver device

The OPC UA protocol is similar to Modbus, but works with more data types, and has no serious limitations, while providing for security, compression, and low latency.

The protocol was developed by the OPC Foundation as an industrial machine-to-machine communication protocol. OPC UA is an improved version of the **Open Platform Communications** (**OPC**) protocol, with one of the major changes being that the new protocol is available free of charge without any restrictions.

In the following table, you can find a more detailed description of the protocol to understand whether it is suitable for your needs:

Key	Value
Open source	Yes
The OSI layer	Transport or application
Data types	Integer, float, string, Boolean, date, time, and so on
Limitations	Not suitable for a complex architecture
Possible operations	Read/write/monitor/query variables
Latency	Low
Usage	IIoT
Security	Yes
Compression	Yes

Table 5: OPC UA protocol specifications

For building the application, we will need the following:

- Required software:
  - Node.js 6+ (https://nodejs.org/en/download/)
  - PostgreSQL (https://www.postgresql.org/download/)
  - The Cloud Foundry CLI (https://github.com/cloudfoundry/cli#downloads)
  - Request (https://www.npmjs.com/package/request)
  - NodeOPCUA (https://www.npmjs.com/package/node-opcua)
  - Async (https://www.npmjs.com/package/async)
  - Docker (https://docs.docker.com/engine/installation/)

- Required hardware:
  - Raspberry Pi 3 (model B)
  - A power adapter (2A/5V)
  - A microSD card (8 GB+) and an SD adapter
  - Ethernet cable for a wired network connection

Preparing an SD card

To prepare an SD card, follow the sequence of actions as described:

1. Download the latest Raspbian LITE image (available at `https://www.raspberrypi.org/downloads/raspbian/`).
2. Connect your SD card to a computer and use Etcher (`https://etcher.io/`) to flash the Raspbian `.img` file to the SD card.
3. Enable SSH:

```
cd /Volumes/boot
touch ssh
```

4. To enable Wi-Fi, create `wpa_supplicant.conf` with the following content:

```
network={
 ssid="YOUR_SSID"
 psk="YOUR_WIFI_PASSWORD"
}
```

 To create a file in a Linux console, you can use the GNU nano editor. It is pre-installed in most Linux distributives. All you need is to run the `nano FILE_NAME` command and follow the displayed instructions.

5. Create the `/home/pi/hub` folder.
6. Create the `/home/pi/hub/package.json` file with the following content:

```
{
  "name": "hub",
  "version": "1.0.0",
  "description": "",
  "main": "index.js",
  "scripts": {
    "start": "node index.js",
    "test": "echo \"Error: no test specified\" && exit 1"
  },
```

```
  "author": "",
  "license": "ISC",
  "dependencies": {
    "async": "^2.4.0",
    "node-opcua": "0.0.64",
    "request": "^2.81.0"
  }
}
```

7. Create the /home/pi/hub/index.js file with the following content, replacing REMOTE-SERVER-ADDRESS.com and REMOTE-SENSOR-ADDRESS with real values:

```
var opcua = require("node-opcua");
var async = require("async");
var request = require("request");

var session, subscription;
var client = new opcua.OPCUAClient();
var sensor = "opc.tcp://REMOTE-SENSOR-
ADDRESS:4334/UA/resourcePath";
var receiver = "http://REMOTE-SERVER-ADDRESS.com:8080";

async.series(
  [
    // establishing connection
    function (cb) {
      client.connect(sensor, function (err) {
        if (err) {
          console.log("Connection to " + sensor + "failed");
        } else {
          console.log("Connection successful");
        }
        cb(err);
      });
    },

    // start session
    function (cb) {
      client.createSession(function (err, res) {
        if (!err) session = res;
        cb(err);
      });
    },

    // read value
    function (cb) {
      session.readVariableValue("ns=1;s=Variable1", function (err,
dataValue) {
```

```
        if (!err) console.log("Variable1 = ",
dataValue.value.value);
        cb(err);
      });
    },

    // write value
    function (cb) {
      session.writeSingleNode("ns=1;s=Variable1", new
opcua.Variant({
        dataType: opcua.DataType.Double,
        value: 100
      }), function (err) {
        cb(err);
      });
    },

    // subscribe to changes
    function (cb) {
      subscription = new opcua.ClientSubscription(session, {
        maxNotificationsPerPublish: 5,
        priority: 5,
        publishingEnabled: true,
        requestedLifetimeCount: 5,
        requestedMaxKeepAliveCount: 3,
        requestedPublishingInterval: 500,
      });

      subscription.on("started", function () {
        console.log("subscription id: ",
subscription.subscriptionId);
      }).on("terminated", function () {
        cb();
      });

      setTimeout(function () {
        subscription.terminate();
      }, 5000);

      // install monitored item
      var monitor = subscription.monitor({
          attributeId: opcua.AttributeIds.Value,
          nodeId: opcua.resolveNodeId("ns=1;s=Variable1"),
        },
        {
          discardOldest: true,
          samplingInterval: 50,
          queueSize: 5,
```

```
        },
        opcua.read_service.TimestampsToReturn.Both
      );

      monitor.on("changed", function (dataValue) {
        console.log("Variable1 = ", dataValue.value.value);

        // send to receiver
        var data = {
          device: "sensor1",
          timestamp: Date.now(),
          Variable1: dataValue.value.value
        };
        request.post({url: receiver, form: data}, function (err) {
          if (err) console.log("Failed to send " +
JSON.stringify(data) + " to " + receiver);
        });
      });
    },

    // close session
    function (cb) {
      session.close(function (err) {
        if (err) console.log("Failed to close session");
        cb();
      });
    }
  ],

  function (err) {
    if (err) {
      console.log("Failed with error:", err);
    } else {
      console.log("Successfully finished");
    }
    client.disconnect(function () {
    });
  }
);
```

8. Create the `/home/pi/hub/Dockerfile` file with the following content:

```
FROM hypriot/rpi-node:boron-onbuild
```

9. Create the `/home/pi/sensor` folder.

10. Create the `/home/pi/sensor/package.json` file with the following content:

```json
{
"name": "sensor",
"version": "1.0.0",
"description": "",
"main": "index.js",
"scripts": {
  "start": "node index.js",
  "test": "echo \"Error: no test specified\" && exit 1"
},
"author": "",
"license": "ISC",
"dependencies": {
  "node-opcua": "0.0.64"
}
}
```

11. Create the `/home/pi/sensor/index.js` file with the following content:

```js
var opcua = require("node-opcua");
var min = 1;
var max = 100;

var host = new opcua.OPCUAServer({
  buildInfo: {
    buildDate: new Date(2018, 8, 8),
    buildNumber: "1234",
    productName: "productName",
  },
  port: 4334,
  resourcePath: "UA/resourcePath",
});

host.initialize(function () {
  var space = host.engine.addressSpace;

  var componentOf = space.addObject({
    browseName: "browseName",
    organizedBy: space.rootFolder.objects,
  });

  var variable1 = 0;

  // generate new value
  setInterval(function () {
    variable1 = Math.floor(max - Math.random() * (max - min));
```

```
  }, 500);

  space.addVariable({
    browseName: "browseName",
    componentOf: componentOf,
    dataType: "Double",
    nodeId: "ns=1;s=Variable1", // a string nodeID
    value: {
      get: function () {
        return new opcua.Variant({dataType: opcua.DataType.Double,
value: variable1});
      },
      set: function (variant) {
        variable1 = parseFloat(variant.value);
        return opcua.StatusCodes.Good;
      }
    }
  });

  host.start(function () {
    var endpoint =
host.endpoints[0].endpointDescriptions()[0].endpointUrl;
    console.log("Endpoint: ", endpoint);
  });
});
```

12. Configure the `min` and `max` values at the beginning of the
    `/home/pi/sensor/index.js` file.

13. Create the `/home/pi/sensor/Dockerfile` file with the following content:

```
FROM hypriot/rpi-node:boron-onbuild
```

Running a simulator application on an RPi

To run a simulator on an RPi, proceed as the following steps suggest:

1. Insert an SD card into the RPi.
2. Connect an Ethernet cable and open an SSH connection.
3. Navigate to `/home/pi/sensor`.

4. Build an image and run a Docker container:

```
# Build an image from a Dockerfile
docker build -t opcua-sensor .
#
# Run container in foreground
docker run -p 4334:4334 --privileged -it --rm --name opcua-sensor-
container opcua-sensor
#
# Run container in background
# docker run -p 4334:4334 --privileged -d  --rm --name opcua-
sensor-container opcua-sensor
#
# Fetch the logs of a container
# docker logs -f opcua-sensor-container
#
# Stop running container
# docker stop opcua-sensor-container
```

```
[em:sensor          ]$ npm start

> sensor@1.0.0 start /Users/                /projects/iot-book/opcua/sensor
> node index.js

Endpoint:  opc.tcp://                   :4334/UA/resourcePath
```

Console output when a simulator app is running

Running a receiver application on a PC

To run a receiver app on a PC, follow the sequence described here:

1. Install and launch a PostgreSQL container:

```
docker run --rm --name postgres-container -e
POSTGRES_PASSWORD=password -it -p 5433:5432 postgres

docker exec -it postgres-container createdb -U postgres iot-book
```

2. Create the `receiver` folder.

3. Create the `./receiver/package.json` file with the following content:

```
{
"name": "receiver",
"version": "1.0.0",
"description": "",
"main": "index.js",
"scripts": {
  "start": "node index.js",
  "test": "echo \"Error: no test specified\" && exit 1"
},
"author": "",
"license": "ISC",
"dependencies": {
  "pg": "^6.2.3"
}
}
```

4. Create the `./receiver/index.js` file with the following content, replacing the database credentials with the correct values:

```
var restify = require('restify');
var server = restify.createServer({name: 'MyApp'});
server.use(restify.bodyParser());

var Pool = require('pg').Pool;
var pool = new Pool({
  database: 'iot-book',
  host: 'host',
  password: 'password',
  port: 5433,
  user: 'postgres',
});

//ensure table exists in db
pool.query('CREATE TABLE IF NOT EXISTS "sensor-logs" (id serial NOT
NULL PRIMARY KEY, data json NOT NULL)', function (err, result) {
  if (err) console.log(err);
});

server.post('/', function create(req, res, next) {
  console.log(req.params);

  //save in db
  pool.query('INSERT INTO "sensor-logs" (data) VALUES ($1)',
[req.params], function (err, result) {
    if (err) console.log(err);
    res.send(201, result);
```

```
    });

    return next();
  });

  server.get('/stats', function search(req, res, next) {
    pool.query('SELECT AVG("Variable1"), MAX("Variable1"),
MIN("Variable1"), COUNT(*), SUM("Variable1") FROM (SELECT
(data->>\'Variable1\')::int "Variable1" FROM "sensor-logs" ORDER BY
id DESC LIMIT 10) data', function (err, result) {
      if (err) console.log(err);
      res.send(result.rows);
    });
    return next();
  });

  server.listen(process.env.PORT || 8080);
```

5. Create the `./receiver/Dockerfile` file with the following content:

```
FROM node:boron-onbuild
EXPOSE 8080
```

6. Build an image and run a Docker container:

```
# Build an image from a Dockerfile
docker build -t opcua-receiver .

# Run container in foreground
docker run -p 8080:8080 -it --rm --name opcua-receiver-container
opcua-receiver

# Run container in background
# docker run -p 8080:8080 -d  --rm --name opcua-receiver-container
opcua-receiver

# Fetch the logs of a container
# docker logs -f opcua-sensor-container

# Stop running container
# docker stop opcua-receiver-container
```

```
em:receiver            $ npm start

> receiver@1.0.0 start /Users/                /projects/iot-book/opcua/receiver
> node index.js

{ device: 'sensor1',
  timestamp: '1533900869892',
  Variable1: '100' }
{ device: 'sensor1',
  timestamp: '1533900870389',
  Variable1: '37' }
{ device: 'sensor1',
  timestamp: '1533900870891',
  Variable1: '55' }
{ device: 'sensor1',
  timestamp: '1533900870891',
  Variable1: '76' }
{ device: 'sensor1',
  timestamp: '1533900871894',
  Variable1: '97' }
{ device: 'sensor1',
  timestamp: '1533900872396',
  Variable1: '92' }
{ device: 'sensor1',
  timestamp: '1533900872396',
  Variable1: '85' }
{ device: 'sensor1',
  timestamp: '1533900873401',
  Variable1: '60' }
{ device: 'sensor1',
  timestamp: '1533900873401',
  Variable1: '17' }
```

Console output when a receiver app is running

Running a receiver application in Predix

To run a receiver app in Predix, follow this sequence:

1. Install and connect the Cloud Foundry CLI to your Predix account.
2. Create a PostgreSQL service and obtain the credentials.

3. Create the `./receiver/manifest.yml` file with the following content:

```
applications:
-
name: receiver
memory: 128M
random-route: true
```

4. Replace the database credentials in `./receiver/index.js`.

5. Deploy to the cloud:

```
cf push
```

6. Change the REMOTE-SERVER-ADDRESS in the hub application on the RPi to the newly deployed receiver.

Running a hub application on an RPi

To run a hub application on an RPi, proceed as follows:

1. Open an SSH connection.
2. Navigate to `/home/pi/hub`.
3. Build an image and run a Docker container:

```
# Build an image from a Dockerfile
docker build -t opcua-hub .
#
# Run container in foreground
docker run --privileged -it --rm --name opcua-hub-container opcua-hub
#
# Run container in background
# docker run --privileged -d  --rm --name opcua-hub-container opcua-hub
#
# Fetch the logs of a container
# docker logs -f opcua-hub-container
#
# Stop running container
# docker stop opcua-hub-container
```

```
[em:hub            $ npm start

> hub@1.0.0 start /Users/            /projects/iot-book/opcua/hub
> node index.js

Connection successful
Variable1 =   24
subscription id:   398664
Variable1 =   100
Variable1 =   37
Variable1 =   55
Variable1 =   76
Variable1 =   97
Variable1 =   92
Variable1 =   85
Variable1 =   60
Variable1 =   17
Successfully finished
em:hub            $
```

Console output when a hub app is running

Getting statistics

To get statistics on sensor data, one needs to open a browser and navigate to
`http://RECEIVER-ADDRESS:8080/stats` or `https://RECEIVER-IN-PREDIX/stats`:

```
[
  {
    "avg": "64.3",
    "max":100,
    "min":17,
    "count":"10",
    "sum":"643"
  }
]
```

 For the source code as shown in this example, go to `https://github.com/Altoros/iot-book/`.

Data management options in Predix

To ensure storing, analyzing, and merging the sensor data we have collected in our Raspberry Pi hubs, we need to use specialized data management solutions. Predix offers a good selection of services for this purpose, as listed here:

- Asset
- Event Hub
- Time Series
- Database as a Service
- Blobstore
- Message Queue (AMQP)
- Key-Value Store:

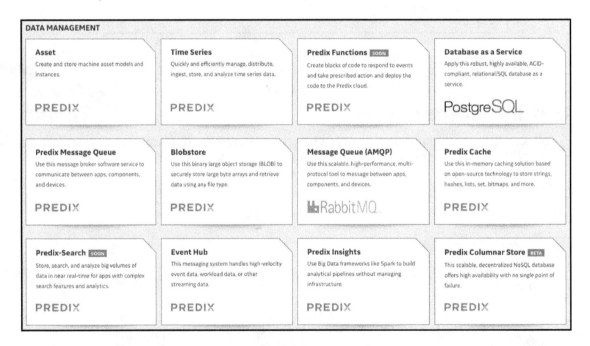

Data management services in the Predix catalog

You can select any of the services, depending on your data type and the operations you need to perform. In particular, for our application that handles time series data, we can use the Time Series storage.

The following subsections describe the data management services offered by Predix (`https://www.predix.io/catalog/services/`) in more detail, highlighting their features and the purposes for which they are usually used.

Asset

The Asset service comprises a REST API layer, a query engine, and a graph database. It allows for creating, updating, and storing asset models describing asset properties and relations between assets, and other elements, in a model. Having created an asset model with the service, you can add your instance data to it in the JSON format.

The service comprises the following features:

- Enhanced security for safe data management
- Advanced analytics based on time series asset data collected from sensors
- Audit history, enabling users to track the operations of creating, updating, and deleting assets and modeling elements
- A scripting engine to define domain-specific business logic for calls to the service
- Data in the JSON format aggregated via a REST API or generated via a user interface

The service can help to enhance performance asset by tracking their changes throughout the life cycle. Based on the audit history, an asset holder can identify components that need to be replaced. Then, the specifications included in the asset model as instance data can be used to choose a proper replacement or an acceptable alternative.

Event Hub

Event Hub is a service for publishing and subscribing. It retrieves data from a variety of sources and streams it to a cloud (the Predix platform) for further processing. The service can also be used to enable communication between applications, devices, and so on.

Event Hub has the following features:

- It is payload-agnostic, enabling users to publish any data and make it available to any subscribers
- It allows for scaling up from a single to multiple subscribers
- It can easily manage large-scale applications for asynchronous message processing
- User authentication and authorization is via UAA or any other OAuth 2.0 provider

Time series

This service is used to collect, store, and analyze time series data from a range of data points (for example, sensors) at preset intervals over a period of time. Each time series dataset includes relevant details about the associated data point (for instance, unit or site).

The service includes the following features:

- Data indexing
- Precision of data up to milliseconds
- Data can be accessed from anywhere, using an HTTP connection
- Horizontal scalability

Database as a Service

This service is actually a relational database management system (PostgreSQL) used for secure storage and retrieval of web app data. It supports a variety of data types (for example, XML, JSON, arrays, geometry, and so on) and can easily cope with managing data from both single-machine apps and applications with many concurrent users.

Database as a Service ensures management of database instances, automatically creating their synchronous replicas in case of a crash. This ensures high availability of stored relational data without user intervention or the need to change the configuration of an app.

The service offers the following features:

- High availability and fault tolerance with automatic **point-in-time recovery (PITR)** to any moment within the preceding seven-day period
- Enhanced data security due to encryption at rest
- Automatically applied patches and updates to address data loss and security issues

Blobstore

The blobstore enables users to upload, store, and retrieve large amounts of binary data-blobs—from any type of sources via HTTP requests. The blobstore can work with data objects (for example, images, video files, and so on) that are larger than those acceptable for Database as a Service.

Some of its major features are the following:

- Possibility to upload objects of up to 5 TB in size, divided in multiple parts
- Secure data transfer via SSL
- Multi-tenancy support
- Easy-to-use and S3-compatible web APIs

Message Queue

Message Queue (AMQP) is a message broker software service designed to enable communication between applications, components, and devices.

The service uses the **Advanced Message Queuing Protocol (AMQP)**, while the **Open Telecom Platform (OTP)** framework ensures clustering and failover capabilities.

Predix cache

This service provides a key-value cache and a storage database. Keys can contain strings, hashes, lists, sets, sorted sets, bitmaps, and the `HyperLogLog` algorithms.

Predix Functions

The Predix Functions service lets you deploy blocks of code to the Predix cloud that can be configured to trigger or respond to events. A code block can be anything from an analytic function to a transformation or a model evaluation.

The code block takes the event information as input, and performs predefined actions in response to those events. Functions can be written in many different languages, depending on the needs of the problem domain and the skill set of the function author.

Predix Message Queue

Predix Message Queue allows reliable delivery of messages by processing messages using an exchange. The service is based on open source RabbitMQ, and supports only Advanced Message Queuing Protocol (AMQP). Predix Message Queue provides persistent, reliable, and durable queuing options.

Predix-Search

Predix-Search, powered by Elasticsearch, can store and index many types of documents, retrieve documents through search keywords, and pull results into a reporting dashboard. Elasticsearch is a highly distributed, readily scalable, open source, full-text search and analytics engine. The service lets you store, search, and analyze big volumes of data quickly and in near real time. Elasticsearch is an underlying technology that powers apps with complex search features and requirements.

Predix Insights

Predix Insights is a big data processing and analytics service. It provides native Apache Spark support and orchestration features using Apache Airflow. Use it to build pipelines and run orchestrations to process analytic data in your runtime environment.

Predix Columnar Store

The Predix Columnar Store uses the Cassandra-distributed NoSQL database to store its data across multiple nodes, or even multiple data centers, providing a highly available, fault-tolerant persistence data layer for your application.

Cassandra handles a high number of writes-per-second, and stores data in a durable fashion that can withstand data center failures, without compromising its data availability or integrity.

 For more information about the Predix storage services, go to `https://www.predix.io/catalog/services/`.

Summary

In this chapter, we gave tips on choosing hardware and a data exchange protocol for a prototype. We also described how to assemble a prototype with different sensors and build and run four types of applications, one for each of the protocols—HTTP, WebSocket, Modbus, and OPC UA. In addition, we overviewed the Predix services for storing, analyzing, and merging the sensor data from the prototypes.

In the next chapter, you will learn about data management techniques and their implementations for the IIoT stack.

4
Data for IIoT

This chapter provides an overview of the considerations for handling data for IIoT effectively and efficiently when solutions are deployed in an enterprise environment.

The following topics are covered in this chapter:

- Challenges in handling data from IIoT solutions for the enterprise
- The recommended data architecture to address these challenges
- The technology stack to implement the recommended architecture
- Best practices and standards for data management and integration
- Sample code and frameworks for data management

Data for IIoT

Handling data is an important (if not the most important) part of any IoT solution. The following figure gives a rough idea of the amount of different types of data that are being generated by various industrial devices and their sensors. Today, we generate at least 1 TB of data per flight in the aviation sector, 500 GB of data per blade of a gas turbine, 35 GB of data from each smart meter, and so on, and these numbers are going to grow exponentially over the next five years. So it is fair to say that the Internet of Things is not actually about things, its about the data that these things are generating.

Hence, it is increasingly going to become a big data and analytics problem:

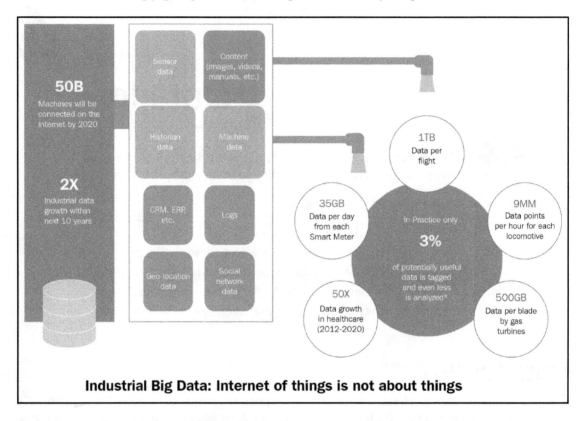

Industrial Big Data: Internet of things is not about things

As data gathering increases rapidly through sensors, especially in the industrial sector, big data technologies and techniques become an integral part of the IIoT stack. These big data technologies help address the challenges related to capture, curation, storage, search, sharing, transfer, analysis, and visualization.

Challenges in handling IIoT data

There are four major challenges in handling IIoT data that we describe here, and also touch upon how enterprises should prepare themselves to address these challenges. In the next section, we will describe the architecture that will help address these challenges:

- The following six characteristics of data captured by IIoT solutions need to be managed in order to make these solutions effective for enterprises:
  - **Volume** (data at rest): Terabytes, exabytes, petabytes, and zettabytes of data.
  - **Velocity** (data in motion): Capturing and processing streaming data in seconds or milliseconds to meet needs or demands.
  - **Variety** (data in many forms): Structured, unstructured, text, multimedia, video, audio, sensor data, meter data, HTML, text, emails, and so on.
  - **Veracity** (data in doubt): Uncertainty due to data inconsistency and incompleteness, ambiguities, latency, deception, model approximations, accuracy, quality, truthfulness, or trustworthiness.
  - **Variability** (data in change): The different ways in which data may be interpreted; different questions require different interpretations. Data flows can be highly inconsistent with periodic peaks.
  - **Value** (data for cocreation): The relative importance of different data to the decision-making process.

- As IIoT solutions generate increased amount of data from various devices, it becomes important that this data be managed in a way that can serve different personnel. The IIoT data will be used to generate reports for management; it can be used by data scientists to build and test their prediction models; or it can be used by field personnel who operate and maintain physical assets. The following figure depicts how this puts strain on the existing enterprise data tools:

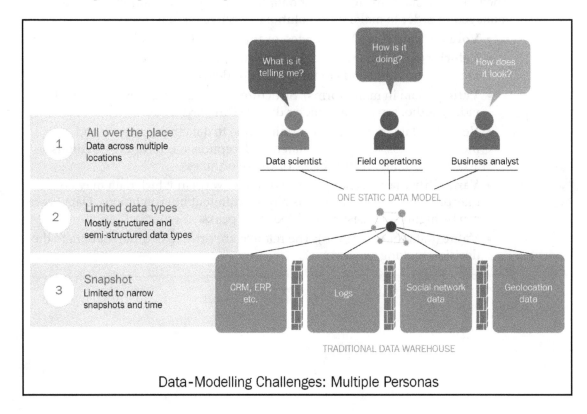

Data-Modelling Challenges: Multiple Personas

- As depicted in the figure, one static model on top of a traditional data warehouse handles limited data types and snapshots over small time frames. Hence, what is required is an approach to data management that will enable the building of custom schemas and models more effectively and dynamically, as depicted here:

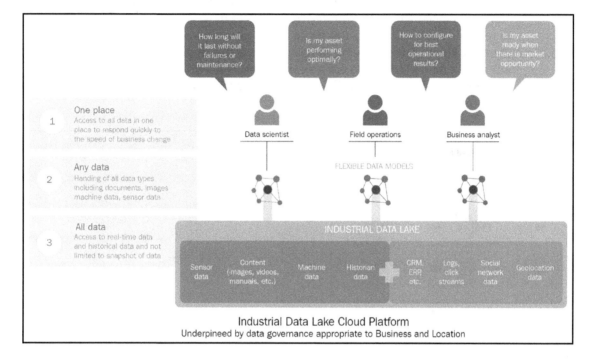

- The existing solutions in enterprises are not geared to support this kind of usage. Moreover, they are a collection of independent tools and technologies in the existing enterprise environment that lead to repetition and extra work when processing this data. This leads to inefficiencies and time lags in getting to the actual analytics that need to be done on the data collected by the IIoT solutions. Hence, we need a more integrated approach to data management that will lead to reduced time and costs, and more agile ways of handling this ever-increasing data workload. The following diagram shows this, highlighting the need for an integrated data platform to achieve this goal. This will help us achieve efficiency and cost-effectiveness, as well as handling the six characteristics of data we mentioned before:

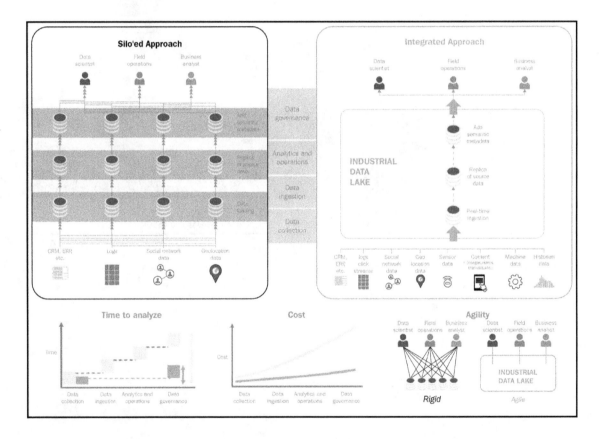

- The data collected by IIoT solutions needs to address different types of use cases and the way to address these different types of use cases will differ. Hence, appropriate technologies will need to be used and supported, enabling each of the different use cases. We can define four high-level use case patterns, which cover most, if not all of the use cases that we will encounter in the IIoT world. The following figure provides a description of these patterns and the relevant details:

Integration and visualization	Structured Data	Batch / CDC-based replication	Simple transformation w/ mastering	Reporting tools
Advanced Analytics	Structured + Unstructured	Batch / CDC-based replication	Machine Learning Predictive Modeling	Reporting tools and self discovery tools
Search + API	Structured + Unstructured	Batch / CDC-based replication	Machine Learning Predictive Modeling	Search & API access to visualization
Real-time analytics	Structured + Unstructured	Real-time ingestion	Simple real-time processing	API based real-time access

Use Case Pattern Summary

The next sections describe what kind of data architecture will help us address the four challenges that we have described in this section.

Data architecture for IIoT

In order to ensure that we are handling data properly and are leveraging the six characteristics of data, we need to have a well-defined data strategy for IIoT solutions. The data strategy should address each layer in the flow of data across the solution. The following diagram captures the overall data architecture for IIoT solutions, followed by a description of each of the layers:

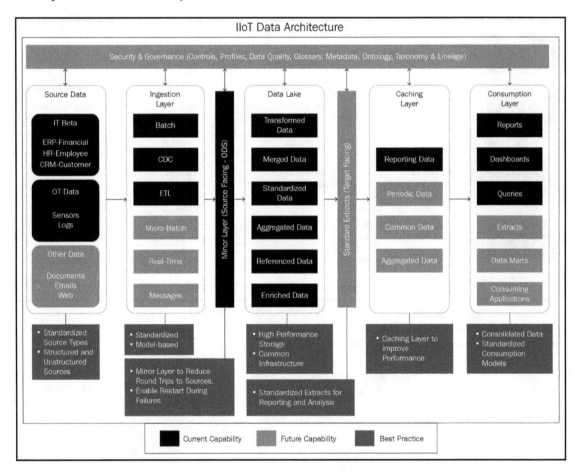

As shown in the preceding figure, it's important to think of the overall data architecture as split into separate layers that interact through interfaces. This is what will add scalability to the architecture, as you can scale each layer up and down as per the overall system requirements. It will also add to the reliability of the system as the failures and issues in one layer can be separated and handled appropriately.

A brief description for each layer is provided here:

- **Data Capture Layer**: In modern IIoT systems, data will be captured from sensors, which will gather logs for operational (OT) data and also from ERP/HR/CRM tools and other enterprise data stores that are more IT-specific. There are other data types, such as documents, emails, and web data/logs that can be captured to combine with the IT/OT datasets to generate meaningful insights. The challenge in capturing datasets is the use of a variety of protocols that are used by various devices and process historians. Companies such as **PTC** and startups such as **Atomiton** provide solutions that abstract out the protocol-specific details so developers can concentrate on the business logic for the applications rather than dealing with the protocol-specific details of these IIoT devices.

- **Data Ingestion Layer**: The ingestion layer needs to be built on technologies that will help move the captured data in its current form to the storage and analytics layers. The first-time transfer of data from the edge to the storage/analytics layer will require something like **Talend** to do a batch transfer. For IT data that resides in existing ERP systems and CRM tools, the bulk transfer of data is possible using tools such as **Sqoop**. Solutions requiring more online analytics applications collecting log data will require something like Flume from the Apache set of technologies. Once the initial transfer of a batch or a large dataset is completed, a solution like *HVR* can be used for **change data capture** (**CDC**). Further data parsing and lineage capture during the ingestion phase is possible using *Informatica* and real-time insights on time series data can be captured using tools like *Druid*.

- **Data Messaging Layer**: In order to optimize data transfer rates and implement high performance use cases, it is essential to put in a messaging infrastructure that will help parallelize and properly direct data loads. The most commonly used messaging infrastructure technologies are **Kafka** and **Rabbit MQ**.

- **Data Storage Layer**: Given that we need to capture a variety of data types that have different profiles and characteristics, we need to leverage more than one technology to provide effective storage for IIoT solutions. Typically, an IIoT solution will capture minimal amounts of data on the edge with most of the data for batch processing being transferred to the cloud. Some form of data lake serves as the landing ground for most data dumped in its raw form, with a schema-on-read rather than schema-on-write methodology being followed. Such a data lake should be built on various technologies to serve different needs. Some are listed here and the details are provided in the following table—HDFS for batch processing, GreenPlum for faster real-time processing, NoSQL storage platforms such as Cassandra for time series, Blobstore for static web content, images and multimedia, and a GraphDB like Neo4j for use cases requiring the storage of highly connected datasets that need to save transformations.

- **Data Analytics Layer**: This layer is where the analytics is performed on the data, and this requires the proper tools depending on what specific analytics need to be performed on the datasets. For example, if there is the need to do real-time analytics on the data, then *Storm* would be a good choice, whereas if the need is to perform more interactive SQL-like analytics, then SparkSQL would be a good choice. If the need is to do data science analysis, then *R Studio*, *Anaconda*, and related data science libraries will be required to build models and train them on the sample datasets collected.

- **Data Caching Layer**: In order to improve performance for reporting periodic, reported, or aggregated datasets, it's important to have a caching layer to provide the in-memory availability of data for consumption. This also provides a layer of abstraction of the consumption layer from the storage layer before it is finally consumed in some form (such as reports).

- **Data Consumption**: Depending on the use case, the consumption of the data will be in the form of dynamically generated reports, dashboards for quick viewing, and real-time actions, as well as queries used for creating data marts and useful extracts. Several tools are available in the market that can be used, such as **Tableau** and **Spotfire**; these can be used to build this layer.

This architecture is the base-level enterprise architecture for IIoT solutions; however, as your IIoT solutions scale and are required to handle petabytes of data from multiple clients, we need to take this architecture one step further and make it capable of being multitenancy and distributed. This can be achieved by leveraging the virtualization and containerization of the caching and analytics (transformation and aggregation) layers. This is depicted in the following figure:

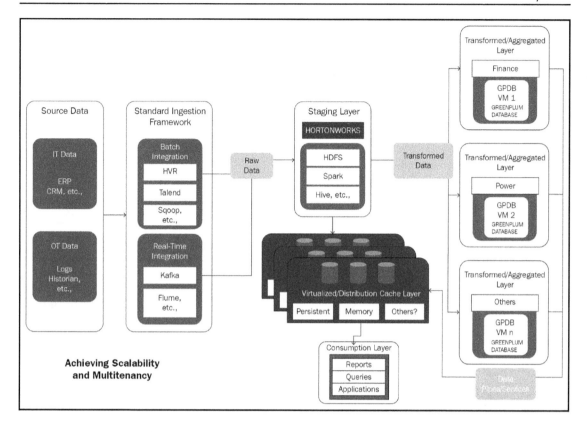

Technology stack to handle data for IIoT

The architecture that we just described can be implemented using a variety of available technologies. Some of this information is summarized in the following diagram, where the choice of technology stack is related to the use case, as well as notes/highlights associated with each one of these:

Platform service	Technology stack	Use case	Highlights
	Talend	Use for first-time ingestion.	Barch and real time.
	Scoop	Bulk data transfer between Hadoop and relational data stores.	Two-way replication with both snapshots and incremental updates.
Ingestion	Flume	Online analytics applications and collects log data to store on HDFS.	Reliable, available, maintains central list of ongoing data flows.
	HVR	Change data capture for sync.	Connects different OLTP in real time and very good replication and refresh capabilities.
	Informatica	Data parsing and lineage.	Integration between different data sources with great parsing and lineage capabilities.
	Druid	Time series data insights.	Aggregation at real-time ingestion.

Messaging	Kafka	Parallel data loads to Hadoop and optimized performance in multi-cluster scenarios; use for high performance use cases.	Distributed pub-sub messaging system; compression and mirroring allows for performance and availability.
	RabbitMQ	Uses more resources, suitable for use cases requiring special features and not so high performance.	More features and worse performance compared to Kafka.
	HDFS	Large data loads for batch processing for cost-effective ETL/storage of raw data/explore data; output data to MPP for consumption. Example: Power Services Fleet Management batch analytics.	Non-relational, block size 64-128 MB, does not use RAID but multiple copies of data.
	GPDB	High performance analytic applications for finance and treasury reporting capabilities.	Analytics object-relational database built on PostGreSQL, MPP but not in-memory; can perform Map-Reduce.
Storage	Cassandra/ Riak TS (NoSQL)	Time series DB, not batch analytics or dynamic ad hoc queries. Use cases requiring high levels of partitioning for distributed storage and performance. Example is the Aviation Time Series data for temperature and pressure trending to predict fault tolerance.	High write throughput (high volume and velocity), well-defined access pattern, point queries, and dynamic schema. Highly denormalized non-relational data model and non-time series machine data requiring scalability.
	BLOB (Amazon S3, OpenStack Swift, ENC Atmos)	Use cases where data is generally read but not written to. Static web content, geographically distributed data backups and archival images, and multimedia (videos, pictures, or music) files are best stored as objects. Example use cases include HealthCare MRI and other image data.	Objects stored along with metadata information. Objects have to be modified as a whole and cannot be handled partly or incrementally. No storage management overhead like block storage.
	Neo4j (GraphDB)	GraphDB for use cases with highly connected data and complex queries. Example use case is Digital Twin where an asset's transformation needs to be persisted.	Stores nodes and edges (relations) for effective querying of complex relations.
	Hadoop and EMR (HDFS, yarn, map-reduce)	Very large datasets requiring batch analytics. Example use case is the Fleet Management for Power Services.	Time is not a constraint, leverage cheap hardware to analyze massive amounts of historically bounded datasets.
Analytics	Storm (topology/ DAGs consisting of Streams, Spouts, and Bolts)	Stream-only processing use cases. Event or message stream processing on continuous data flow. The use case is for Brilliant Manufacturing for alerting and logging of machine data (low latency).	Enables at-least-once processing for each stream item but not necessarily in order, Trident enables exactly once processing but adds state as well as micro-batching and hence latency. Ecosystem of libraries for machine learning, high productivity. Not good for low latency use cases (buffering).
	Spark (RDDs)	Hybrid batch and stream processing use cases requiring reacting to thresholds and trends over time periods. Example use case is the identification of faulty wind turbines for GE Renewables (throughput over latency).	In-memory batch processing engine that also does micro-batching for Spark Streaming—Lambda architecture. RDDs are immutable datasets that can be transformed to new RDDs (hence maintaining lineage without maintaining state or persisting to disk). Complete representation of all tasks as DAGs beforehand.
	Flink (Streams, Operators, Sources and Sinks)	Hybrid batch and stream processing use cases requiring low latency, high throughput, item-by-item processing. Example use case is the GE Energy use case for fault tolerance of inverters.	Stream first extensible to batch - Kappa architecture (streams with bounded datasets). Lots of automatic features, such as partitioning, caching, memory management, and adjustment to changes in input data.
	R, MATLAB, TAMR	Data Science algorithm development and publishing.	Notebooks such as Jupyter and Zeppelin.
Search	SOLR	All forms of search.	Based on Lucene; input formats: XML, CSV, JSON.
	Elastic Search	All forms of search.	Input format: JSON. Very suitable for use with REST APIs. It is a schemaless database and provides for efficient automatic as well as manual indexing.

Visualization	Tableau	Use cases requiring high quality visualization and drill-down capabilities. Also, a broader set of integration with data sources is possible.	Cost concerns from clients.
		Use cases requiring data cleansing and analytics enabled through integration with R, SAS, and other packages.	Issues using it with GPDB.

Best practices and standards

There are two main focus areas for which enterprises need to define a good strategy in order to handle the growth of data due to IIoT solutions. These are described in this section:

- **Data Integration**: Since there are varied sources from which the IIoT solution gets data, having a proper integration strategy is important. An IIoT data integration solution should have an architecture. If you don't fully embrace the existence of the data integration architecture, you can't address how the architecture affects scalability, staffing, cost, and the ability to support real-time capabilities, MDM, services, and interoperability with other tools. Although it may overlap with the data-warehousing architecture and interacts with the entire BI technology stack in the enterprise, the integration architecture is an autonomous structure required for an autonomous practice. A good integration practice ensures the building of common data models that will address one of the concerns that we highlighted in the challenges that arise out of the use of IIoT solutions in the enterprise.

The following figure shows this for enterprise systems that are fed by our IIoT solutions:

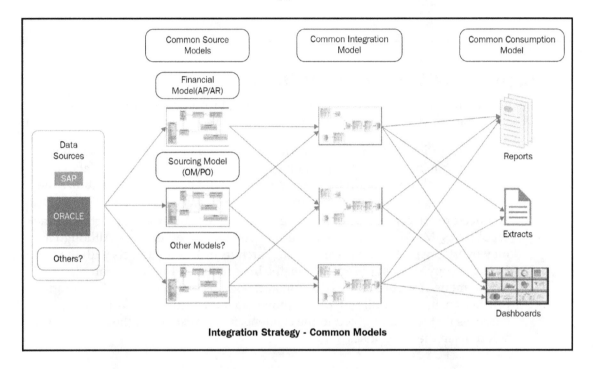

Integration Strategy - Common Models

What integration type and pattern you choose will depend on the use of your IIoT data in your enterprise. We present the following tables that list the different types of integrations that you can choose from:

Batch Data Integration	Real-Time data Integration	Big data Integration	Data Virtualization
Large data sets	Small amounts of data transfer	Very Large data sets	Across data stores and data sets
Point to point	Point to point	Not Point to point	Not Point to point
Groups of data	Single business transactions	Processing to the data	No intermediate persistent store
Asynchronous - sent periodically	Synchronous	Only smaller sets of results get integrated	In memory integration
Tightly coupled	Tightly coupled	Loosely coupled	Loosely coupled
Careful orchestration of changes required	Logical design solutions to reduce P2P limitations	Master data/keys in structured and metadata tags in un-structured	Truly cross data platform and store integration in-memory

Data Integration Types

Based on the integration type, there are certain patterns that can be applied and the relevant technologies to implement these patterns can be used. The following table categorizes four major patterns:

Hub and Spoke	Request and Reply	Pub and Sub	Two-Phase Commits
Used for real-time data integration	Point to point or through hub	Pub and sub information	All effected systems update together or fail
One interface created for each additional system	Synchronous or asynchronous	Requires orchestration system	Leveraged for transactional systems
All data transformed into canonical model	Need not have a common model	Requires tracking of requests	
Canonical model definition requires careful design	Get information or acknowledgement back		

Data Integration Types

The following data integration operational best practices should be followed:

- Understand the technical and business aspects of data
- Requirements and design exercise for developing interfaces
- **Extract**: The `src` system support staff creates w/o Ops inefficiencies
- **Staging**: Audit trail of the data extracted and loose coupling
- **Security**: Profiling for access layers, data masking, and so on
- **Transformation**: Lookups, mapping, matching, aggregation, normalization
- **Load**: Use application code, data validation rules at the target data structure
- **Big data**: Lack of metadata (schema on read) means governance is important

- **Data Governance**: It's important to build a data governance practice that will ensure the proper management and tracking of data and its attributes. Since IIoT solutions bring data from various sensitive sources that go through several transformations, this becomes very important and relevant. We will not go through the details of governance, but we provide a high-level framework that should be used as a reference while defining your governance strategy. As depicted in the following figure, it should span policy, profile, quality, metadata, security, and compliance management:

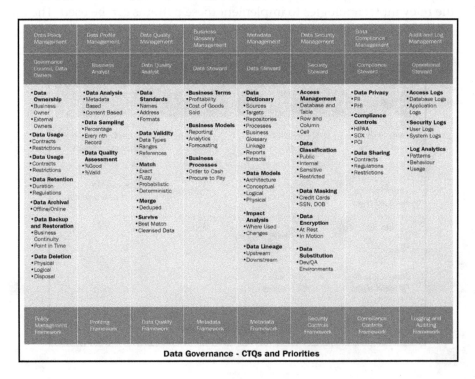

Data Governance - CTQs and Priorities

Sample code and frameworks for handling data

As we close this chapter, we will list the source code that we have used elsewhere in the book and summarize how you can connect to some of the data stores in order to persist the data. This will act as a reference for the reader, and can be used as easy access to the source code required for handling the IIoT data. Now, let's look at the following steps:

1. Connecting to Liquibase using Spring Framework (from Chapter 2, *IIoT Application Architecture and Design*):

```xml
<persistence xmlns="http://java.sun.com/xml/ns/persistence"
        xmlns:xsi="http://www.w3.org/2001/XMLSchema-instance"
version="2.0"
xsi:schemaLocation="http://java.sun.com/xml/ns/persistence
http://java.sun.com/xml/ns/persistence/persistence_2_0.xsd">
    <persistence-unit name="iiotSamplePersistentUnit"
                transaction-type="RESOURCE_LOCAL">

    <description>Persistence Unit</description>
<provider>org.eclipse.persistence.jpa.PersistenceProvider</provider
>
        <mapping-file>META-INF/custom-orm.xml</mapping-file>

      <exclude-unlisted-classes>false</exclude-unlisted-classes>

    <properties>
        <property name="eclipselink.logging.level" value="FINE"/>
        <property name="eclipselink.logging.level.sql"
value="INFO"/>
        <property name="eclipselink.weaving" value="static"/>
        <property name="eclipselink.profiler"
value="QueryMonitor"/> <!-- probably disable this in prod -->
        <property name="eclipselink.jdbc.native-sql"
value="true"/>
        <property name="javax.persistence.query.timeout"
value="10000"/>
    </properties>
  </persistence-unit>
</persistence>
```

2. Liquibase configuration and DDL scripts are given next; we are reading from an env property file and Spring automatically wires these properties to the appropriate bean. We will use the env property only when running locally; in a cloud deployment, we will use manifest.yml to bind to appropriate PostgreSQL instances, but the code does not need to change:

```
@Configuration
public class LiquibaseConfiguration {
    private final DataSource dataSource;
    @Value("${spring.datasource.driver-class-
name:org.postgresql.Driver}")
    private String dataSourceDriverClassName;

    @Value("${vcap.services.${iiot_sample_postgres_name:iiot-
sample-postgres}.credentials.uri}")
    private String dataSourceUrl;

    @Value("${vcap.services.${iiot_sample_postgres_name:iiot-
sample-postgres}.credentials.username}")
    private String dataSourceUsername;

    @Value("${vcap.services.${iiot_sample_postgres_name:iiot-
sample-postgres}.credentials.password}")
    private String dataSourcePassword;
    @Autowired
    public LiquibaseConfiguration(DataSource dataSource){
        this.dataSource = dataSource;

    }

    @Bean
    public SpringLiquibase liquibase(TenantDataSourceConfig
tenantDataSourceConfig) {
        SmarterSpringLiquibase liquibase = new
SmarterSpringLiquibase(tenantDataSourceConfig);
        liquibase.setChangeLog("classpath:db/changelog.xml");
        liquibase.setDataSource(dataSource);
        liquibase.setDefaultSchema("iiot-sample");
        liquibase.setDropFirst(false);
        liquibase.setShouldRun(true);
        return liquibase;
    }
}
```

3. DDL Scripts for Liquibase; all the DB scripts are saved in the `resources/db` directory:

```
CREATE TABLE alerts
(
   id bigserial NOT NULL,
   alerts_uuid text NOT NULL,
   severity integer,
   alert_name text,
   alert_info text,
   created_by text NOT NULL,
   created_date timestamp with time zone NOT NULL DEFAULT now(),
   updated_by text,
   updated_date timestamp with time zone,
   tenant_uuid text NOT NULL,
   CONSTRAINT alerts_pkey PRIMARY KEY (id)
);


CREATE UNIQUE INDEX ALERTS_TENANT_IDX ON Alerts(alerts_uuid,
tenant_uuid);
```

4. From `Chapter 3`, *IIoT Edge Development*. Connecting to Postgres using Node.js, create the `./receiver/index.js` file with the following content, replacing the `database` credentials with the correct values:

```
var http = require('http');
var querystring = require('querystring');
var Pool = require('pg').Pool;
var pool = new Pool({
 user: 'user',
 database: 'database',
 password: 'password',
 host: 'host',
 port: 5432
});

//ensure table exists in db
pool.query('CREATE TABLE IF NOT EXISTS "sensor-logs" (id serial NOT
NULL PRIMARY KEY, data json NOT NULL)', function (err, result) {
 if (err) console.log(err);
});

http.createServer(function (req, res) {
 req.on('data', function (chunk) {
   var data = querystring.parse(chunk.toString());
   console.log(data);
```

```
      //save in db
      pool.query('INSERT INTO "sensor-logs" (data) VALUES ($1)',
[data], function (err, result) {
          if (err) console.log(err);
      });
  });
  req.on('end', function () {
    res.writeHead(200, 'OK', {'Content-Type': 'text/html'});
    res.end('ok')
  });
}).listen(process.env.PORT || 8080);
```

5. Covered in Chapter 6, *Developing Your First Application for IIoT*. Connecting to and using InfluxDB:

```
var restify = require('restify');
var server = restify.createServer({name: 'MyApp'});
var Influx = require('influx');
var alertEmail = require('./alert-email');
var slack = require('slack-incoming-webhook')({url: '{webhook
url}', });

var min = 0;
var max = 100;
var alertFrom = 90;
var interval = 1000;
var alertSlack = slack({
  url: 'https://hooks.slack.com/services/xxx/yyy/zzz',
  channel: '#channel-name',
  icon: ':warning:'
});

// create connection
const influx = new Influx.InfluxDB({
  host: 'localhost',
  database: 'mydb',
  schema: [
    {
      measurement: 'sensor1',
      fields: {
        variable1: Influx.FieldType.INTEGER
      },
      tags: [
        'device'
      ]
    }
  ]
});
```

```
// simulate receiving data from sensors
setInterval(function () {
  var variable1 = Math.floor(max - Math.random() * (max - min));

  if (variable1 >= alertFrom) {
    var msg = 'variable exceeded ' + variable1 + ' rpm';
    alertEmail(msg);
    alertSlack(msg);
  }

  influx.writePoints([
    {
      measurement: 'sensor1',
      tags: {device: 'raspberry'},
      fields: {variable1: variable1}
    }
  ]).then(function () {
    console.log(variable1);
  }).catch(function (err) {
    console.error(err);
  });
}, interval);

server.use(function search(req, res, next) {
  res.header('Access-Control-Allow-Origin', '*');
  res.header('Access-Control-Allow-Headers', 'X-Requested-With');
  return next();
});

server.get('/last', function search(req, res, next) {
  influx.query('select * from sensor1 WHERE time > now() -
5m').then(function (result) {
    res.json(result)
  }).catch(function (err) {
    res.status(500).send(err.stack)
  });
  return next();
});

server.get('/stats', function search(req, res, next) {
  influx.query('SELECT COUNT(*), MEAN(*), MEDIAN(*), MODE(*),
SPREAD(*), STDDEV(*), SUM(*), FIRST(*), LAST(*), MAX(*), MIN(*),
PERCENTILE(*, 5) FROM "sensor1" WHERE time > now() -
1h').then(function (result) {
    res.json(result)
  }).catch(function (err) {
    res.status(500).send(err.stack)
  });
```

```
    return next();
});

server.get(/\/public\/?.*/, restify.plugins.serveStatic({
    directory: __dirname
}));

server.listen(8080);
```

Summary

In this chapter, we covered the essentials of data as it relates to IIoT. We described why data management is at the center of any IIoT solution and is critical in order for these solutions to be successfully deployed and to show ROI in an enterprise environment. The details of a properly scalable data architecture and the corresponding stack were covered, as well as the associated best practices and standards. Finally, we included the source code that pertains to connecting with some of the different data stores for the reader.

In the next chapter, we look at how to use this data to perform analytics and also build a sample end-to-end application.

Advanced Analytics for the IIoT 5

In this chapter, we will cover the concepts of advanced analytics and how it helps in IIoT use cases to provide insights, and to efficiently run manufacturing process and control systems for better productivity. Analytics that come under the category of complex data analysis, using techniques such as machine learning, are referred to in this chapter as advanced analytics. By the end of this chapter, you will have learned some of the IIoT business use cases and how machine learning techniques help in solving them. From the technical side, we will cover machine learning concepts at a high level, and frameworks such as Apache Spark ML and TensorFlow, as well as other tooling that is available to us.

In this chapter, we will cover the following topics:

- IIoT business use cases and analytics
- IIoT analytics classification—reliable, efficient, and profitable
- IIoT analytics—cloud and edge
- IIoT analytics—architecture

IIoT business use cases and analytics

In this section, we will discuss some of the IIoT use cases and the analytics needed for measuring the outcomes. Some of them are common and are used across industries including mining, aviation, oil and gas, power, healthcare, and semiconductors, and can be broadly classified into areas such as asset performance, operations optimization, and supply chain management.

In general, enterprises measure the performance of plants and run them efficiently by monitoring the health of the equipment, as well as business needs and targets. The following are some of the measures that provide an ability to get an insight into plant performance and efficiency:

- Asset reliability and availability
- Monitoring mission-critical events
- Reducing unplanned downtime
- Optimization of the manufacturing process
- Optimization of fleet operations

Power plant performance using heat rate

Heat rate is one of the metrics that can be used to measure the performance of a power plant. Heat rate is defined as the amount of energy needed as input to produce a unit of power output. In addition to heat rate, there are other parameters, such as efficiency, fuel costs, and emissions levels, that are considered. For more details about heat rate, please refer to `https://www.eia.gov/tools/faqs/faq.php?id=107t=3`

Typically, to calculate the heat rate or any other metric, various data points of various parameters need to be collected over a period of time. In other words, these can be referred to as **Key Performance Indicators** (**KPIs**). To calculate metrics from various dimensions, large datasets need to be gathered; that's one of the reasons why analyzing such large volumes of datasets is referred to as a big data problem. These KPIs will provide an insight into efficiency and also an opportunity to improve the power plant efficiency for various persona to make key decisions, by comparing metrics over time and over different sites:

- Is there a performance degradation in an asset over time?
- Is there an opportunity to change the operating setting of an asset?
- Compare the asset performance across the sites with similar assets.
- Forecast the power consumption by asset, plant, and site.

Manufacturing process

The **manufacturing process** is broadly classified into two areas: **discrete** and **continuous** manufacturing. In continuous manufacturing, products are manufactured based on the recipes and processes in an efficient way applicable to healthcare (drug) and food/beverages manufacturing; discrete manufacturing is all about producing a final product by the assembly of various products. In these areas, data and analytics can play a key role in enabling the manufacturers to predict or forecast the events based on the real-time data, or to control the equipment in realtime for efficient manufacturing through a simple aggregation of the data to a complex analytic that can be used to train and build a machine learning model.

IIoT analytics types

IIoT analytics primarily falls under the following types:

- Reliable analytics
- Efficient analytics
- Profitable analytics

Reliable analytics

Reliable analytics provides insights into metrics such as failure events, and maintenance events over a period of time to determine the reliability of the plant. Each process of the plant collects a set of metrics that feeds to continuously running analytics, so that the respective analytics can identify anomalies and generate alarms and notifications. Based on the notification, the plant operators can schedule maintenance events for tuning the system, with or without any downtime.

Efficient analytics

Efficiency analytics provides an opportunity for plant operators to run efficiently through various procedures, such as tuning the operating settings at peak load or downtime. Efficiency analytics requires more data for providing insightful recommendations for the plant operators using machine learning models. Some of the analytics that fall into this category include forecasting, predictions, load factor, and cycle time.

Profitable analytics

Profitable analytics, which provide an additional dimension to the given types, such as how efficiently the plant can be run and still be profitable for business success, are referred to as profitable or financial analytics. For example, the mining industry often needs to extract and ship the ore that is more in demand and make decisions about which ore they can expect or suggest to the back office based on demand. To enable such use cases, running a number of forecasting algorithms based on historical data to make the necessary bidding, or, in manufacturing, to measure the yield, is often required.

Digital twins

Digital twins is the digital representation of a physical asset. It is comprised of data and analytics that provide the state at a given point in time. Digital twins can provide various metrics by running the various types of analytics discussed previously, using the data captured historically and in realtime. Digital twins provides an opportunity to compare and contrast similar assets within or across enterprises. For more details about digital twins, please refer to `https://www.ge.com/digital/applications/digital-twin`.

What-if – analysis and simulations

Digital twins, to a large extent, provides a means to get insights into various aspects by running simulations. For instance, it enables users to execute the related and applicable analytics together. In a what-if scenario, we can get some insight into the performance of an asset by tuning the operating parameters and getting a holistic view of the plant performance. Typically, to get an optimized setting, we need to run various simulations with different operating condition combinations. The what-if scenarios help plant operators to get insights about how the real asset performs under different operating parameters, so that the operator can plan for preventive measures or plan for improvements which, at times, would lead to a fatal state of the asset and impact productivity.

Recommendation, notifications, and alarms

A recommendations system needs to be part of the analytics strategy to make data-driven recommendations leveraging analytics. Continuous monitoring of physical assets provides real-time insights into health and performance that can be tagged and represented in the respective digital twins via recommendations, notifications, and alarms to help the field operators make the necessary decisions.

Analytics catalog and market opportunity

Analytics catalog is defined as the set of analytics available at an enterprise level to visualize the state of the assets in various dimensions, such as reliability, efficiency, and financial. It is a means of organizing related analytics and operationalizing and monetizing the analytics. Typically, in an industry, not all assets are manufactured by a single vendor; usually, different vendors provide various equipment for the final product. It is always helpful for the end customer if the vendors can collaborate and exchange the data to run the plant efficiently and be part of customer success, as each vendor has their own skill set and expertise in the understanding of their equipment.

It is also an opportunity for third-party vendors in extending the capabilities of digital twins to build various algorithms by leveraging the data and to contribute to the overall efficiency of the industry.

IIoT analytics – cloud and edge

Based on the IIoT use cases, the analytics need to be executed on the edge device closer to the controller so that it can react using a standard operation procedure based on the mission -critical events. On the other hand, there are analytics that typically run for a longer time and need to process large amount of datasets, which is at a fleet level. Such analytics fall under big data analytics and require high computing power to distribute the data computation generally preferred to run in a cloud environment for scalability and cost reasons. In this section, we will discuss both the cloud-based and edge-based analytics and technologies that can be used.

Cloud-based analytics

As mentioned earlier, large datasets often need to be analyzed in IIoT. Cloud-based deployments are a great solution for such large volumes of data to run analytics at scale. Based on the requirements of the enterprise, it can be run in a public or private cloud. All major cloud providers, such as **Amazon Web Services** (**AWS**), **Azure**, and **Google Cloud Platform** (**GCP**), provide the big data environment backed with Hadoop infrastructure to run the analytics at cloud scale.

Edge-based analytics

To gain real-time insights and to control the hardware for efficiency, analytics needs to be run closer to the control systems. Edge-based analytics needs to detect and respond to the mission-critical events in realtime. It is also important to note that the edge-based analytics typically apply the logic on a single or small set of time-based events to provide the outcome, due to limited resources on an edge device.

Cloud and edge–analytics combined

For better accuracy in predicting events, it is more valuable to use the analytics in combination with the cloud and edge strategy. For example, we can train machine learning models using the big data infrastructure to build better predictive models, and eventually deploy them at the edge level, so that we can predict the outcomes in real-time with better accuracy in near realtime.

IIoT data for analytics

In this section, we will discuss some of the core datasets of IIoT, such as time series, and asset data, and its role in analytics.

Time series data

Sensor and control systems are the core elements of the IIoT that produce enormous amounts of data through which we can determine various aspects of the physical system in various dimensions, such as performance, health, and anomalies. Typically, the sensor data is stored in a time series format. For example, temperature sensor reading at a timestamp of 12p.m. with a value of 15° can be referred to as a tag (temperature sensor), timestamp (time at which the reading happened), and value (actual value observed) respectively. In IIoT, there will be thousands of tags (aka sensor names) and its values need to be monitored to measure the overall system behavior of turbo machinery equipment for a holistic view of the machine health and performance. There can be a variety of analytics deployed to monitor the entire equipment performance and chain the analytics together for different metrics. Based on the performance metrics and anomaly detection pattern observed, the analytics generate alerts to the field engineers automatically using a feedback loop mechanism.

The analytics can be extended to forecast and predict the events based on the time series data using some of the well-known machine learning models such as **ARIMA** and others.

Asset data

Asset data acts as contextual and static data for the analytics. Analytics can leverage the combination of sensor data and the static asset data to provide more meaningful outcomes and analysis, based on the asset classification and observed data from the sensor.

Process, recipes, and steps

In some manufacturing domains, for example, drug manufacturing, production will typically involve a process with recipes and manufacturing the drugs in batches in a discrete fashion. Analytics can leverage the data observed from the sensors attached to the bioreactors, and the process data in producing the batch provides insights into the overall efficiency and quality of the batches, and tunes the recipes and setting accordingly to product better outcomes.

Manufacturing Execution System (MES) data

On the factory floor, MES provides a means to collect a variety of data from various systems, such as work orders, tracking the process, performance, and schedule. Manufacturing analytics takes advantage of the MES data in providing more insightful predictions and KPIs of the floor operations, yield, and optimization. An integrated analytics analyzing MES data with ERP, including supply chain data, will provide an opportunity to run the manufacturing operations in an efficient way, combining the real-time data from the MES operations data. For more details about the MES system, please refer to `https://www.sap.com/products/execution-mes.html`.

IIoT analytics – architecture

In this section, we will discuss architecture for building analytics in IIoT, using popular open source technologies as a reference for running the analytics at ultra scale on the cloud and on-premise.

Big data and analytics – technology stack

Based on the needs of the business, the big data platform needs to be run in various deployment models, such as public and private clouds, or sometimes it needs to be run on the same stack in a customer environment. Occasionally also, platforms need to be built that are cloud agnostic, so that the stack can be portable across the cloud environments. In various business cases such as this, it is always good to have a strategy of building a platform that is suitable for different deployment modes. In this section, we will discuss a generic data and analytic platform architecture that relies more on open source technologies.

The following diagram illustrates various technologies available for building an analytics platform. It is broadly categorized into three layers and the respective technology stack for reference:

- Infrastructure
- Big data and analytics platform
- Application platform

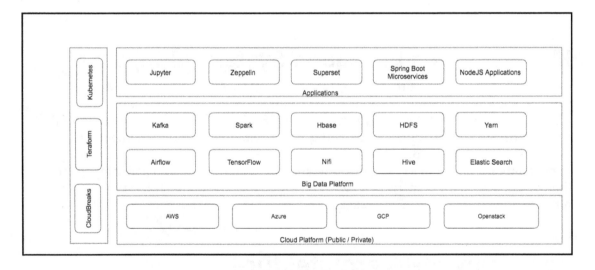

Automation and cloud provisioning

CloudBreaks, which is referenced in the diagram, is a cluster provisioning tool. It helps to build the cluster based on the cloud preference, and also provides an ability to autoscale the cluster based on the data volume and other criteria to provision the resources. It is extensible via blueprints.

Big data and analytics – architecture

In this section, we will discuss the data flow from data ingestion, storage, analysis, and consumption. The following diagram illustrates different technologies that are integrated to run the analytics at scale, and the data flow between the different components:

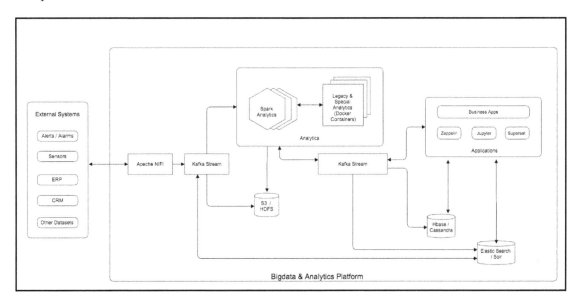

Data ingestion

The data can be ingested from various external systems, such as sensors, and financial systems, into the cloud-based data platform for analysis. **Apache Nifi** is one of the widely-used technologies that ingests the data from external systems into the cloud at scale. It also provides the ability to execute transformations of the ingested data and can be synced to various data sources, such as S3 and Kafka.

Data streaming

Kafka is a widely used messaging system for streaming the data at cloud scale. It provides a variety of connectors for integration with various data sources. It enables you to build data pipelines for streaming the data in a pub-sub model.

Data computing

Spark is a widely-used framework that can process large datasets using distributed computing. The data-ingested stream from Kafka can be consumed, and provides the ability to run streaming analysis for use cases, such as anomaly detection and other mission critical events, and to raise alarms in realtime based on the business requirements.

Spark can support a wide variety of analytics, such as simple math through machine learning using statistics and physics-based models. It can run the data transformations such as for **extract**, **transform**, and **load** (**ETL**) purposes before the business analytics can execute for the insights. Spark analytics can be configured to run in batch for long processing jobs in order to analyze multiple data points by querying the data from object storage such as S3, and databases such as **Cassandra**, and **HBase**.

After analyzing the data, the results produced can be streamed to Kafka for eventual persistence and also enable the application to stream the results for real-time dashboards.

Data persistence

As discussed in previous chapters, S3 is an object storage for large files and a combination of S3, HDFS, and databases such as Cassandra, and HBase enable us to store the IoT datasets in a distributed way. S3 provides the ability to query the data with high performance and persist the data efficiently, as discussed in previous chapters. AWS provides an S3 API to enable the object storage in public cloud deployments and Scality is another option that provides an S3 compatible API to store large files, somethings that comes in handy for on-premises deployments. For more details on Scality S3, please refer to `https://www.scality.com/topics/s3-compatible-storage/`.

Data search

The ingested data can be stored in a filesystem and indexed data can be stored in search tools such as **Solr** or **Elasticsearch** for looking up the actual data. The search tools also enable the applications to look up the data using metadata. We can leverage Spark to store the analyzed results in the search tools, so that the applications can access the data for fast access and make simple calculations such as the moving average based on the criteria selected by users.

Applications

Jupyter and Zeppelin Notebooks provide web-based capability to explore the datasets and author the machine learning algorithms in an interactive mode and build the models by training, as well as test the algorithms using the commonly used libraries, such as **scikit-learn**, **TensorFlow**, and **Spark ML**. They also provide an ability to visualize the results. Superset is another rich visualization tool for plotting the data by query from various types of data sources and for building the dashboard. The purpose-built business applications can be used to query the data for interactively executing the analytics, and integrating with the Notebooks, such as Jupyter, which provide an ability to build the application platform. For more details about the Jupyter Notebook, please refer to `https://jupyter-notebook.readthedocs.io/en/stable/`.

Analytics definition

Analytics is a composition of an input dataset, a logical engine, and derived dataset. The logic unit analyzes the data and produces a set of outcomes. The logical unit can range from aggregation to complex statistical analysis. Analytics can be configured with different settings based on the equipment, environment, and various factors.

The following diagram illustrates the analytics blueprint:

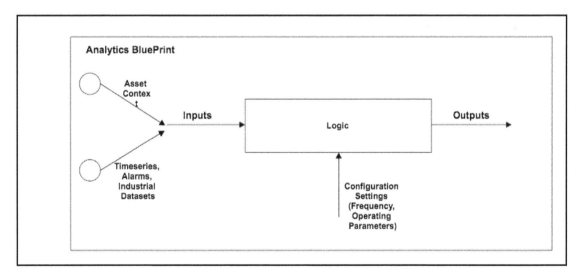

Streaming and batch analytics

Streaming analytics run continuously on incoming data streams, otherwise known as hot data, to provide real-time analysis and outcomes. Streaming analytics comes in handy for detecting mission-critical events and streaming the results in real-time for further action. Typically, streaming analytics runs analysis on a single data point, or a small number of data points arrived in realtime for high throughput. On the other hand, batch analytics runs the analysis on large datasets, including historical datasets, also known as **cold data** or **warm data**, to provide meaningful insights in a scheduled fashion. Typically, batch analytics takes longer compared with streaming analytics, due to the complexity involved in analyzing large volumes of data for different dimensions pertaining to an asset.

Lambda architecture facilitates the process of large volumes of data in a distributed fashion with low latency and fault tolerance. In Lambda architecture, as mentioned in the following diagram, it primarily consists, two pipelines with **Batch Analytics** and **Stream Analytics** (real-time), which provides the process the data in incremental and store the data in a persistent store, such as Cassandra in a batch pipeline. In a stream pipeline (real-time, aka fast analytics), the data will be processed with live data for real time analysis and the data streamed to the applications. In the IIoT, it is very common for data to be duplicated. Where the data arrives late in such scenarios, the Lambda architecture helps to process the data eventually in a reliable manner in batch mode, while still keeping the live stream data available for the applications with exactly once semantics. Lambda architecture can be implemented using the **Spark**, **Spark Streaming**, **Kafka**, and **Cassandra** technologies as mentioned in the following diagram.

For more details about Lambda architecture, please refer to `https://mapr.com/developercentral/lambda-architecture/`.

Lambda architecture can be depicted as follows:

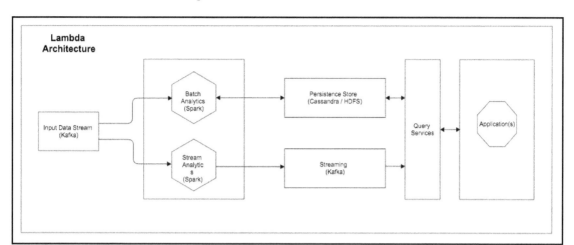

Event-driven analytics

Event-driven analytics provides a way to run the analytics based on the events rather than executing the logic for all the data points. This provides a way to run the analytics efficiently and trigger them based on events. In the IIoT, we can classify various sets of events based on the classification of assets and configure the analytics to react to the events.

ETL pipelines

ETL pipelines facilitate the extraction, transformation, and loading of the data, and the running of the IIoT analytics. Typically, the legacy systems data needs to be ingested and transformed before running the operational analytics. In such scenarios, the data needs to be extracted and loaded into the data storage, such as S3 buckets and Cassandra, and eventually transformed in the database systems for running the analytics on the data collected.

Analytics orchestration

In the IIoT, usually, a chain of analytics must be run to calculate the metrics. For example, KPIs are one kind of performance metrics that often need to be calculated at an enterprise level, and also calculated at a different asset level in the asset hierarchy. In such a scenario, it is necessary to chain the analytics together to calculate the KPIs at a site or enterprise level. To orchestrate the analytics, **Apache Airflow** is one of the open source orchestration frameworks that can be used to chain the analytics.

Advanced analytics – artificial intelligence, machine learning, and deep learning

Advanced analytics is classified as the set of analytics that requires complex statistical analysis, physics-based models, neural networks, and so on; in other words, the analytics that falls under the category of **artificial intelligence** (**AI**) for building machine learning models and predicting outcomes based on the machine models using observed data. AI-based analytics are all about learning from the observed data and eventually predicting the outcomes for the new data, or classifying the data based on the models built using the knowledge-based systems. In this section, we will primarily discuss machine learning and deep learning methods in building the AI algorithms.

Building a model

An algorithm is a technique that will be trained with some data for fitting. For example, a linear regression technique is an algorithm and fitting the data with the algorithm is the process of training. The output of the training will generate an output called a model, for example, y = 4x + 9, where 4 and 9 are the coefficients in calculating y when x is given as input.

Exploratory data analysis

Exploratory data analysis provides a way to analyze the data interactively and build a machine learning model. This will be the first step in the life cycle of building a model. It also helps the data scientist to better understand the datasets and trends to come up with the best technique for predicting the outcome and building the model. Some of the most frequently used open source tools, such as Zeppelin, and Jupyter, are being used in the industry for exploratory analysis and for building the Notebooks. Some of these technologies are discussed later in this chapter.

Analytics life cycle

In a typical analytics life cycle, the first step involves developing an analytics leveraging a number of interactive analysis tools such as Zeppelin, and Jupyter, and eventually publishing the analytics to a catalog for operationalizing. This involves configuring and running in a computing environment such as Apache Spark at cloud scale, based on the volume of data. The configuration of the analytics, for example, includes the asset instance (also known as an equipment running in site) of the asset classification (also known as an asset type). We will discuss further the development of industrial analytics using the Spark Framework in later sections of the chapter.

In the following diagram, we see the steps of developing and operationalizing a machine learning-based analytic:

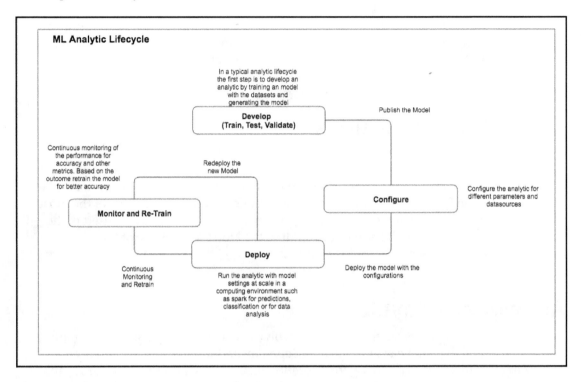

After the model is developed using tools such as Jupyter, the next step in the life cycle is to configure it with the correct settings for data sources, operation settings, conditions, and frequency. This is so that when the model is deployed, it can collect the data from the configured data sources and execute the model with the correct settings and conditions, and also stipulate how frequently to execute the model on the incoming data or the data at rest. After the model is configured, it will be deployed in the runtime execution environment where the model can be executed at scale using technologies such as Apache Spark for analyzing the data and eventually executing the model using TensorFlow. The other important step in the life cycle is the ability to monitor performance as well as the ability to auto-retrain the model for better accuracy, which was discussed in detail in other sections.

Machine learning model life cycle

The life cycle of a machine learning model goes through multiple phases:

- Training
- Testing
- Validation
- Prediction
- Retraining

Training a model

The first step in building a model is to train a model with a dataset. To make it simple to understand the steps here, I am referring to a linear regression technique. Typically, the linear regression technique ($Y = mX + c$) will be trained with a sample dataset. The dataset can be divided into training and testing datasets to train the linear equation to come up with the best possibility for m and c. By using the training dataset, the model can be fitted with various data points from the training dataset that will end up, for example, something like $Y = 4X + 10$.

Testing a model

The second step is to test the model using the dataset from the observed dataset and to test the model $Y = 4X + 10$ for correctness, measuring various performance metrics of the model by running a number of tests against the model.

Validating a model

After the model is trained and tested using the observed sample dataset, the next step is to validate by testing the model with a dataset that is not part of the observed sample data, but taking a number of real dataset and testing the model for the predictions and measuring the performance metrics.

Predictions using a model

After the model is validated, and provided the performance metrics are met, the final step is to deploy the model in production for real predictions. Once the model is deployed, the new data can be run against the model for realtime predictions. Typically, if the model requires a large dataset for providing predictions, the model is likely to be executed in the offline mode.

Retraining a model

Retraining the model with the latest datasets will help to build a more accurate model over time. Typically, continuous monitoring of the deployed model performance will give an opportunity for retraining the model. Automating the process of retraining the model and continuous deployment of better models for real-time predictions with better predictions saves millions of dollars. In the retraining step, typically it goes through the same phase of training, testing, and validation of the model, but the sophisticated retraining process identifies the outliers to produce a better model from the previous history of the model's performance.

Model performance

In practice, due to various factors such as operating settings and environment conditions, model performance starts to degrade. It's always good practice to monitor the performance of the model by tracking the predictions of the model and the real observed data over a period of time. This can provide an insight into model performance to take the necessary actions on the acceptance of the model. In some IIoT use case scenarios, it is critical to refrain from accepting model predictions if the prediction goes out of range with an offset limit. In such cases, the performance metrics play a significant role

Hypertuning parameters, or the optimization of model parameters

In some of the machine learning model generation processes, simulations should be run with a different parameter setting along with an input dataset that can produce a better model. Typically, such a process is referred to as an optimization process or identification of the hypertuning parameters.

Model performance metrics

During the process of building a model or the models being used in production for real-world predictions, performance metrics are used to determine the correctness of the predictions over a period of time. The performance metrics differ from model to model but here are some of them for measuring the **goodness of fit** (**GOF**). For further details, please refer to `https://www.mathworks.com/help/curvefit/evaluating-goodness-of-fit.html`,

- SSE (Sum of Squares due to error)
- RMSE (Root Mean Squared Error)
- R- Square

Determining outliers and offset management

In the real world, it is not always guaranteed that the models receive the good and expected datasets. There is always the possibility of human error or unexpected events that can produce the bad sets that can cause the models to produce bad predictions. It is always good practice to consider large datasets and identify the outliers during the process of building a model, and also to have a way of identifying the outliers in the incoming stream of data, which will typically be done as part of the model pipeline processing for the model predictions.

Continuous training of a model

In the IIoT, to manage a fleet of equipment, it is often required to control the processes using machine learning techniques. The machine learning models help to predict and control the outcome. In such scenarios, model prediction performance often needs to be kept high. In a number of special scenarios, due to bad datasets or some unexpected events or changes in control settings, the performance of the model may drift. In such a setup, it is always advantageous to have the capability of continuous training of machine learning models and automation of deployment with little or no human intervention. Continuous training of a model provides a way of listening to the latest data and adjusting the model coefficients accordingly. It also produces a better model for users to make recommendations or to automatically control the edge processes, or for control systems to automatically produce better throughput.

ML pipelines and orchestration

A ML model orchestration is a logical flow of multiple steps required to produce a machine learning model. In the process of building a machine learning model, it includes multiple steps as discussed in previous sections. In addition to these, the orchestration often entails some preprocessing of the datasets and also leveraging a combination of techniques for producing a model based on the domain and use cases. In such situations, it is good practice to create a logical flow of steps that can be orchestrated to produce a model. The first step is always to analyze a variety of datasets during which multiple types of transformations and extractions will be executed, which is referred to as feature engineering. In such a process, it often gets complex if there are too many steps and it is difficult to keep track of the feature extraction process. It is helpful to have a way of configuring and executing in a more organized way. For that reason, the Spark machine learning pipeline comes in very handy.

The ML pipeline flow diagram is as follows:

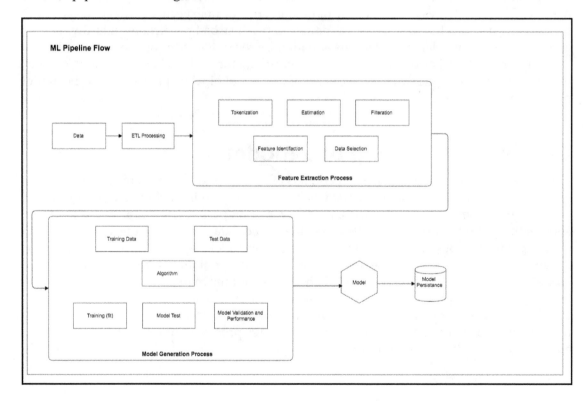

IIoT data

Data is the core of model building. In IIoT use cases, most of the models are dependent on the asset context, time series data, images for building models and predicting the outcomes. The data referred to is the raw data being ingested from various data sources such as edge systems, ERP, business applications, alerts, and alarms from control systems.

ETL

In most of the IIoT use cases, the data needs to be transformed for various reasons, such as the modern data architecture using NoSQL technologies, deduplication, Lambda, and data transformations from a legacy data model to a newer model. Typically, the ingested raw data goes through an ETL pipeline that can archive, extract, transform, and load the data into the new systems. The operations can happen interchangeably and with more cycles, based on the use case. After the data is transformed into the final format, it can be streamed to the next step of the pipeline processing.

Feature extraction process

Feature extraction is the first step of model building. Typically, data scientists leverage some of the common tools, such as Jupyter and Zeppelin, for data exploration and for the feature extraction process, and eventually deploy the model as an ML pipeline to operationalize. In this step, the incoming transformed data as a stream, or the data at rest in the database or filesystem, will be analyzed for tokenizing, along with the transformation for identifying the features that are relevant to the business use case. Once the relevant features are identified, the sample dataset can be identified from the explored data for the next steps of the pipeline.

Model generation process

During the model generation step as discussed in the previous section, the sample data will be divided into training and test data for building the model in ratios such as 70:30 or 80:20. Once data is identified, the next step is to identify the relevant algorithm applicable for the business use case and train the algorithm with the dataset, test, and then validate the model to the performance. This may take multiple iterations. Also, in some scenarios, multiple algorithms may be needed for the final outcomes.

Storing the model

After the model performance is satisfied, the model generated can be stored in a filesystem or a block store, so that the model can be used for the predictions and the entire pipeline also reused for retraining the model with new datasets.

Developing an ML pipeline

The following example provides steps required for creating the machine learning pipeline and is used in the training process. After the model is trained, it is used for predictions that retrain the entire pipeline to automatically extract the features and predict the input data using Spark.

Create a Spark data frame for the input data by doing the following:

```
from pyspark.ml import Pipeline
from pyspark.ml.classification import LogisticRegression
from pyspark.ml.feature import HashingTF, Tokenizer
from pyspark.sql import SparkSession

training = spark.createDataFrame([
        (0, "test iiot", 1.0),
        (1, "validate", 0.0),
        (2, "train iiot validate", 1.0),
        (3, "gartner test", 0.0)
    ], ["id", "data", "label"])

training.show()
```

The training data is as follows:

```
+---+-------------------+-----+
| id| data|label|
+---+-------------------+-----+
| 0| test iiot| 1.0|
| 1| validate| 0.0|
| 2|train iiot validate| 1.0|
| 3| gartner test| 0.0|
+---+-------------------+-----+
```

The feature extraction is as follows:

```
tokenizer = Tokenizer(inputCol="data", outputCol="iiot")
hashingTF = HashingTF(inputCol=tokenizer.getOutputCol(),
outputCol="features")
 lr = LogisticRegression(maxIter=20, regParam=0.001)
pipeline = Pipeline(stages=[tokenizer, hashingTF, lr])
```

Training using a pipeline:

```
model = pipeline.fit(training)
```

Predict using the model as follows:

```
 test = spark.createDataFrame([
        (1, "iiot new test")
    ], ["id", "data"])
test.show()
prediction = model.transform(test)
selected = prediction.select("id", "data", "probability", "prediction")
for row in selected.collect():
        rid, text, prob, prediction = row
        print("(%d, %s) --> prob=%s, prediction=%f" % (rid, text,
str(prob), prediction))
```

The results are as follows:

```
(1, iiot new test) --> prob=[0.005793730834978676,0.9942062691650213],
prediction=1.000000
```

IIoT data variety

The industrial internet is a network of various types of analytics that work together to produce better productivity, efficiency, and reliability. In this section, we will discuss some of the most frequently used types of analytics and applicable use cases in the IIoT:

- Geospatial
- Image analysis
- Acoustics

Spatial analytics

Spatial analytics provides a way of locating and tracking the equipment and provides a means to predict the estimation. It provides the ability to predict the potential risk based on the location of the equipment and the nearest entities and so on. Spatial analytics provides a way of integrating industries with the supply chain ecosystem in terms of inventory, schedule, orders, and predicting the maintenance cycle. Spatial analytics, in combination with weather-based data, provide a means for industrial equipment to generate the power efficiently using renewables with wind turbines. It also helps to simulate the water flooding behavior associated with oil production.

Spatial analytics analyzes large datasets to form grids and neighbors to analyze the data and identify the equipment and classify the behavior. For such large-scale analysis and simulations, Apache Spark with the Magellan Framework will provide an abstract API for building the spatial analytics.

Image analysis

Image analysis offers a way to identify the objects in an image using an AI leveraging deep learning technique. Deep learning is a process in which it forms a multilayer neural network to identify and classify the objects in an image. For learning about the images and building a model, it runs various simulation procedures that require large computing power such as GPUs. IIoT use cases include identifying the grinding size of the ore in mining, water flooding, drilling procedures for oil production, and metrology measurements in the semiconductor fabrication process, as well as X-rays, MRI scans, and skin cancer tests and so on, in healthcare.

TensorFlow is a popular framework developed by Google and has been widely adopted in the IIoT to build the complex neural network-based models for classifying images at a cloud scale.

Acoustics – based analytics

In the IIoT, condition-based monitoring is more efficient than scheduled monitoring as it reduces the cost of maintenance significantly. In condition-based monitoring, equipment maintenance is required only when there is a potential degradation in performance, instead of running the maintenance in a scheduled fashion, which also increases the reliability of the equipment. At the same time, condition-based monitoring requires a very sophisticated setup to detect the state of the equipment under all possible scenarios. Typically, condition-based monitoring needs to monitor the equipment in a variety of means based on the type of equipment. The types of datasets include vibration data generated from the rotating equipment, such as turbo machinery and will help to determine the state of the equipment. Acoustics-based analytics provides a way to determine the state by measuring the wavelength and frequency using physics and statistical-based modeling to determine the state of the equipment. It also needs to combine, in other words chain, the related set of analytics to determine the overall state of the equipment connected for identifying the fault and alerting the field engineers ahead of time to take the necessary action prior to an outage.

Machine learning types

There are two types of machine learning: supervised and unsupervised learning.

Supervised learning

In supervised learning, the model is built by learning from the data observed. The observed data is well known and created in the past by giving inputs and generated output, so that the data can be used and fitted with a function to build a model by splitting the data into training and testing. Typically, in IIoT, predicting the anomalies, classifying the type, analyzing the size of the ore, and forecasting the time series data can be done using supervised learning. Classification and regression are among the supervised learning methodologies for building the models.

Unsupervised learning

In unsupervised learning, there is no labeled data for modeling. Instead, it will use various characteristics for grouping the data and forming a cluster of related data. It can also be used for dimensionality reduction in the context of feature extraction and identifying related features. In the IIoT, unsupervised learning provides an opportunity to identify and analyze new outcomes and related patterns. It also comes in especially handy for filtering the dependent variables. As IIoT is a very complex environment, it requires a larger effort in identifying the related features.

PMML for predictive analytics

PMML is an acronym for Predictive Model Markup Language. PMML is an XML-based schema definition of defining the predictive model. It provides various types of techniques and respective parameters. PMML provides a standard way of storing the model so that it can ported across different systems and of loading the models for predictions.

The PMML schema is as follows:

```
<xs:simpleType name="MINING-FUNCTION">
  <xs:restriction base="xs:string">
    <xs:enumeration value="associationRules"/>
    <xs:enumeration value="sequences"/>
    <xs:enumeration value="classification"/>
    <xs:enumeration value="regression"/>
    <xs:enumeration value="clustering"/>
    <xs:enumeration value="timeSeries"/>
    <xs:enumeration value="mixed"/>
  </xs:restriction>
</xs:simpleType>
```

Spark provides the ability to persist the generated model in PMML format:

```
<xs:element name="ExampleModel">
  <xs:complexType>
    <xs:sequence>
      <xs:element ref="Extension" minOccurs="0" maxOccurs="unbounded"/>
      <xs:element ref="MiningSchema"/>
      <xs:element ref="Output" minOccurs="0"/>
      <xs:element ref="ModelStats" minOccurs="0"/>
      <xs:element ref="Targets" minOccurs="0"/>
      <xs:element ref="LocalTransformations" minOccurs="0" />
      ...
      <xs:element ref="ModelVerification" minOccurs="0"/>
      <xs:element ref="Extension" minOccurs="0" maxOccurs="unbounded"/>
```

```
        </xs:sequence>
        <xs:attribute name="modelName" type="xs:string" use="optional"/>
        <xs:attribute name="functionName" type="MINING-FUNCTION"
use="required"/>
        <xs:attribute name="algorithmName" type="xs:string" use="optional"/>
      </xs:complexType>
    </xs:element>
```

The following is an API provided by Spark for saving the model in PMML format to a specific file:

```
testModel.toPMML("/tmp/testmodel-pmml.xml")
```

Event – driven machine learning model

In the process of building a machine learning model, an interface needs to be designed on how to interact with the model. One of the approaches discussed here is an event-driven machine learning model that can be triggered based on different kinds of event data and where the necessary action can be triggered for predict, train, retrain, and validate.

In a event-driven model, the event definition will determine the type of action that needs to be triggered and also provides the flexibility on how to fetch the data. Typically, for real time model predictions, it needs to provide the predictions in real-time in continuous mode, for which the model can receive a stream of events from a messaging channel, such as Kafka. On the other hand, if the model needs to fetch and run the model predictions on data at rest based on the action of the event, it can query the data with the range to provide the predictions. Also, in another scenario, the user can trigger the model on-demand which requires the model execution to be run immediately and to provide the prediction results.

Event – driven model architecture

In the following diagram, the on-demand events are the user-driven events that are typically generated by the user action and needs, and the criteria used:

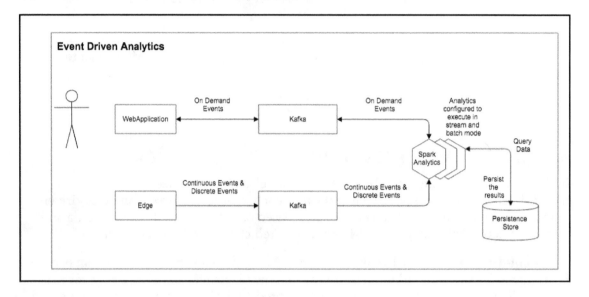

So, based on the type of events, the models running in production will react to the event by querying the data from the appropriate data sources and provide the predictions as a stream to the applications, so that the users can view the predictions on an on-demand basis. Also, in an IIoT world of what-if scenarios, it is important to see the overall plant efficiency if any of the settings have changed, and in such scenarios, it is important to run a cluster of a multiple chain of models to provide insights for field engineers. It can be categorized as on-demand analytics. On the other hand, continuous or discrete events are generated by automated processes so that they can be streamed to the models that are running in production and generate the results, so that the application can query the results and visualize them by reading the results on dashboards. In both scenarios, the results of the predictions can either be streamed asynchronously or get persisted over time.

Building models in offline mode

In the process of building models, the latest data often needs to be accessed for better model accuracy. Typically, in such scenarios, running the analysis on production data is an overhead for any production system that necessitates the setting up of an offline data cluster that is in sync with the real production data cluster, with commodity hardware, and with eventual consistency. This is so that the analysts can run the data analysis on the warm data for the purpose of long-running analysis and simulations for building a machine learning model.

Reference architecture

As shown in the following diagram, the hot data cluster is the operational cluster running in production for serving the enterprise applications:

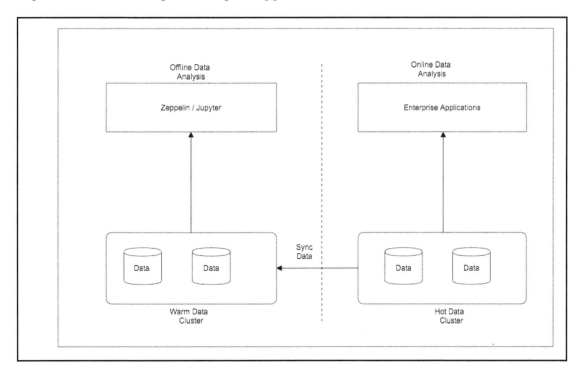

Also, for the purpose of aiding offline data analysis, in other words, for analysts to run data simulations with no overhead for the customer SLA, the data can be synchronized from the hot data cluster to the warm data cluster using daemons. This is so that analysts can run their analysis and build models using the latest datasets. The warm data cluster will be analogous to the hot data cluster in terms of the technology stack to keep it in sync and consistent, so that the models can be promoted to production and operationalize seamlessly through a continuous process.

Real-time model tuning and deployment

In the IIoT, for some of the mission-critical equipment, it is necessary to produce models with better accuracy during predictions. For building such models, we need to continuously monitor and train and build models in realtime, or near realtime, based on complexity. In real-time model tuning, we continuously stream the live data for which the models will be continuously trained and monitor the accuracy and other performance parameters.

The machine learning code that can be used to train with the dataset can be stored in a registry and can expose it as an endpoint. So that the code can be scheduled to continuously train up on the latest datasets, generate a new model and persist in a common location. For most algorithms, continuous model training consumes a lot of resources in building a model that can affect the performance metrics of the production system. It is recommended that you run separate data pipelines for continuous model training so that the pipeline preprocess steps can cleanse the data automatically before building the models and, based on the performance metrics and the criteria defined, the models can be published for the operations. The operational data pipeline that is being used by the applications in a real system can constantly retrieve the latest models published to service predictions, with recommendations for the applications.

The following diagram illustrates real-time model training and deployment:

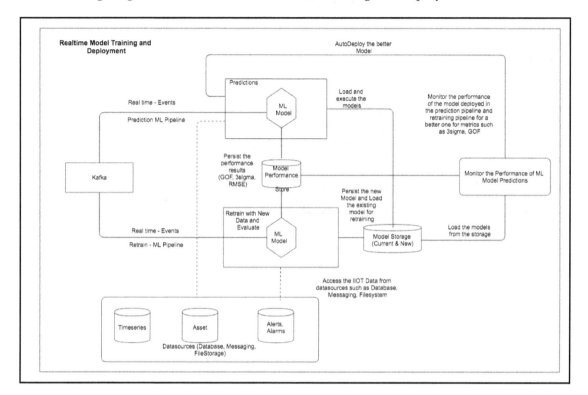

Kafka is used for streaming the events for the models running in production. The ML models shown in the preceding diagram are shown logically as two instances looking for streaming events for predictions and retraining. The analytics running in the cluster has the ability to load the models from the storage system and execute the models when the new event arrives and then query the appropriate datasets. Once the models execute upon the data for predictions, the results are persisted. In parallel, the ML monitoring system can measure the performance of the models over a period of time with real datasets and what the real outcome was when it was observed can provide the actual performance of the model. This is so that the monitoring system can compare the results and deploy the models to the production automatically or through the gate keeping process in order to approve the newer version of the model.

Machine learning as a service

At an enterprise level, multiple systems often need to be integrated to exchange the data between different systems. In such scenarios, service-oriented architecture provides a better flexibility in the integration of the systems for various reasons, such as the type of language and platform. After the model is built, the ML model as a service endpoint provides a way to integrate with the external system and can interact with the model for predictions. It provides a greater flexibility and extensibility of ML models to interact with various other models instead of execution in a silo. Now, we can have an network of ML models working together, exchanging the predictions across the enterprises with multi-tenancy that provides better outcomes working through the systems across the vendors.

The following diagram illustrates building a machine learning model as a service:

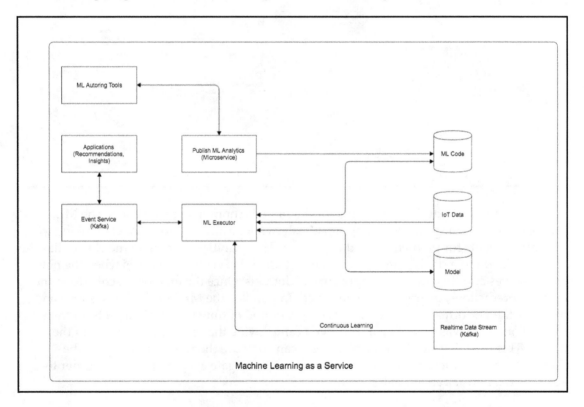

Creating an ML model endpoint

In this section, we will be creating an ML model endpoint:

Step 1

Deploy the analytics as a service that can automatically generate the endpoints with which the external applications can interact with the model. When a machine learning code is written and published to a registry, it can provide the following endpoints automatically, so that the client applications can send events such as train, test, and predict to the respective endpoint.

The following are a set of endpoints for a machine learning model:

- **model <x>/train:** For training the model so that the external system can send a train event
- **model <x>/test:** For testing the model so that the external system can send a test event
- **model <x> /validate:** For validating the model so that the external system can send a validate event
- **model <x>/predict:** For predictions from the model so that the external system can send a predict event
- **model <x>/performance:** For measuring the performance model and obtaining metrics according performance event
- **model <x>/configure:** For configuring the model with the datasource so that at runtime, the model can collect datasets.

Step 2

The analytics is deployed as a streaming endpoint so that the client applications can stream the events for the respective models. The analytics can listen to the events and react to the event type.

Step 3

The ML-based analytics can leverage the Kafka as an event server for various types of events, as depicted in the preceding diagram. The ML-based analytics can load the respective model coefficients from the registry and provide the predictions. After processing the events, analytics can publish the results (predictions) to Kafka, which can then be streamed to the clients. Likewise, the analytics can also publish the newly generated models to the registry.

Containerization of machine learning models

In the real world, machine learning models can be developed in different languages, libraries, and technologies based on the use case to accelerate their development. In such a complex environment, containerization of the models provides a greater flexibility in the process of model operationalization. It provides a freedom for the developers to choose the right technology for the use case and also enables interaction with the legacy analytics under the same data infrastructure. It also provides the ability to execute the models at ultra scale with high availability and resiliency

Legacy analytics and challenges

In the IIoT, one of the common challenges is how to deploy and run the legacy analytics in modern data infrastructure. Typically, the legacy analytics can be a large number and the engineers who developed them may not have been with the company. However, to rewrite such analytics and deploy them in modern infrastructure can be a nightmare, as some of them can be mission critical. In such scenarios, it will be challenging to rewrite them in one go and to keep up with the cloud scale data requirements and scalability reasons. One option is the containerization of legacy analytics and deployment in modern infrastructure. The following is a reference architecture on how to Dockerize and run the legacy analytics at scale with out rewriting, including a number of caveats, such as the limitations in leveraging distributed computing, which can be a phased approach to rewrite and run, leveraging modern technologies.

Containerization for legacy analytics

Legacy analytics can be containerized using the Docker containers, so that the analytics can be deployed and run at scale based on the traffic. The container scan includes all the necessary libraries and software components for running the legacy analytics as a standalone process.

Data for legacy analytics

In order to make the data available for legacy analytics, one approach is to pull the data closer to logic based on the volume of data. The other approach is to push the data into the analytics, based on how the analytics are built. To provide the integration messaging, the framework can be leveraged to exchange the data between modern data infrastructure and containers. Also, schedule execution of the processes to pull the data and make it available for the analytics.

Analytic Orchestration - Architecture

The ingested data stored in S3 buckets can be streamed to Kafka and trigger the analytics running in a container approach, so that the analytics can run the analysis and write the results back to the modern data infrastructure, as depicted in the following architecture:

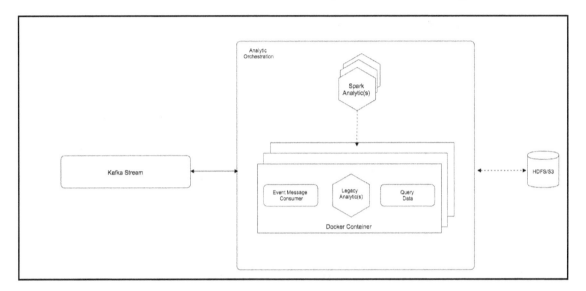

Analytics orchestration

In real-world scenarios, for business outcomes, the analytics need to be executed in a combination of legacy and newly-developed analytics. In such cases, open source technologies such as Apache Airflow can be leveraged to orchestrate multiple analytics as a single pipeline. In this way, the analytics can be orchestrated and executed sequentially or in parallel based on the use cases and finally, the results can either be streamed to the messaging channel or persisted into a storage such as S3, or eventually HBase or Cassandra.

Data flow

As shown in the analytics orchestration architecture diagram mentioned in the previous section, the data is streamed via Kafka as input data to the legacy analytics running using container technology, such as a Docker container to scale based on the data volume. The containers can embed a messaging consumer and publisher channel to exchange the data between the modern data infrastructure so as to read and write the results. The other option is to read and write the results based on business requirements to the respective data storage.

Pros and cons of this approach

This approach would accelerate the adoption of modern data infrastructure and run the legacy analytics at scale and be part of the same ecosystem. It would also help to phase the rewriting of the legacy analytics and better understand the logistics. The downside is that the legacy analytics will not be leveraging the distributed computing approach if they need to run for a very large dataset immediately. Based on immediate business needs, the respective analytics that need to analyze very large datasets can be rewritten and orchestrated with the legacy analytics that can run the enterprise analytics at scale.

Time series data-based analytics

As discussed in the previous topic, for most of the IIoT use cases, the time series data needs to be analyzed. Windows-based operations on continuous time series data provides a way to calculate moving averages, rollups to measure asset performance, and anomaly detection in realtime.

Windows-based calculations

Spark provides the ability to run Windows-based operations by aggregating the data for a feature continuously. Here is an example where the KPI average of heat rate is being calculated on a weekly basis over time. Windows-based calculations can be applied to both batch and streaming data to calculate the average:

```
powerDF.groupBy(window(powerDF.col("Date"),"1
week")).agg(avg("heatrate").as("weekly_average"))

+-------------------+-------------------+-------------------+
|start |end |weekly_average |
+-------------------+-------------------+-------------------+
|2017-04-13 17:00:00|2017-04-20 17:00:00|208.5694 |
```

```
|2017-04-20 17:00:00|2017-04-27 17:00:00|203.5780 |
|2017-04-27 17:00:00|2017-05-04 17:00:00|299.5316 |
|2017-05-04 17:00:00|2017-05-11 17:00:00|292.5935 |
|2017-05-11 17:00:00|2017-05-18 17:00:00|291.5799 |
+------------------+------------------+-----------------+
```

Forecasting of time series data points

The forecasting of time series data points is a very common requirement for business needs such as sales and profit. In the IIoT for instance, in the power domain, one of the use cases is to forecast the power generation in future so that it can be used for financial outcomes, and how to meet the targets. In a mining domain, it helps the sales team to forecast the kind of ore that can be extracted over time for trading reasons, so that they can commit to the orders.

There are multiple ways to forecast the time series endpoint based on the use case and nature of the data, variables, and dependencies. In this section, we will discuss the ARIMA model for forecasting the time series data. ARIMA is an acronym for Auto Regression Integrated Moving Average. The following is an example of how Spark provides the ability to forecast the time series data using the ARIMA model:

```
val lines = spark.read.option("testdata.csv").getLines()
val ts = Vectors.dense(lines.map(_.toDouble).toArray)
val arimaModel = ARIMA.fitModel(1, 0, 1, ts)
val forecast = arimaModel.forecast(ts, 20)
```

Developing a neural network using Keras and TensorFlow using Jupyter

Keras is a high-level API framework for developing deep learning models. Keras is a well-designed API for integrating with a variety of deep learning frameworks such as TensorFlow. Due to its simpler and abstract APIs, it helps developers to accelerate development. It also provides the ability to extend the underlying language capabilities and plug in to the Keras APIs too.

Environment setup

For authoring the analytics Anaconda provides an easier way to develop and test machine learning models using tools such as Jupyter and it also provides a simpler way to create virtual environments to manage different Python packages.

Download and set up Anaconda: `https://www.anaconda.com/download/#macos`.

Create a virtual environment as shown in the following screenshot:

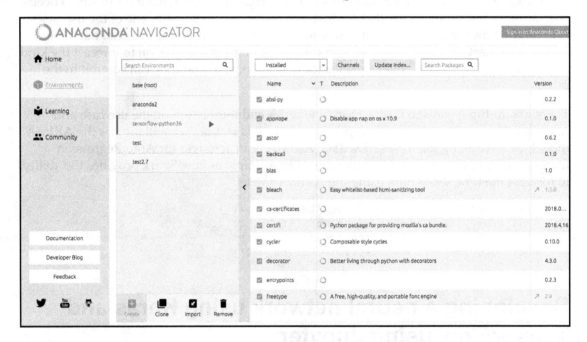

Install the required Keras Python modules, as shown in the following screenshot:

Browse the Jupyter App in Anaconda, as shown in the following screenshot:

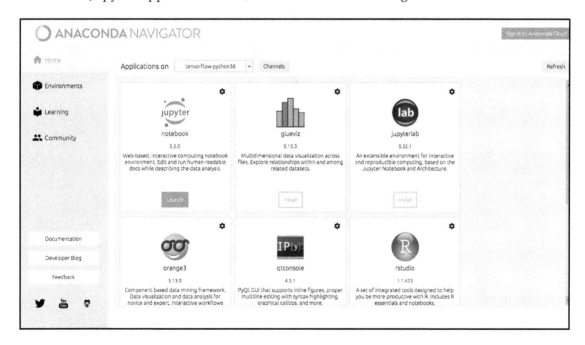

Create a Jupyter Notebook, as shown in the following screenshot:

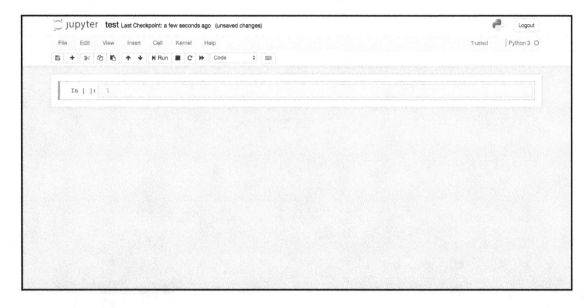

Developing the neural network

The following sections depict the steps for building a neural network using the Keras framework.

The step for creating a sequential model is as follows:

```
# Create your first MLP in Keras
from keras.models import Sequential
from keras.layers import Dense
import numpy
# Load Data
dataset = numpy.loadtxt("population.csv", delimiter=",")
# split into input (X) and output (Y) variables
X = dataset[:,0:10]
Y = dataset[:,10]
# create model
model = Sequential()
```

The step for adding layers to a model is as follows:

```
model.add(Dense(12, input_dim=10, activation='relu'))
model.add(Dense(10, activation='relu'))
```

The step to compile a model is as follows:

```
model.compile(loss='binary_crossentropy', optimizer='adam',
metrics=['accuracy'])
```

The step to fit a model with data is as follows:

```
model.fit(X, Y, epochs=50, batch_size=5)
```

The step to evaluate a model is as follows:

```
scores = model.evaluate(X, Y)
```

The step to predict using the model is as follows:

```
predictions = model.predict(X)
```

The output of the model is as follows:

```
Epoch 1/50
768/768 [==============================] - 0s 568us/step - loss: 3.6841 -
acc: 0.5964
Epoch 2/50
768/768 [==============================] - 0s 170us/step - loss: 0.9283 -
acc: 0.6003
Epoch 3/50
768/768 [==============================] - 0s 166us/step - loss: 0.7414 -
acc: 0.6380
```

The performance metrics of the models in terms of accuracy are as follows:

```
acc: 79.69%
```

Developing an analytics for analyzing time series data using Spark

In this section, we will discuss the creation of a Spark-based analytics for time series analysis and we will discuss some of the Spark concepts. We will be using the following tools for its development:

- **Zeppelin**: We will be using Zeppelin for data exploration, authoring the analytic and executing the analytic and visualizing the data. For more details on Zeppelin, go to https://zeppelin.apache.org/docs/0.8.0/.

- **Spark**: Spark is used as the computing platform for analyzing the data. We will also be leveraging the Spark SQL and other Spark APIs for loading the data and analyzing the data in-memory
- **Time series data**: We will have sample time series data that we can use for analyzing the data for the business outcomes. For this section, we will just do a simple Avg of the data, but it has the potential to expand to include various use cases and analyze outcomes.

Environment setup

Install and start the Zeppelin instance and access the Zeppelin Notebook browser:

```
https://zeppelin.apache.org/
```

Creating a Spark-based Notebook and creating the Spark session

Zeppelin out of the box comes with a Spark interpreter that will automatically create a Spark session for the Notebook. You can access the Spark session by using Spark as shown in the following lines:

Load the time series data in CSV file format and create a Spark data frame:

```
val tempDF = spark.read.option("header",
"true").csv("/Users/k/samples/testdata/temperature.csv")
```

After the data is loaded, Spark creates a data frame. A data frame is a columnar representation of the data in-memory that provides the flexibility to run the SQL statements.

Selecting the data from a Spark data frame:

```
val data = tempDF.select(tempDF("Date").as("timestamp"),
tempDF("temperature").as("temperature"), tempDF("pressure") as
("pressure"), tempDF("speed") as ("speed"))
```

Creating a temporary view of the data:

```
tempDF.createOrReplaceTempView("temp")
```

Executing a Spark SQL:

```
val data =  spark.sql("select * from temp")
```

Printing the data in the Spark data frame:

```
data.show()

+-------+-----------+----------+----------+
| Date|Temperature| Pressure| Speed|
+-------+-----------+----------+----------+
|1/18/16| 703.299988|728.130005| 673.26001|
|1/25/16| 723.580017| 744.98999|694.390015|
| 2/1/16| 750.460022|789.869995|680.150024|
| 2/8/16| 667.849976|701.309998|663.059998|
|2/15/16| 692.97998|712.349976|685.049988|
|2/22/16| 707.450012|713.429993|680.780029|
|2/29/16| 700.320007| 720|697.679993|
| 3/7/16| 706.900024|726.919983|685.340027|
|3/14/16| 726.809998|743.070007| 724.51001|
|3/21/16| 736.5|745.719971| 731|
|3/28/16| 736.789978|757.880005| 728.76001|
| 4/4/16| 750.059998|752.799988|735.369995|
|4/11/16| 743.02002| 761| 731.01001|
|4/18/16| 760.460022|769.900024|713.609985|
|4/25/16| 716.099976|725.765991| 689|
| 5/2/16| 697.630005|711.859985| 689.01001|
| 5/9/16| 712| 724.47998| 709|
|5/16/16| 709.130005| 721.52002|696.799988|
|5/23/16| 706.530029|733.935974|704.179993|
|5/30/16| 731.73999| 739.72998|720.559998|
+-------+-----------+----------+----------+
```

Filtering the data using Spark SQL:

```
val filterData = spark.sql("select date, temperature from temp where
temperature > 700.0")
filterData.show()

+----------+----------+
| date| temperature|
+----------+----------+
|2016-01-18|703.299988|
|2016-01-25|723.580017|
|2016-02-01|750.460022|
|2016-02-22|707.450012|
|2016-02-29|700.320007|
|2016-03-07|706.900024|
|2016-03-14|726.809998|
|2016-03-21|736.500000|
|2016-03-28|736.789978|
|2016-04-04|750.059998|
```

```
|2016-04-11|743.020020|
|2016-04-18|760.460022|
|2016-04-25|716.099976|
|2016-05-09|712.000000|
|2016-05-16|709.130005|
|2016-05-23|706.530029|
|2016-05-30|731.739990|
|2016-06-06|724.909973|
|2016-06-13|716.510010|
|2016-07-11|708.049988|
+----------+----------+
```

Visualizing the data in the data frame using SQL in Zeppelin:

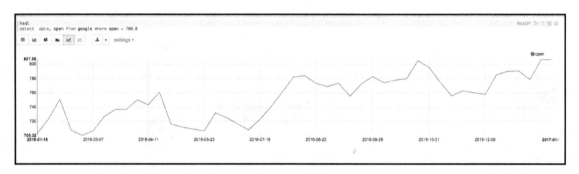

Write the results to the filesystem:

```
filterData.write.format("csv").save("/Users/k/samples/testdata/filtereddata
1.csv")
```

Developing streaming analytics using Spark

In this section, we will discuss the steps required in developing a streaming analytics using Spark and Kafka.

Kafka is a streaming platform for real time message streaming. It is a highly scalable distributed platform that enables the client and servers to publish and subscribe for messages.

Spark has a Kafka connector that supports real-time streaming analysis. It supports the analysis of the incoming stream for anomaly detection or any other use cases for real time notifications and alerts in mission-critical events.

Environment setup

Install Kafka and Spark from the following URLs:

- `http://kafka.apache.org/documentation/#producerapi`
- `https://spark.apache.org/downloads.html`

Developing the streaming analytics

Spark is a microbatch-based streaming engine that processes the data in batches. In the following example, it is configured to process the batch data acquired within one second. If the data points are ingested at a rate of 100 ms, then within one second, 10 data points can be accumulated by the time the batch is processed.

Creating a streaming context using spark API:

```
sc = SparkContext(appName="IIoTSparkStreamingApp")
ssc = StreamingContext(sc, Seconds(1))
```

Configure the Kafka brokers and topic to listen for the input stream:

```
brokers = "localhost:9092"
topic = "test"
```

Create a direct stream for the input stream data:

```
message = KafkaUtils.createDirectStream(ssc, [topic],
{"metadata.broker.list": brokers})
```

Transform the input stream data from Kafka and collect the data:

```
counts = lines.flatMap(lambda line: line.split(",")).map(lambda word:
(word, 1)).reduceByKey(lambda a, b: a+b)
```

Start the streaming context:

```
ssc.start()
```

Summary

In this chapter, we covered the concepts of advanced analytics and how it plays a major role in the IIoT use cases for running the industrial equipment and manufacturing plants efficiently. We also discussed some of the real-world challenges in running the legacy analytics at scale and how big data plays a major role in building better models to predict the outcomes with more accuracy. We also looked at some of latest technologies, such as Apache Spark ML, the Keras framework, and the APIs available for the development of machine learning models. In the next chapter, we will look at how to develop an IIoT application.

6
Developing Your First Application for IIoT

In this chapter, you will learn about the S95 standard (https://www.isa.org/isa95/) and how it applies to the exchange of asset data. We also provide an overview of databases to store asset data and a comparison of time series storage. Then, we demonstrate how to build a Node.js application that simulates the reading of time series data from sensors and how to enable analytics and visualizations of the data reads. Finally, we provide instructions on configuring Grafana alerts with visualizations, and email and Slack notifications about database values exceeding limits.

This chapter covers the following topics:

- S95 standard and exchange of asset data according to the S95 standard
- Choosing a database management system to store asset data
- Comparison of the most common time series storage
- Using InfluxDB as a time series storage
- Building a Node.js application to simulate reading of time series data
- Types of analytics
- Using InfluxDB to enable descriptive analytics for time series data
- Using Highcharts and Grafana to enable visualization of time series data
- Configuring notifications via email and Slack and setting up alerts from Grafana

Developing and modeling assets using the S95 standard

The S95 standard, otherwise known as ANSI/ISA-95 (and in Europe IEC 62264), was developed by the **International Society of Automation** (**ISA**) to provide guidelines on integrating an enterprise system with a control one. The standard is applicable to all industries and all types of processes within them—batch, continuous, and repetitive.

S95 consists of the following parts, describing different aspects of integrating an enterprise control system:

- **ANSI/ISA-95.00.01-2000, Enterprise-Control System Integration, Part 1: Models and Terminology**: The document overviews the object models that can help to identify the information to exchange and provides standard terminology
- **ANSI/ISA-95.00.02-2001, Enterprise-Control System Integration, Part 2: Object Model Attributes**: This part of the standard relates to the attributes of the objects as defined in *Part 1*
- **ANSI/ISA-95.00.03-2005, Enterprise-Control System Integration, Part 3: Models Of Manufacturing Operations Management**: The document explores the production (manufacturing execution) level in more detail, giving recommendations on a standardized approach to describing it
- **ISA-95.04, Object Models and Attributes, Part 4: Object Models and Attributes For Manufacturing Operations Management** (still in development): This part of the standard addresses the object models and attributes that define the information exchange flows between different activities at the manufacturing execution level
- **SA-95.05, B2M Transactions, Part 5: Business-To-Manufacturing Transactions** (still in development): The document looks into the transactions between an enterprise management and a production automation system

The total of the documents provide a consistent terminology to facilitate manufacturer-supplier communication and a hierarchical system model representing control levels within an enterprise.

The standards distinguish five types of reference models that help to define the boundaries between an enterprise and a control system:

- Context models
- Hierarchy models (scheduling and control, equipment hierarchy)
- Functional data flow models (manufacturing functions, data flows)

- Object models (objects, object relations, object attributes)
- Operation activity models (operation elements, operation functions, operation flows)

The S95 models can aid in determining the responsibilities of various business functions and the types of information to be exchanged between applications on different control levels.

ISA-95 control levels

Each of the control levels is associated with different activities and time frames as illustrated in the following diagram:

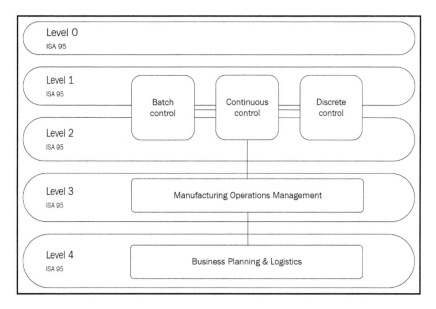

Activities on different S95 enterprise control levels

Software systems used at each of the levels will vary, too. For instance, **Level 4** can also include an ERP (enterprise resource management) system, as well as apps for supply chain management or customer relationship management. In addition to a **manufacturing execution system** (**MES**), **Level 3** can comprise a laboratory information management system. **Level 1** and **Level 2** embrace commonly used control systems, while **Level 0** corresponds to physical assets.

Exchange of asset data as represented in S95

The enterprise and the control systems exchange information that can be divided into four categories: product definition, production capability, production schedule, and production performance. Each of the categories includes data describing resources, that is, personnel, material, equipment, and process segments.

To exchange information, the **Business-To-Manufacturing Markup Language** (**B2MML**) is used. Messages are transferred as a set of XML files. The following diagram illustrates the data exchange between Level 4 (an ERP system) and Level 3 (MES):

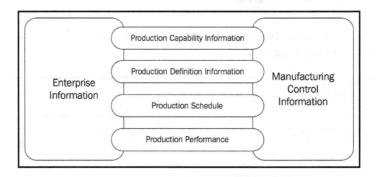

Information exchange between control Levels 3 and 4

Information exchange within an enterprise control system can embrace the following types of asset data:

- Personnel
- Departments
- Facilities
- Shifts
- Shift assignment
- Machines
- Employees
- Employee qualifications
- Production orders
- Processes
- Articles
- Resource vectors
- Process steps
- Production phases

- Sensors
- Sensor-to-machine communication
- Alerts

The following XML message illustrates the exchange of data about the `Engines` asset:

```
<?xml version="1.0" encoding="UTF-8"?>
<ProductionCapability xmlns="http://www.mesa.org/xml/B2MML-V0600"
xmlns:xsi="http://www.w3.org/2001/XMLSchema-instance"
xsi:schemaLocation="http://www.mesa.org/xml/B2MML-V0600 file:/[PATH ON THE
COMPUTER]/Schema/B2MML-V0600-ProductionCapability.xsd">
  <ID>L303</ID>
  <Description>List of Engines</Description>
  <CapabilityType>Used</CapabilityType>
  <EquipmentCapability>
    <EquipmentID>E304</EquipmentID>
    <Description>A turbofan engine</Description>
    <CapabilityType>Used</CapabilityType>
    <HierarchyScope>
      <EquipmentID>GE CF34</EquipmentID>
      <EquipmentElementLevel>Area</EquipmentElementLevel>
      <HierarchyScope>
        <EquipmentID>Turbofan engine GE CF34</EquipmentID>
        <EquipmentElementLevel>EquipmentModule</EquipmentElementLevel>
      </HierarchyScope>
    </HierarchyScope>
    <EquipmentCapabilityProperty>
      <ID>Priority</ID>
      <Value>
        <ValueString>1</ValueString>
      </Value>
    </EquipmentCapabilityProperty>
  </EquipmentCapability>
  <EquipmentCapability>
    <EquipmentID>E211</EquipmentID>
    <Description>An turbofan engine</Description>
    <CapabilityType>Used</CapabilityType>
    <HierarchyScope>
      <EquipmentID>GE GE90</EquipmentID>
      <EquipmentElementLevel>Area</EquipmentElementLevel>
      <HierarchyScope>
        <EquipmentID>Turbofan engine GE GE90</EquipmentID>
        <EquipmentElementLevel>EquipmentModule</EquipmentElementLevel>
      </HierarchyScope>
    </HierarchyScope>
    <EquipmentCapabilityProperty>
      <ID>Priority</ID>
```

```
      <Value>
        <ValueString>1</ValueString>
      </Value>
    </EquipmentCapabilityProperty>
  </EquipmentCapability>
</ProductionCapability>
```

The following XML message illustrates the of data about the `Employees` asset:

```
<?xml version="1.0" encoding="UTF-8"?>
<PersonnelInformation xmlns="http://www.mesa.org/xml/B2MML-V0600"
xmlns:xsi="http://www.w3.org/2001/XMLSchema-instance"
xsi:schemaLocation="http://www.mesa.org/xml/B2MML-V0600 file:/[PATH ON THE
COMPUTER]/Schema/B2MML-V0600-Personnel.xsd">
  <Description/>
  <PublishedDate>2017-09-01T08:00:00</PublishedDate>
  <Person>
    <ID>M145</ID>
    <PersonName>William Mouton</PersonName>
  </Person>
  <Person>
    <ID>H323</ID>
    <PersonName>Abigail Embry</PersonName>
  </Person>
</PersonnelInformation>
```

The following XML message illustrates the exchange of data about the `Order` asset:

```
<?xml version="1.0" encoding="UTF-8"?>
<ProductionSchedule xmlns="http://www.mesa.org/xml/B2MML-V0600"
xmlns:xsi="http://www.w3.org/2001/XMLSchema-instance"
xsi:schemaLocation="http://www.mesa.org/xml/B2MML-V0600
file:/C:/Users/Angelo/Documents/Xlab%20Progetti/ARTISAN/WP5/Task%205.2%20In
teroperability%20Data%20Exchange%20Mod
el%20Definition/B2MML%20versione%20600/Schema/B2MML-V0600-
ProductionSchedule.xsd">
  <ID>PS122643</ID>
  <Description>Planned Order</Description>
  <ProductionRequest>
    <ID>O-10342</ID>
    <Description>Order for 10 turbofan engines GE GE90</Description>
    <ProductProductionRuleID>O10342</ProductProductionRuleID>
    <EndTime>2017-09-01T08:00:00</EndTime>
    <SegmentRequirement>
      <ID>S53</ID>
      <LatestEndTime>2017-10-01T08:00:00</LatestEndTime>
      <ProductionParameter>
        <Parameter>
```

```
        <ID>Release date</ID>
        <Value>
          <ValueString>2017-09-01T80:00:00</ValueString>
        </Value>
      </Parameter>
    </ProductionParameter>
    <MaterialRequirement>
      <Quantity>
        <QuantityString>10</QuantityString>
        <UnitOfMeasure>units</UnitOfMeasure>
      </Quantity>
    </MaterialRequirement>
  </SegmentRequirement>
 </ProductionRequest>
</ProductionSchedule>
```

 For additional information about the S95 and its applications, read this publication: https://www.isa.org/isa95/.

Selecting a storage

Each manufacturing facility contains a huge number of assets, from screwdrivers to machines. To track all of them, observing the S95 requirements, you need a suitable database storing asset data. Available storage options can be subdivided into the following groups.

Relational DBMS

A relational DBMS is a table-oriented store based on the relational model (originally described by Edgar F. Codd). Such databases comprise a number of records (entities), each corresponding to a row in a table. The records (entities) contain attribute values.

Relation schemas within a database table are defined by the table name, a fixed number of attributes, and fixed data types. The schemas are the product of normalization in the course of data modeling.

Operations within such databases are performed using a database language—most commonly SQL.

Examples of relational DBMS are Oracle, MySQL, Microsoft SQL Server, PostgreSQL, and DB2.

Key-value stores

The databases of this type store pairs of keys and values. When required, data can be retrieved based on a known key. Such stores are mostly used in embedded systems or as in-process databases.

The major advantage of key-value stores is their simplicity, though this also makes them unsuitable for complex applications.

Examples of key-value stores are Redis, Memcached, Microsoft Azure Cosmos DB, Hazelcast, and Ehcache.

Advanced forms

This is an extended form of a key-value store with an additional capability of sorting the keys. Moreover, it provides a possibility to range queries and perform the ordered processing of keys.

Examples of advanced form stores are Redis, Memcached, Hazelcas, Microsoft Azure Cosmos DB, and Riak KV.

Document stores

Document stores—also known as **document-oriented database systems**—have a non-uniform, often nested, record structure. Their columns can contain more than one value, while value types in individual columns can vary from record to record.

In addition, document stores often use internal JSON notations that can be processed directly in applications.

Examples of document stores are MongoDB, Amazon DynamoDB, Couchbase, CouchDB, and MarkLogic.

Graph DBMS

Graph DBMS (graph-oriented/graph database) represent data in the form of graph structures—nodes and edges (relations between nodes). Graph DBMS usually do not index all nodes, which makes it impossible to access nodes directly based on attribute values.

The main advantage of such databases is that they allow for easy processing of graph data and calculating specific graph properties (for example, how many steps are required to get from one node to another).

Examples of graph databases are Neo4j, Microsoft Azure Cosmos DB, OrientDB, Titan, ArangoDB, and MongoDB.

Time series DBMS

The databases of this type are used specifically to handle time series data (for example, from sensors, smart meters, and RFIDs). Each entry in such a storage has a timestamp.

Examples of times series databases are InfluxDB, RRDtool, Graphite, OpenTSDB, and Kdb+.

RDF stores

These stores are based on the **Resource Description Framework** (**RDF**) methodology that was initially meant for describing IT resource metadata. Today, the application area of such databases is more generic, mostly for semantic and some other types of web applications.

In a RDF database, information is stored in the form of subject-predicate-object triples.

Examples of RDF stores are MarkLogic, Jena, Virtuoso, AllegroGraph, and Stardog.

Object-oriented DBMS

Object-oriented DBMS—also known as **object databases**—appeared following the rise of object-oriented programming. Accordingly, these data stores are based on the object-oriented data model, comprising classes, properties, and methods.

Objects are managed as single and indivisible units and stored the way they are represented in a programming language, without conversion or decomposition. For operations with objects, such databases often use specific SQL-like query languages.

Examples of object-oriented databases are Caché, Db4o, ObjectStore, Versant Object Database, and Matisse.

Search engines

Search engines are NoSQL solutions specifically designed for data search. This type of databases supports complex search expressions, full-text search, distributed and geo-based search, and stemming techniques. They also provide a possibility to range and group search results.

Examples of search engines are Elasticsearch, Solr, Splunk, MarkLogic, and Sphinx.

MultiValue DBMS

In a MultiValue DBMS, data is stored in tables, which is similar to relational databases. However, unlike in the case of relational solutions, a record attribute in a MultiValue store can be assigned more than one value.

For storing information, such databases use two separate files—one for raw data and the other for the format to display the raw data.

Examples of MultiValue DBMS are Adabas, UniData, UniVerse, and jBASE.

Wide column stores

Wide column stores—a type of key-value stores—ensure data storage in records and can contain large numbers of dynamic columns. In such a store, names and record keys can vary within the same table.

Examples of wide column stores are Cassandra, HBase, and Microsoft Azure Cosmos DB.

Native XML DBMS

Native XML database management systems use a data model similar to that of an XML document. These systems must not be confused with XML-enabled databases that can only store data as XML documents. A native XML database can use formats other than XML to store data, if appropriate, and offers wider capabilities, including the following:

- Hierarchical representation of data
- Reading embedded PCDATA declarations in XML elements
- Support of XML-specific query languages, for example, XPath, XQuery, or XSLT

Examples of native XML DBMS are MarkLogic, Oracle Berkeley DB, and Virtuoso.

Content stores

Content stores, sometimes referred to as content repositories, are designed to manage various digital content (for example, text, pictures or videos, including metadata).

For queries, such databases mostly use SQL or XPath. Other features include the following:

- Full-text search
- Versioning
- Hierarchical structuring of content

Examples of content stores are Jackrabbit and ModeShape.

Event stores

Based on the event sourcing concept, such stores are used to keep time series records of all events that change the state of an individual object. This is what makes them different from other types of database management systems, where only the current state of an object is stored.

Event stores support such manipulations as the insertion of new events and querying event time series for an object. However, modifications or deletions of existing events are not possible. The feature is of special value for distributed systems, where consistency is very important.

Examples of event stores are Event Store and NEventStore.

Navigational DBMS

Navigational DBMS were developed back in the 1960s to handle large amounts of data. Their peculiarity is that they provide access to datasets via linked records. Depending on the flexibility of linking, such databases can use hierarchical- or network-type database interfaces.

Examples of navigational DBMS are IMS and IDMS.

In addition to the aforementioned DBMS, we would like to mention one more new and fast-growing type of data storages—blockchain.

Blockchain

A blockchain (or a chain of blocks) is actually a distributed database that stores a list of records (or blocks) with timestamps. The concept of blockchain was first introduced by Satoshi Nakamoto in 2008, with the bitcoin cryptocurrency becoming its first implementation.

Each of the blocks in a chain is directly linked to the preceding one, which makes data modifications impossible. Making changes to a block after data is recorded into it would require altering all the subsequent blocks.

The list of records is continuously expanded as new blocks are added to the chain and validated. The validation is ensured through a collectively managed peer-to-peer network based on a specific validation protocol.

Due to such design, blockchains are inherently secure. They provide high Byzantine fault tolerance, thereby allowing for decentralized consensus. Considering all of the above, blockchain can be potentially used for recording events, maintaining medical records, and other data management activities, such as managing identities, processing transactions, and documenting provenance.

It is possible to distinguish public or private blockchains. Public solutions are more trusted because data is available to any user on the network. However, this type of blockchain could be too expensive for IoT since they charge per transaction payment.

Private blockchains can be used free of charge, but they are less trusted. This is due to the fact that their participants are less numerous than in a public network. So, cheating is more probable.

Examples of blockchains are ChromaWay Postchain, Bitcoin, Ethereum, Emercoin, EOS, Tezos and Steem/Golos.

Important considerations

When selecting a database, make sure it is suitable for your needs, in particular, in terms of data types it can store. For example, if you work with time series data and would like to have statistics, consider using databases with analytical functions (for example, InfluxDB or Graphite). If you are using a cloud, pay attention to the availability of as-a-service solutions. If you do not use a cloud, you may need to create a database cluster.

Performance is also critical. A database must be able to handle all data you want to save, plus a safety margin, at an acceptable speed. As most databases require using a fixed schema of fields, it may be difficult to ensure updates without a downtime.

Usually, databases can work with any programming language. However, to avoid unpleasant surprises, check if there is a client available for the selected database in the package repository of your preferred programming language.

When you install a database on top of your own infrastructure, keep in mind that you need to update it to the latest version within the shortest time possible for security reasons, provide its network availability, scaling capabilities, and a functional backup system.

> The 451 Research company created a database landscape for 2016, covering the existing DBMS. For more details, go to `https://451research.com/state-of-the-database-landscape`.

Time series storage

When we need to store information describing the operation of assets at certain moments over a period of time (for example, information from asset sensors), the best choice is a time series storage. Currently, there are dozens of such databases to choose from. The table here features a comparison of the most widely used ones:

	DalmatinerDB	InfluxDB	Prometheus	Elasticsearch	Graphite (Whisper)

Data types	`float62, int56`	`int64,`
		`float64,`
		`bool,` and
		`string`
			`float64`	`string,`
				`int32, int64,`
				`float32,`
				`float64,`
				`bool, null`
					`float64`

Data compression ratio	1	2.2	1.3	22	12
Precision	millisecond	nanosecond	millisecond	millisecond	second
Ingest performance (metrics/sec)	3m	470k	800k	30k	300k
Data source	TCP (binary protocol), OpenTSDB (text), Graphite (text), Prometheus (text), Metrics 2.0 (text), InfluxDB (HTTP)	InfluxDB (HTTP), InfluxDB (UDP), OpenTSDB (text), OpenTSDB (HTTP), Graphite (text), etc.	scraping (text, protobuf)	HTTP	UDP (text protocol), TCP (text protocol, pickle), pickle
Authorization	No	Yes	No	Yes	No

Comparison of time series storage

Using InfluxDB as a time series storage

For our purposes, as described in the subsequent section, we will use InfluxDB, because it is fast and mature, and allows us to perform analytical operations. The easiest way to start InfluxDB locally is by using a Docker container. All you need to do is to run the following command:

```
docker run -p 8086:8086 -v $PWD:/var/lib/influxdb influxdb
```

The $PWD value stands for the default path to the folder for saving the database data (current working dir). To specify another path, change the value as appropriate.

The return of the command will be as shown in the following screenshot:

```
em:timeseries             $ docker run -p 8086:8086 -v $PWD:/var/lib/influxdb influxdb

  8888888          .d888 888                    8888888b.  888888b.
   888            d88P"  888                    888   "Y88b 888  "88b
   888            888    888                    888    888 888  .88P
   888   88888b.  888888 888 888  888 888  888  888    888 8888888K.
   888   888 "88b 888    888 888  888 Y8bd8P'   888    888 888  "Y88b
   888   888  888 888    888 888  888   X88K    888    888 888    888
   888   888  888 888    888 Y88b 888 .d8""88b. 888  .d88P 888   d88P
  8888888 888  888 888    888  "Y88888 888  888 8888888P"  8888888P"

[I] 2017-07-11T11:02:48Z InfluxDB starting, version 1.3.0, branch master, commit 76124df5c121e411e99807b9473a03eb785cd43b
[I] 2017-07-11T11:02:48Z Go version go1.8.3, GOMAXPROCS set to 4
[I] 2017-07-11T11:02:48Z Using configuration at: /etc/influxdb/influxdb.conf
[I] 2017-07-11T11:02:48Z Using data dir: /var/lib/influxdb/data service=store
[I] 2017-07-11T11:02:48Z reading file /var/lib/influxdb/wal/_internal/monitor/1/_00001.wal, size 5616229 engine=tsm1 service=cacheloader
[I] 2017-07-11T11:02:48Z /var/lib/influxdb/data/mydb/autogen/2/000000004-000000003.tsm (#0) opened in 1.694784ms engine=tsm1 service=filestore
[I] 2017-07-11T11:02:48Z /var/lib/influxdb/data/mydb/autogen/2/000000005-000000001.tsm (#1) opened in 9.925612ms engine=tsm1 service=filestore
[I] 2017-07-11T11:02:48Z reading file /var/lib/influxdb/wal/mydb/autogen/2/_00007.wal, size 0 engine=tsm1 service=cacheloader
[I] 2017-07-11T11:02:48Z /var/lib/influxdb/data/mydb/autogen/2 opened in 36.63897ms service=store
[I] 2017-07-11T11:02:48Z reading file /var/lib/influxdb/wal/_internal/monitor/1/_00002.wal, size 0 engine=tsm1 service=cacheloader
[I] 2017-07-11T11:02:49Z /var/lib/influxdb/data/_internal/monitor/1 opened in 375.409264ms service=store
[I] 2017-07-11T11:02:49Z opened service service=subscriber
[I] 2017-07-11T11:02:49Z Starting monitor system service=monitor
[I] 2017-07-11T11:02:49Z 'build' registered for diagnostics monitoring service=monitor
[I] 2017-07-11T11:02:49Z 'runtime' registered for diagnostics monitoring service=monitor
[I] 2017-07-11T11:02:49Z 'network' registered for diagnostics monitoring service=monitor
[I] 2017-07-11T11:02:49Z 'system' registered for diagnostics monitoring service=monitor
[I] 2017-07-11T11:02:49Z Starting precreation service with check interval of 10m0s, advance period of 30m0s service=shard-precreation
[I] 2017-07-11T11:02:49Z Starting snapshot service service=snapshot
[I] 2017-07-11T11:02:49Z Starting continuous query service service=continuous_querier
[I] 2017-07-11T11:02:49Z Starting HTTP service service=httpd
[I] 2017-07-11T11:02:49Z Authentication enabled:false service=httpd
[I] 2017-07-11T11:02:49Z Listening on HTTP: [::]:8086 service=httpd
[I] 2017-07-11T11:02:49Z Starting retention policy enforcement service with check interval of 30m0s service=retention
[I] 2017-07-11T11:02:49Z Listening for signals
[I] 2017-07-11T11:02:49Z Storing statistics in database '_internal' retention policy 'monitor', at interval 10s service=monitor
[I] 2017-07-11T11:02:49Z Sending usage statistics to usage.influxdata.com
```

Console output after starting InfluxDB

If you prefer installing without Docker, follow the instructions on the InfluxData website (https://www.influxdata.com/). You can also use the database in a cloud (for example, Amazon, Aiven, and so on).

Now, we have a container running in the foreground. However, if it is not a cloud, we will need to create a database instance, naming it mydb. To do this, run the following:

```
curl -i -XPOST http://localhost:8086/query --data-urlencode "q=CREATE
DATABASE mydb"
```

The return will be as shown in this screenshot:

```
em:timeseries melnikaite$ curl -i -XPOST http://localhost:8086/query --data-urlencode "q=CREATE DATABASE mydb"
HTTP/1.1 200 OK
Connection: close
Content-Type: application/json
Request-Id: a3fb7a41-6628-11e7-8001-000000000000
X-Influxdb-Version: 1.3.0
Date: Tue, 11 Jul 2017 11:03:59 GMT
Transfer-Encoding: chunked

{"results":[{"statement_id":0}]}
```

Creating an InfluxDB database instance

Now, we have a database named `mydb` ready for data posting.

Creating instances of assets and adding time series data

In this section, we will build a Node.js application that simulates reading of time series data from sensors. To store the data, we will use the InfluxDB time series database.

For building the application, we will need the following software:

- Node.js 6+ (`https://nodejs.org/en/download/`)
- `restify` (`https://www.npmjs.com/package/restify`)
- `node-influx` (`https://www.npmjs.com/package/influx`)
- `slack-incoming-webhook` (`https://www.npmjs.com/package/slack-incoming-webhook`)
- Docker (`https://docs.docker.com/engine/installation/`)

To build a Node.js application that simulates reading of time series data from sensors, proceed as follows:

1. Create a `package.json` file, describing software dependencies. If you use a cloud, specify `localhost` and `mydb` as the credentials for the host and database accordingly:

```
{
  "name": "timeseries",
  "version": "1.0.0",
  "description": "",
  "main": "index.js",
```

```
"scripts": {
  "start": "node index.js",
  "test": "echo \"Error: no test specified\" && exit 1"
},
"author": "",
"license": "ISC",
"dependencies": {
  "emailjs": "^1.0.10",
  "influx": "^5.0.7",
  "restify": "^5.0.0",
  "slack-incoming-webhook": "^1.1.0"
}
}
```

 To create a file in a Linux console, you can use the GNU nano editor. It is pre-installed in most of Linux distributives. All you need is to run the `nano FILE_NAME` command and follow the displayed instructions.

2. Create an `index.js` file containing the main code of the application:

```
var restify = require('restify');
var server = restify.createServer({name: 'MyApp'});
var Influx = require('influx');
var alertEmail = require('./alert-email');
var slack = require('slack-incoming-webhook')({url: '{webhook
url}', });

var min = 0;
var max = 100;
var alertFrom = 90;
var interval = 1000;
var alertSlack = slack({
  url: 'https://hooks.slack.com/services/xxx/yyy/zzz',
  channel: '#channel-name',
  icon: ':warning:'
});

// create connection
const influx = new Influx.InfluxDB({
  host: 'localhost',
  database: 'mydb',
  schema: [
    {
      measurement: 'sensor1',
      fields: {
        variable1: Influx.FieldType.INTEGER
      },
```

```
        tags: [
          'device'
        ]
      }
    ]
});

// simulate receiving data from sensors
setInterval(function () {
  var variable1 = Math.floor(max - Math.random() * (max - min));

  if (variable1 >= alertFrom) {
    var msg = 'variable exceeded ' + variable1 + ' rpm';
    alertEmail(msg);
    alertSlack(msg);
  }

  influx.writePoints([
    {
      measurement: 'sensor1',
      tags: {device: 'raspberry'},
      fields: {variable1: variable1}
    }
  ]).then(function () {
    console.log(variable1);
  }).catch(function (err) {
    console.error(err);
  });
}, interval);

server.use(function search(req, res, next) {
  res.header('Access-Control-Allow-Origin', '*');
  res.header('Access-Control-Allow-Headers', 'X-Requested-With');
  return next();
});

server.get('/last', function search(req, res, next) {
  influx.query('select * from sensor1 WHERE time > now() -
5m').then(function (result) {
    res.json(result)
  }).catch(function (err) {
    res.status(500).send(err.stack)
  });
  return next();
});

server.get('/stats', function search(req, res, next) {
  influx.query('SELECT COUNT(*), MEAN(*), MEDIAN(*), MODE(*),
```

```
SPREAD(*), STDDEV(*), SUM(*), FIRST(*), LAST(*), MAX(*), MIN(*),
PERCENTILE(*, 5) FROM "sensor1" WHERE time > now() -
1h').then(function (result) {
    res.json(result)
  }).catch(function (err) {
    res.status(500).send(err.stack)
  });
  return next();
});

server.get(/\/public\/?.*/, restify.plugins.serveStatic({
  directory: __dirname
}));

server.listen(8080);
```

3. Create an `alert-email.js` file with a configuration of email notifications as shown here. Make sure to specify the address of your SMTP server as the credentials (user, host):

```
var email = require('emailjs');

var server = email.server.connect({
  user: 'username@gmail.com',
  password: 'password',
  host: 'smtp.gmail.com',
  ssl: true
});

// send the message and get a callback with an error or details of
the message that was sent
function alertEmail(msg) {
  server.send({
    text: msg,
    from: 'username@gmail.com',
    to: 'username@gmail.com',
    subject: 'Alert'
  }, function (err, message) {
    console.log(err || message);
  });
}

module.exports = alertEmail;
```

4. Create a `mkdir` public folder to store files enabling Highcharts visualizations of analytics for sensor data.

5. Create a `public/index.html` file with the following content:

```html
<script src="https://code.jquery.com/jquery-3.1.1.min.js"></script>
<script src="https://code.highcharts.com/highcharts.js"></script>
<script
src="https://code.highcharts.com/highcharts-more.js"></script>
<script
src="https://code.highcharts.com/modules/solid-gauge.js"></script>
<script
src="https://cdnjs.cloudflare.com/ajax/libs/toastr.js/2.1.3/toastr.
min.js"></script>
<link
href="https://cdnjs.cloudflare.com/ajax/libs/toastr.js/2.1.3/toastr
.min.css" rel="stylesheet" type="text/css"/>
<link href="./chart-style.css" rel="stylesheet" type="text/css"/>
<link href="./gauge-style.css" rel="stylesheet" type="text/css"/>
<script src="./chart-script.js"></script>
<script src="./gauge-script.js"></script>

<div id="chart-container"></div>

<div class="gauge-container">
  <div class="flex-item" id="gauge-container-count"></div>
  <div class="flex-item" id="gauge-container-mean"></div>
  <div class="flex-item" id="gauge-container-median"></div>
  <div class="flex-item" id="gauge-container-mode"></div>
  <div class="flex-item" id="gauge-container-spread"></div>
  <div class="flex-item" id="gauge-container-stddev"></div>
  <div class="flex-item" id="gauge-container-sum"></div>
  <div class="flex-item" id="gauge-container-first"></div>
  <div class="flex-item" id="gauge-container-last"></div>
  <div class="flex-item" id="gauge-container-max"></div>
  <div class="flex-item" id="gauge-container-min"></div>
  <div class="flex-item" id="gauge-container-percentile"></div>
</div>
```

6. Create a `public/chart-script.js` file with following content:

```javascript
$(document).ready(function () {
  var stats = [{}];
  var alertFrom = 90;
  var interval = 1000;

  $.getJSON('http://localhost:8080/last', function (response) {
    var data = [];
    for (var i = 0; i < response.length; i++) {
      data.push({
        x: new Date(response[i].time).getTime() * 1000,
```

```
          y: response[i].variable1
        });
    }

  Highcharts.chart('chart-container', {
    chart: {
      type: 'spline',
      animation: Highcharts.svg, // don't animate in old IE
      marginRight: 10,
      events: {
        load: function () {
          // set up the updating of the chart each second
          var series = this.series[0];
          setInterval(function () {
            $.getJSON('http://localhost:8080/stats', function
(response) {
              stats = response;
              var x = (new Date()).getTime() * 1000;
              var y = response[0].last_variable1;
              series.addPoint([x, y], true, data.length > 300);

              if(y >= alertFrom) toastr['warning']('variable1
exceeded ' + y + ' rpm');
            });
          }, interval);
        }
      }
    },
    credits: {
      enabled: false
    },
    title: {
      text: 'sensor1'
    },
    xAxis: {
      type: 'datetime',
      tickPixelInterval: 150
    },
    yAxis: {
      title: {
        text: 'variable1'
      },
      plotLines: [{
        value: 0,
        width: 1,
        color: '#808080'
      }]
    },
```

```
            tooltip: {
              formatter: function () {
                return '<b>' + this.series.name + '</b><br/>' +
                  Highcharts.dateFormat('%Y-%m-%d %H:%M:%S', this.x) +
'<br/>' +
                  Highcharts.numberFormat(this.y, 2);
              }
            },
            legend: {
              enabled: false
            },
            series: [{
              name: 'variable1',
              data: data,
              zones: [{
                value: alertFrom
              }, {
                color: 'red'
              }]
            }]
          });
        });
      });
```

7. Create a `public/chart-style.css` file with the following content:

```css
#chart-container {
  min-width: 300px;
  height: 400px;
  margin: 0 auto;
}
```

8. Create a `public/gauge-script.js` file with the following content:

```js
$(document).ready(function () {
  var stats = [{}];
  var gauges = {};
  var min = 0;
  var max = 100;
  var interval = 1000;

  var gaugeOptions = {
    chart: {
      type: 'solidgauge'
    },

    credits: {
      enabled: false
```

```
      },

   title: null,

   pane: {
     center: ['50%', '85%'],
     size: '140%',
     startAngle: -90,
     endAngle: 90,
     background: {
       backgroundColor: (Highcharts.theme &&
Highcharts.theme.background2) || '#EEE',
       innerRadius: '60%',
       outerRadius: '100%',
       shape: 'arc'
     }
   },

   tooltip: {
     enabled: false
   },

   // the value axis
   yAxis: {
     stops: [
       [0.1, '#55BF3B'], // green
       [0.5, '#DDDF0D'], // yellow
       [0.9, '#DF5353'] // red
     ],
     lineWidth: 0,
     minorTickInterval: null,
     tickAmount: 2,
     title: {
       y: -70
     },
     labels: {
       y: 16
     }
   },

   plotOptions: {
     solidgauge: {
       dataLabels: {
         y: 5,
         borderWidth: 0,
         useHTML: true
       }
     }
```

```
        }
    };

    var gaugeTypes = [
      {name: 'count', suffix: ' changes'},
      {name: 'mean', suffix: ' rpm'},
      {name: 'median', suffix: ' rpm'},
      {name: 'mode', suffix: ' rpm'},
      {name: 'spread', suffix: ' rpm'},
      {name: 'stddev', suffix: ' rpm'},
      {name: 'sum', suffix: ' rpm'},
      {name: 'first', suffix: ' rpm'},
      {name: 'last', suffix: ' rpm'},
      {name: 'max', suffix: ' rpm'},
      {name: 'min', suffix: ' rpm'},
      {name: 'percentile', suffix: ' rpm'}
    ];

    for (var i = 0; i < gaugeTypes.length; i++) {
      var name = gaugeTypes[i].name;
      var suffix = gaugeTypes[i].suffix;
      gauges[name] = Highcharts.chart('gauge-container-' + name,
Highcharts.merge(gaugeOptions, {
        yAxis: {
          min: min,
          max: max,
          title: {
            text: name
          }
        },

        series: [{
          name: name,
          data: [0],
          dataLabels: {
            format: '<div style="text-align:center"><span
style="font-size:25px;color:' +
            ((Highcharts.theme && Highcharts.theme.contrastTextColor)
|| 'black') + '">{y}</span><br/>' +
            '<span style="font-size:12px;color:silver">' + suffix +
'</span></div>'
          },
          tooltip: {
            valueSuffix: suffix
          }
        }]
      }));
    }
```

```
    // Bring life to the dials
    setInterval(function () {
      $.getJSON('http://localhost:8080/stats', function (response) {
        stats = response;
        for (var i = 0; i < gaugeTypes.length; i++) {
          var name = gaugeTypes[i].name;
          if (!gauges[name]) return;
          var newVal = stats[0][name + '_variable1'];
          if (!newVal) return;
          newVal = parseFloat(newVal.toFixed(2));
          var point = gauges[name].series[0].points[0];
          point.update(newVal);
        }
      });
    }, interval);
});
```

9. Create a `public/gauge-style.css` file with the following content:

```css
.gauge-container {
  display: flex;
  flex-flow: row wrap;
  justify-content: space-around;
}

.flex-item {
  padding: 5px;
  width: 300px;
  height: 200px;
  margin-top: 10px;
}
```

10. Create a Docker file for running the application inside a container with the following content:

```
FROM node:boron-onbuild
EXPOSE 8080
```

The source code for the sample above is available at `https://github.com/Altoros/iot-book/tree/master/timeseries`. You can also get all the source code with one command:
`git clone https://github.com/Altoros/iot-book.git`

Understanding the analytics

Big data analytics aims at revealing patterns, correlations, and providing other valuable insights based on processing of large data quantities. By capturing and analyzing big data—large and varied datasets—businesses can better understand their workflows, customer behavior, market trends, growth opportunities, and so on.

Previously, to take an informed decision, a company would have to first gather data, then analyze it, and integrate it into the decision-making process. The whole cycle could take quite a long time to complete. With big data analytics, businesses can speed it up, which gives them the competitive advantage of being more agile.

It is possible to distinguish the following four types of analytics:

- **Descriptive analytics**: It helps you to get a historical overview of events over a given period and prepare the resultant data for further analysis, if required. The most common tools are Google Analytics, Omniture, and so on.
- **Diagnostic analytics**: It is provided by business intelligence tools, allowing for deeper insights into data to understand the causes of events or behavior.
- **Predictive analytics**: It goes beyond simply extracting and examining data from a variety of sources, enabling users to predict occurrence of events or behavior.
- **Prescriptive analytics**: It provides the ability to understand what should be done to address certain issues in a given situation and minimize adverse events.

In the subsequent sections, we describe how to enable descriptive analytics of time series data using InfluxDB.

Exploring descriptive analytics with InfluxDB

In the following section, we give two examples of InfluxDB analytical functions that can be used to process time series data from sensors. The examples are taken from `https://docs.influxdata.com/influxdb/v1.2/query_language/functions/`.

Example – count the field values associated with a field key

The COUNT(*) function returns the number of non-null field values:

```
> SELECT COUNT("water_level") FROM "h2o_feet"

name: h2o_feet
time                    count
----                    -----
1970-01-01T00:00:00Z    15258
```

The output is the number of non-null field values for the water_level field key in the h2o_feet measurement.

Example – calculate the mean field value associated with a field key

The MEAN(*) function returns the arithmetic mean (average) of field values:

```
> SELECT MEAN("water_level") FROM "h2o_feet"

name: h2o_feet
time                    mean
----                    ----
1970-01-01T00:00:00Z    4.442107025822522
```

The output is the average field value for the water_level field key in the h2o_feet measurement.

 For more examples and detailed information, go to https://docs.influxdata.com/influxdb/v1.2/query_language/functions/.

Deploying your first analytics

In this section, we provide a selection of examples, illustrating how to apply some of the InfluxDB analytical functions to process the time series data from sensors collected using the Node.js application we built earlier.

To enable the analytics for the time series data from sensors read with the Node.js application, proceed as follows:

1. Run a `git clone` command to copy the source code of the application:

    ```
    git clone https://github.com/Altoros/iot-book.git
    ```

2. Start the application, running the following command:

    ```
    docker build -t timeseries
    docker run -p 8080:8080 -it --rm --name timeseries-container
    timeseries
    ```

    The return will be as shown in this screenshot:

```
em:timeseries            $ npm start

> timeseries@1.0.0 start /Users/           /projects/iot-book/timeseries
> node index.js

26
82
62
9
18
17
91
95
24
{ attachments: [],
  alternative: null,
  header:
   { 'message-id': '<1499771164791.0.33523@em.local>',
     date: 'Tue, 11 Jul 2017 14:06:04 +0300',
     from: '              .com',
     to: '            .com',
     subject: '=?UTF-8?Q?Alert?=' },
  content: 'text/plain; charset=utf-8',
  text: 'variable1 exceeded 91 rpm' }
17
{ attachments: [],
  alternative: null,
  header:
   { 'message-id': '<1499771165813.1.33523@em.local>',
     date: 'Tue, 11 Jul 2017 14:06:05 +0300',
     from: '             .com',
     to: '            .com',
     subject: '=?UTF-8?Q?Alert?=' },
  content: 'text/plain; charset=utf-8',
  text: 'variable1 exceeded 95 rpm' }
8
55
17
75
63
69
33
62
13
```

Console output after starting the Node.js app

3. Now, you can start querying data with analytical functions. Data will be retrieved, using InfluxQL, which is a SQL-like query language for interacting with InfluxDB.

Examples of queries with InfluxDB analytical functions

In the following section, you will see some examples with the SELECT statement, querying data from one or more measurement(s). All of the examples are taken from https://docs.influxdata.com/influxdb/v1.3/query_language/data_exploration/.

Example – select all fields and tags from a single measurement

The query will select all fields and tags from the h2o_fee measurement:

```
> SELECT * FROM "h2o_feet"

name: h2o_feet
---------------
time level description location water_level
2015-08-18T00:00:00Z below 3 feet santa_monica 2.064
2015-08-18T00:00:00Z between 6 and 9 feet coyote_creek 8.12
[...]
2015-09-18T21:36:00Z between 3 and 6 feet santa_monica 5.066
2015-09-18T21:42:00Z between 3 and 6 feet santa_monica 4.938
```

 If you are using a CLI, you will need to enter USE NOAA_water_database before running the query. Otherwise, the HTTP API will automatically query the DEFAULT retention policy of the database.

Example – group query results by a single tag

The GROUP BY clause groups query results based on a user-specified set of tags or a time interval. This example is for the InfluxQL function calculating the average water_level for each tag value of location in the h2o_feet measurement. The returned results are grouped into two series—one for each tag value of location:

```
> SELECT MEAN("water_level") FROM "h2o_feet" GROUP BY "location"

name: h2o_feet
tags: location=coyote_creek
time mean
---- ----
1970-01-01T00:00:00Z 5.359342451341401


name: h2o_feet
tags: location=santa_monica
time mean
---- ----
1970-01-01T00:00:00Z 3.530863470081006
```

 Fore more examples with other statements, go to https://docs. influxdata.com/influxdb/v1.3/query_language/data_exploration/.

Running a query

To run a query, you need to send a GET request to a query endpoint. To do this, in the following code, you should specify the target database (mydb) as the value for the db URL parameter and add the query you want to run as the q URL parameter:

```
curl -G 'http://localhost:8086/query?pretty=true' --data-urlencode
"db=mydb" --data-urlencode "q=SELECT \"value\" FROM \"cpu_load_short\"
WHERE \"region\"='us-west'"
```

InfluxDB will return a response in the JSON format, with the results displayed in the results array. In the case of an error, the database will generate an error key, explaining the cause of the error:

```
{
    "results": [
        {
```

```
    "statement_id": 0,
    "series": [
        {
            "name": "cpu_load_short",
            "columns": [
                "time",
                "value"
            ],
            "values": [
                [
                    "2015-01-29T21:55:43.702900257Z",
                    2
                ],
                [
                    "2015-01-29T21:55:43.702900257Z",
                    0.55
                ],
                [
                    "2015-06-11T20:46:02Z",
                    0.64
                ]
            ]
        }
    ]
}
```

 Running multiple queries to InfluxDB in a single API call will return multiple results in the same response.

Visualizing time series data and charts

In this section, we describe how to enable visualization of the time series data from sensors collected using the Node.js application we built earlier.

To prepare for visualizing the data from the application, perform the following actions:

1. Run the following git clone to copy the source code of the application:

   git clone https://github.com/Altoros/iot-book.git

2. To start the application, run the following command:

```
docker build -t timeseries
docker run -p 8080:8080 -it --rm --name timeseries-container
timeseries
```

Visualizing time series data with Highcharts

Highcharts is a popular library for representing information in the form of charts and gauges. We will use it to visualize the time series data from the Node.js application we built earlier in this chapter.

To do this, you need to type `http://localhost:8080/public/index.html` in a browser. After that, you will see the chart as shown in the following screenshot, visualizing the output of the MEAN function based on the time series data from the Node.js application:

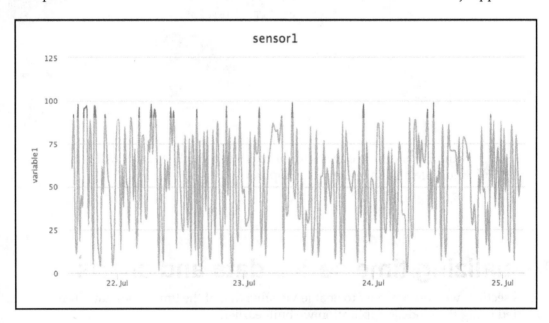

Highcharts visualization of the MEAN function for time series data

If you need to get raw data in JSON format, use the following URL:
`http://localhost:8080/stats`:

Browser output with raw data

In the following screenshot, you can see an example of how Highcharts can visualize the current values for an analytical function:

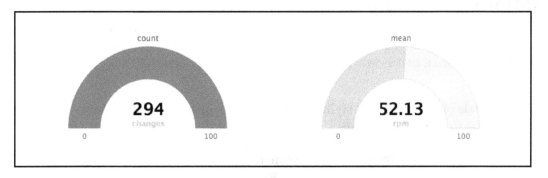

Highcharts visualization of the current values for the COUNT and MEAN functions

Visualizing time series data with Grafana

As an alternative to Highcharts, you can also use Grafana—an open source tool, featuring analytics and visualization of metrics. Most commonly, Grafana is used for visualizing time series data based on the infrastructure and application analytics. However, it is also suitable for working with data from industrial sensors, home automation, weather, and process control devices.

The tool has a large community and offers a lot of plugins, enabling users to visualize data from almost any source in the form of charts, gauges, and even maps.

Out-of-box Grafana supports the following data sources:

- Graphite
- Prometheus

- Elasticsearch
- InfluxDB
- OpenTSDB
- MySQL
- AWS CloudWatch

 You can find additional data sources in Grafana's plugin repository: `https://grafana.com/plugins`.

Grafana building blocks

The main building block of Grafana is a dashboard. Each dashboard can comprise a number of panels, arranged on rows. Rows are logical dividers within a dashboard used for arranging individual panels into groups. Their width is automatically scaled to fit a browser.

Grafana panels offer a variety of styling and formatting options, enabling users to build visualizations to match their needs. Users can drag and drop panels to change their position within rows or resize them. To set a time period for dashboard visualizations, use the time picker located in the upper-right corner.

 For more details about Grafana and its building blocks, go to `https://grafana.com/`.

Running Grafana

Grafana is available in two versions, one for running in a cloud and the other for running locally.

To run the tool locally, use the following command:

```
docker run -it --rm --name=grafana -p 3000:3000 -e
"GF_SECURITY_ADMIN_PASSWORD=secret" -e "GF_SMTP_ENABLED=true" -e
"GF_SMTP_HOST=smtp.gmail.com:587" -e "GF_SMTP_USER=username@gmail.com" -e
"GF_SMTP_PASSWORD=" -e "GF_SMTP_FROM_ADDRESS=username@gmail.com" -v
~/grafana:/var/lib/grafana grafana/grafana
```

For SMTP authentication, make sure to substitute the
`username@gmail.com` value of the `GF_SMTP_FROM_ADDRESS` with your
actual email address.

After that, you can open Grafana, pasting the following URL in the browser:
`http://localhost:3000`.

To sign in, type `admin` in the **User** field and `secret` in the **Password** field.

Configuring a Grafana visualization

First of all, we need to add a data source. To do this, carry out the following:

1. On the displayed Grafana home page, open the side menu by clicking the
   Grafana icon in the upper-left corner of the top header:

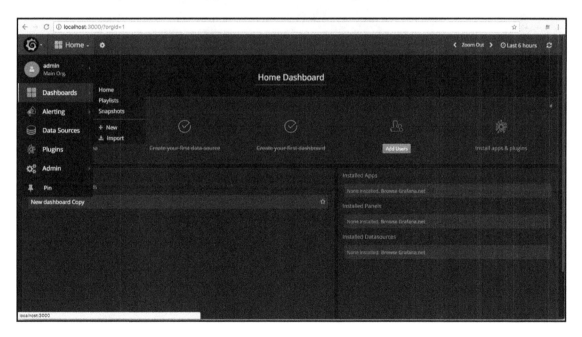

Side menu on the Grafana home page

2. On the side menu, click **Data Sources**.

3. Click the + **Add data source** button in the top header.

4. Select **InfluxDB** from the **Type** drop-down list. After clicking the **Add** button, you will see the following window displayed on the screen:

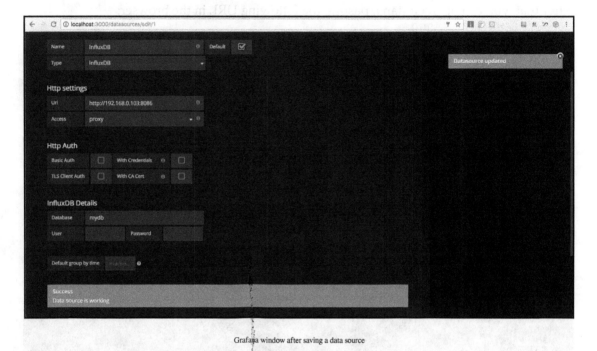

Grafana window after saving a data source

5. After that, you can start adding panels and rows to the displayed Grafana dashboard. To add a panel, click **+ADD ROW** and select a panel type by clicking one of the buttons in the panel type pane:

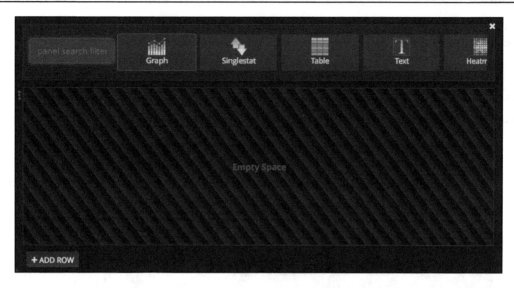

+ADD ROW button (in the lower-left corner) and panel type pane (in the upper part)

6. To configure a panel, you need to open a configuration page for that panel. To do that, left-click **Panel Title** and select **Edit** in the displayed menu:

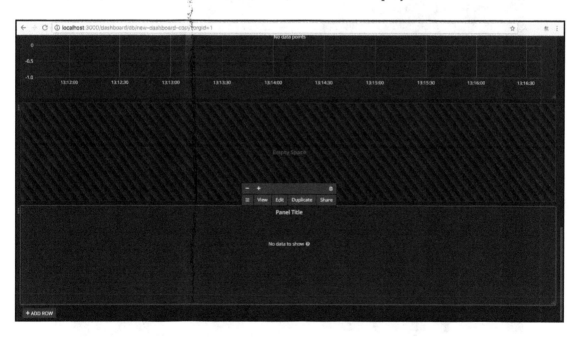

Opening a configuration page for a panel

The following subsection describes the Graph panel in more detail, while providing some basic configuration tips.

Graph panel

To configure a Graph panel, proceed as follows:

1. On the **Metrics** tab of the configuration page, select **sensor1** for the FROM statement.
2. For the SELECT statement, select **variable1**. The rest of the settings can be left as they are:

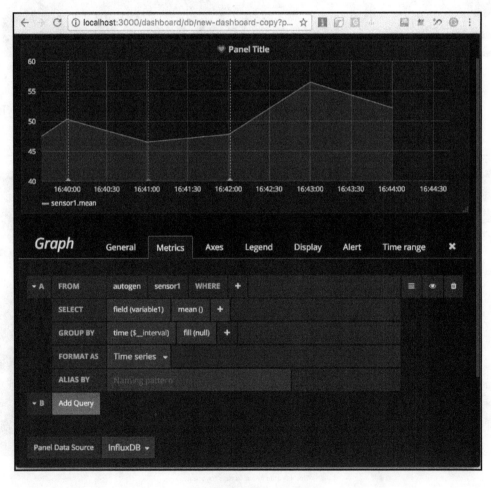

A Graph panel with a configuration page

3. You will also need to set up an auto updating period, opening the appropriate menu in the upper-right corner of the displayed dashboard:

The menu for setting up an auto updating period

Soon after that, you will start getting new values from the database at preset intervals (auto updating periods).

Once you have set up an auto updating period, it will be applied to all the panels added to a current dashboard.

4. On the **Alert** tab of the same configuration page, you can configure a visualization to warn about the values in a graph exceeding the admissible maximum. To do this, specify an appropriate value in the **IS ABOVE** statement:

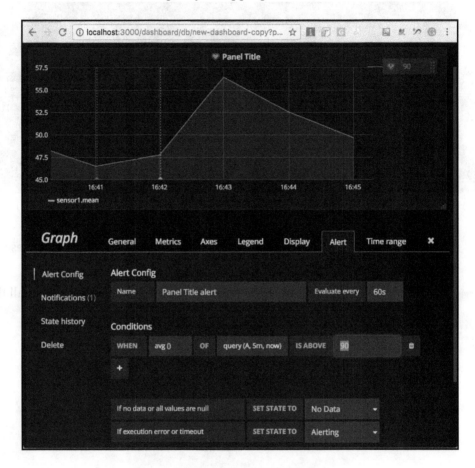

Setting an admissible maximum for alerts

In addition to Graph, Grafana also includes the following types of panel:

- Heatmap (allows for grouping values by timestamps, with the resultant groups highlighted in different colors)
- Table (displays the last N values of a time series retrieved from a database)
- Alert List (can be used to monitor whether the displayed values are okay or out of an admissible range)
- Singlestat (displays only the latest value of a time series)

For more information about these panels and their configuration, go to `http://docs.grafana.org/features/panels`.

Here, you can see an active Grafana dashboard with multiple panels added to it:

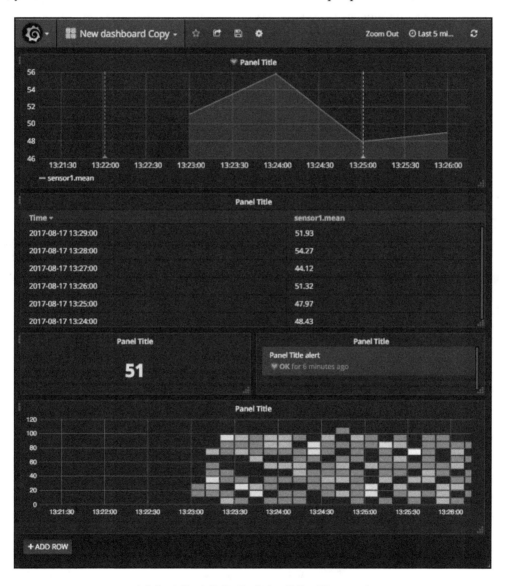

A Grafana dashboard with Alert List, Singlestat, Table, and Heatmap panels

Visualizing the outcomes of the analytics as alerts

This section outlines the procedure for setting up the notifications about database values exceeding preset limits. Such notifications can be received in one of the following ways—by email or via a Slack channel. Additionally, you can configure alerts in Grafana.

Configuring email notifications

To configure email notifications, proceed as follows:

- Specify the credentials (email address, host) of the SMTP server
- Change the **alertFrom** value in the `index.js` file to a required limit value

Once you have completed this configuration, you will start getting emails, whenever some of the values exceed a specified limit:

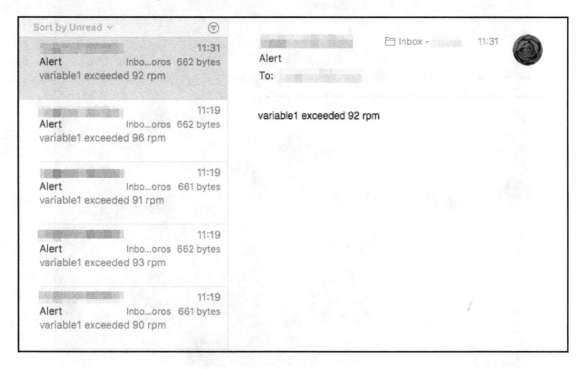

An alert displayed in a mail client

Configuring notifications via Slack

To configure notifications via Slack, you need to create a Slack Webhook. To do this, carry out the following:

1. Go to `https://my.slack.com/services/new/incoming-webhook/`.
2. Select a channel for notifications in the **Post to Channel** drop-down list. The generated Webhook will be displayed in the Webhook URL field:

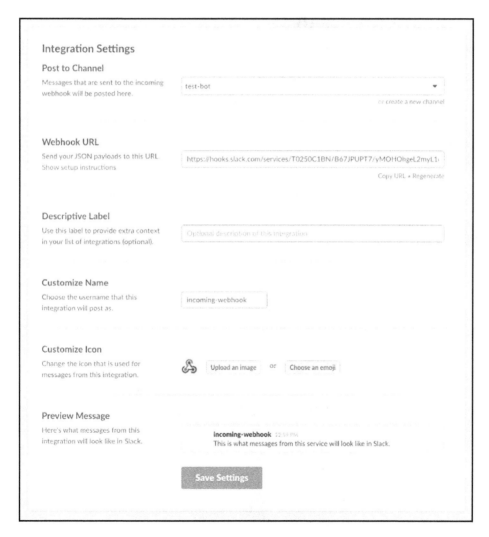

The page for configuring and customizing a Webhook

3. To customize the default bot name, specify a new name in the **Customize Name** field. To change the avatar, click the **Upload an image** or **Choose an emoji** button.

4. Once the configuration process is over, paste the Webhook URL to `alertSlack.url` in the `index.js` file and run the application once again. After that, you will start getting notifications to Slack.

Configuring alerts in Grafana

To configure alerts in Grafana, you need to create a notification channel.

Grafana supports a range of default notification channels, including the following:

- Email
- Slack
- HipChat
- Telegram

To create a notification channel, proceed as follows:

1. Open the **Alerting** menu and select **Notification channels**:

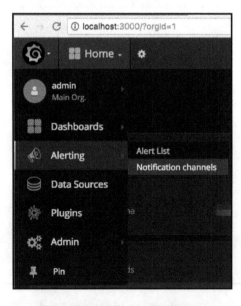

Opening the Notification channels page

2. On the **Notification channels** page, click the **New Channel** button.
3. On the displayed **New Channel** page, add an email channel and check **Include image**.
4. To add a Slack channel, repeat the actions as described in *Step 1* to *Step 4*.

For configuring a Slack channel, use the Webhook URL we got in Slack in the beginning of this section (see the *Configuring notifications via Slack* section).

5. Open the configuration page for the Graph panel by clicking the **Panel Title**.
6. On the **Alert** tab, add email and Slack channels in the **Send to** field by clicking the + button:

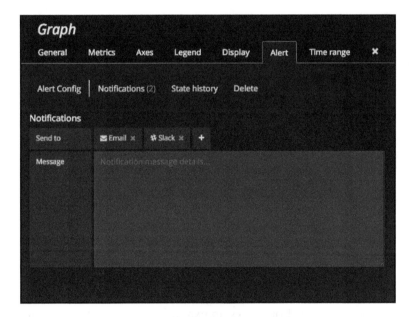

Configuring alerts for the Graph panel

7. Now, you will start getting alerts with Graph visualizations via the preset email and Slack channels.

8. Here, you can see an example of a Slack alert with a Graph visualization and a message about a value exceeding its maximum:

An example of a Slack alert with a Graph visualization

9. The following screenshot shows an example of an email alert from Grafana with a Graph visualization:

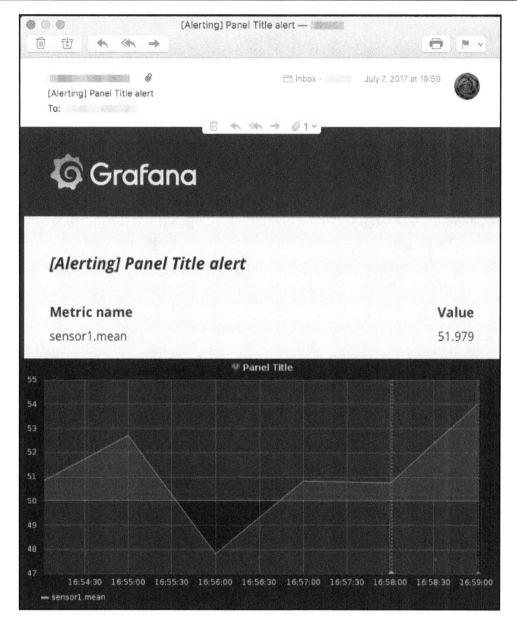

An example of an email alert with a Graph visualization

Once a value is back to normal, you will get one more notification about it.

Summary

In this chapter, we looked into how the S95 standard addresses asset modeling and exchange of asset data between different levels of an enterprise control system. Then, we overviewed the existing database management systems (including blockchain) with a focus on the data types they can store. Furthermore, we compared the most widely used time series storage.

We provided a detailed instruction and a sample code to build a Node.js application that simulates reading of time series measurements. Touching upon different types of analytics, we highlighted the analytical functions of the InfluxDB database. Then, we demonstrated how to enable descriptive analytics with InfluxDB for the Node.js app we had previously built. In addition, we showed how to set up time series visualizations with Highcharts and Grafana and to configure email and Slack notifications and alerts from Grafana.

The next chapter will address the most common issues related to security, deployment, and scalability of IoT cloud applications, such as scaling of microservices, Continuous Integration and deployment, and secure communication with devices using UAA and OAuth.

Deployment, Scale, and Security

7

In the previous chapter, we looked at how to develop an end-to-end **Industrial Internet of Things (IIoT)** application. In this chapter, we will go over securing, deploying, and finally scaling various components of an IIoT application.

The following topics will be covered in depth:

- Securing cloud-based microservices
- Securing edge-to-cloud connectivity
- Continuous deployment of microservice options, such as Docker and Cloud Foundry
- Scaling your microservices, databases, and so on

This chapter provides a framework for developing secure IIoT software, makes a case for adopting continuous deployment, and finally closes with guidelines on how to scale different components.

IIoT security practices

Consider the **Distributed Denial of Service (DDoS)** attack of October 16th, 2016, which almost brought down the internet on the east coast of the USA due to its attack on DYN's servers. This was later identified as having been due to a Mirai botnet attack using **Internet of Things (IoT)** devices, such as cameras, home routers, and so on. The Mirai bot targeted devices that used a stripped-down Linux OS by scanning the internet for open Telnet ports and logging into the device using one of the default passwords, thereby taking over the devices and using them for the DDoS. This is a very clever and effective way to implement a bot that rides on IoT devices. With billions of IoT devices around, these types of attacks have become common and it is natural that some of these attacks will be targeted toward IIoT devices as well, which could have a devastating impact on industrial plants and plant operations.

Therefore, securing IIoT applications is paramount for large-scale deployment, and security should not be an afterthought, but rather should be part of the application development life cycle. But securing IoT implementations and deployments are essentially complex due to the nature of the IoT ecosystem, which is essentially made up of meshes of simple devices that run on different operating systems, and security concerns and possible breaches are common. In addition, IoT implementations consist of several devices across the stack, possibly offered by various vendors. Hence, when we talk about IoT security, we are essentially talking about securing every layer of the stack and addressing the vulnerability of the entire solution as a whole. To recap, a typical IIoT application consists of three tiers, namely devices, the gateway, and the cloud tier, as shown here:

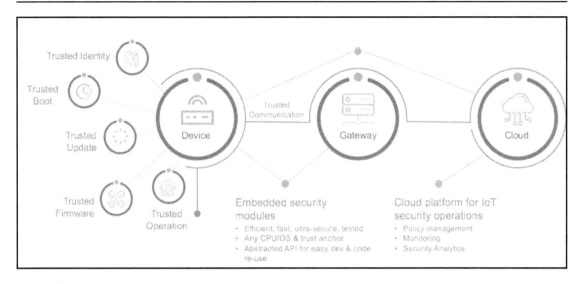

The three-tier architecture of a typical IIoT application

Securing IoT applications involves securing all three tiers. To do this, we need to consider all key aspects, such as the security of the IoT devices, communication between the tiers, security on the cloud, and finally, the life cycle management of these components, as shown here:

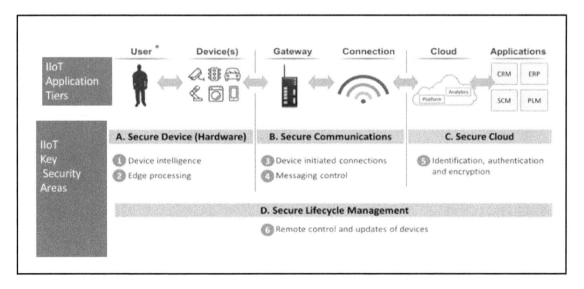

Various key IoT components and key security considerations

Securing IoT tiers will require us to adopt various different security strategies, such as making the IoT device smart so that it can use secure booting to run only authorized software, making sure that the device initiates communication to the cloud, and making the cloud data encrypted. Let's start our security journey by looking at the key practices involved in securing IIoT applications.

Key principles of securing IIoT applications

Securing an IIoT application needs to be done in a methodical way and should be implemented throughout the entire life cycle of the application. The following is a blueprint for developing secure IIoT applications:

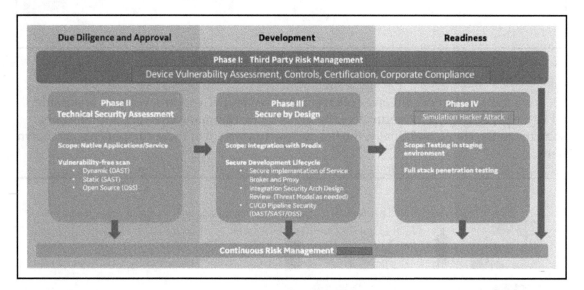

A framework for the secure development of IIoT applications

The IIoT secure blueprint recommends starting with proper due diligence toward the third-party components being used, such as other devices, networks, and regulatory guidelines, followed by an in-depth technical review of the software that is being developed using various static and dynamic scans to identify vulnerabilities. Developers should continue to incorporate these practices during the life cycle of the products, and finally, before release, should do a full-scale penetration test before going to production. To summarize, the security blueprint consists of the following activities:

- Third-party/external risk assessment
- Technical security assessments
- Ongoing secure-by-design practices
- Simulation of hacker attacks (otherwise known as **penetration testing**)

Essentially, we start off by understanding the risks associated with existing IIoT devices, and the regulatory situation, then move on to getting a good picture of the technical assessment of the software and hardware. Once the assessments are completed, we implement a secure-by-design strategy that builds security into every aspect of the development and design. Finally, we test the software and hardware with penetration testing to identify and fix issues before releasing the application for production. We will go into more depth on these stages in these following sections.

Phase 1 – third-party and architecture risk assessments

An IIoT application typically includes many IIoT devices from many different vendors. Take, for example, a typical power plant—it may have a generator built by GE, but instrumentation equipment from Siemens, and so on, that function together to perform the intended operation—but having these diverse and highly critical components poses many security risks.

The goal of this phase is to access the security vulnerabilities of these devices by gaining a deeper understating of the device architecture, such as whether or not these devices use secure protocols, secure authentication, and authorization models. Also, a good understanding of the device software and network location needs to be acquired.

We should develop a comprehensive **threat model** of the entire system to correctly identify vulnerabilities. A thread model helps capture the network topology and architecture of the existing system and can help us identify and understand the threats and vulnerabilities. The threat model should capture all the different components in the system, including the network endpoints and data centers, cloud providers used, hardware components, both internal and external endpoints, versions of the software and hardware used, third-party components such as databases, and protocols such as HTTPS, firewalls, and open ports. An example threat model is given here for reference:

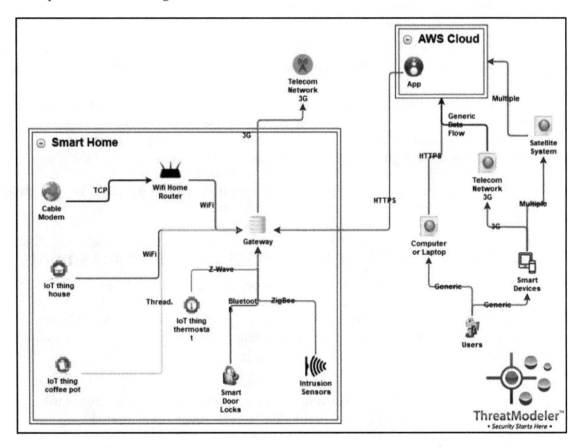

A sample threat model

A good threat model will provide enough information to help us focus on the vulnerabilities in the IIoT application and to plug them successfully. The **Open Web Application Security Project** (**OWASP**) provides a good amount of detail to help us build a comprehensive threat model, and provides useful guidelines that can be followed to build a good threat model.

In addition to system vulnerabilities, we need to focus on the compliance aspects in an industrial internet application that will be deployed in multiple geographical regions. It is very important to get a good understanding of the current regulatory laws, such as GDPR and HIPAA, and depending on the application domain (for example, healthcare, oil and gas applications, and so on), we need to make sure that the application is compliant to the regulations. The company's legal team will be very helpful in identifying regulatory challenges, and a compliance audit should be undertaken to review the application's adherence to regulatory guidelines.

Phase 2 – technical security assessments

The goal of phase 2 is to run many different security tools to perform static and dynamic code analyses to identify vulnerabilities in the IIoT application code. Before we dive into the tools, let's look at a recap of the top vulnerabilities, as defined by OWASP, given here for reference:

- **Injection issues**: These happen when additional query parameters are added as part of the API query by an attacker. Issues such as SQL injections and LDAP injections fall into this category.
- **Cross-site scripting (XSS)**: XSS occurs whenever an attacker takes over the end user's browser and enables the attacker to execute scripts in the user's browser, which can hijack user sessions, among other things.
- **Broken authentication and session management**: In this situation, the hacker is able to get hold of the account credentials and session tokens of other users and can then assume other users' identities to access information.
- **Sensitive data exposure**: Many healthcare and financial applications have APIs that do not properly protect sensitive data. Attackers could steal or modify such weakly protected data for fraudulent use, such as credit card fraud, and so on.
- **Broken access control**: This is a big problem, as in this case, due to the lack of access control, the hacker is able to get hold of other users' data. This is especially important in the case of multi-tenant applications, where one tenant user can get hold of another tenant's information due to improper access controls.
- **Using components with known vulnerabilities**: Since using open source software is very prevalent in IIoT applications, using components such as libraries, frameworks, and other software modules with vulnerabilities in their applications will expose your application to the same vulnerabilities.

- **Insufficient logging and monitoring**: Insufficient logging and monitoring is a big issue in modern applications since is it highly distributed, which allows the attacker to extract the data. Studies show that the time to detect a breach is over 200 days, and the breach is typically detected by external parties, rather than internal processes or monitoring.

We typically use a variety of tools to detect these vulnerabilities. These tools can be grouped into the following categories:

- Static analysis security testing
- Dynamic analysis security testing
- Open source scans for vulnerabilities

We will go in depth about these categories in the following section.

Static analysis security testing (SAST)

Static code analysis (also known as source code analysis) is usually performed on the source code from the repo as part of the CI/CD pipeline during the software development. It finds many different security vulnerabilities, and is usually called **white box security testing**, since it looks at the internals of the code to detect security vulnerabilities. These tools can also monitor code smells, code coverage, and other parameters. An example of a good tool is SonarQube. Have a look at this sample SonarQube report:

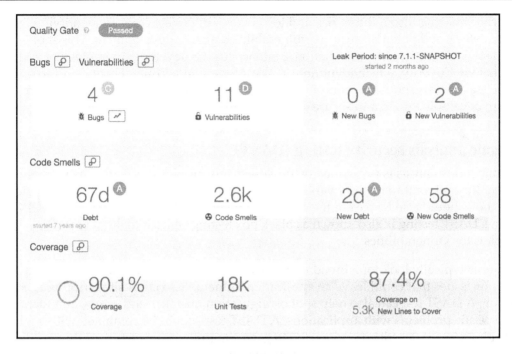

The SonarQube dashboard, detailing the code quality and vulnerabilities

The following is an example of the security vulnerability caused by a lack of validation of the variable spec, which could result in an injection issue:

```
// dumpObj:
dumpObj: function( spec ) {
  var val = "<undefined>";
  try {
    val = eval( "this."+spec ).toString();
```

Review the arguments of this "eval" call to make sure they are validated. ···   7 months ago ▾ L989 %

🔒 Vulnerability ◎ Critical ○ Open ▾ Not assigned ▾ 30min effort Comment   ◈ cwe, owasp-a3 ▾

```
  } catch( exception ) {
  }
  this.dump( spec + "=" + val + "\n" );
},
```

Detail of an injection bug identified by the SonarQube tool

Static code analysis also reduces risk and lowers overall project costs by identifying critical quality defects and potential security vulnerabilities during development. This should provide reliable, actionable remediation guidance for the developer to implement. Other tools include Coverity, which identifies the OWASP vulnerabilities, Fortify, and so on. Static code analysis should be part of IIoT development practices and will provide immense value in developing good and secure software.

Dynamic analysis security testing (DAST)

Dynamic code analysis is performed on deployed and running software. The purpose is to hammer the endpoint to identify various security issues during the development cycle. These tools should also be part of the daily run and should be integrated with the CI/CD pipeline. DAST testing is also known as black box testing, since it looks at the API endpoints for vulnerabilities.

DAST tests typically look for a broad range of vulnerabilities, including input/output validation issues that could leave an application vulnerable to cross-site scripting or SQL injection. A DAST test can also help spot configuration mistakes and errors, and identify other specific problems with applications. A DAST test should be combined with a white box testing tool, as described previously, to get a comprehensive picture of the vulnerabilities in an IIoT application. The following is an example of the output from the Tinfoil tool, which identifies top vulnerabilities:

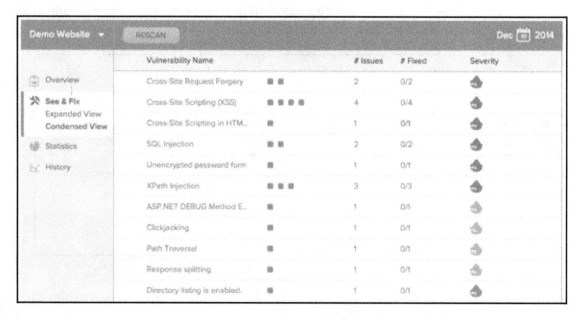

An example of a Tinfoil report detailing various vulnerabilities

Other tools for dynamic testing include Burp Suite, Qualys, and WebInspect, all of which can be used as part of the software life cycle. It is very important to plan for reviewing the output of these tools, and then add user stories to address the vulnerabilities before release, otherwise it is not going to help with secure development practices.

Open source scans

A typical IIoT application uses many different open source software components, libraries, or frameworks. Identifying and fixing software vulnerabilities in the open source software components and utilizing correct versions of the components are both necessary steps for essential protection against exploitation and a potential breach.

The open source software security assessment helps to do the following:

- Identify open source software used throughout the product code base
- Map vulnerabilities to the open source components used in the software
- Recommend software versions, including alternative versions, that can be used inside the application

BLACK DUCK is a tool that is heavily used in enterprises for open source scans. The following is a sample report that both identifies the open source components used in a sample IIoT application, and provides a detailed readout of the vulnerabilities and recommendations:

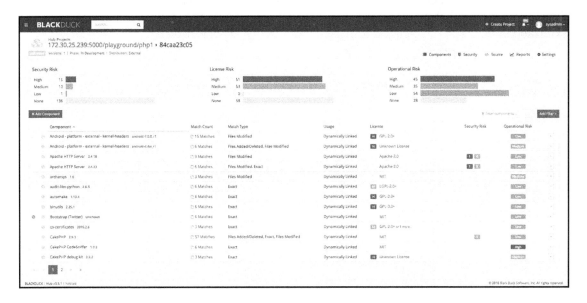

A sample BLACK DUCK report, identifying open source software libraries and their vulnerabilities

BLACK DUCK should also be integrated as part of the CI/CD pipeline and should be periodically reviewed by the team. Any exceptions to the standard libraries need to be approved by the legal department.

Phase 3 – secure by design

Secure by design means designing software to be secure from the ground up. It is assumed that there will be bad actors who will try to hack the software, hence we should bake in the general guidelines, such as authentication, authorization, logging, monitoring, and so on, as part of the design. We will go into detail about different secure architectures in the following section.

Securing an IIoT application is an ongoing activity and is fundamentally about protecting the applications and services that make up the IIoT application, while protecting your sensitive data. Security should include design and architecture, in addition to fixing the issues identified on an ongoing basis.

Phase 4 – penetration testing

Finally, before we release the software, penetration testing needs to be completed by the Red Team. Here, the Red Team try to hack into the software by simulating a hacker attack. The Red Team may identify various vulnerabilities that need to be resolved by the development team before going live. If your organization does not have a Red Team, external vendors can be engaged to perform the penetration testing.

IIoT device security design and architecture

An IIoT device is at the center of the IIoT application, and innovations such as smart cities, smart grids for utilities, and smart homes all rely on robust and resilient IIoT devices. Safe operations and securing the IoT device tier should be paramount in any IIoT application. Furthermore, the diversity of the devices in an IIoT solution is huge—a typical IIoT solution may consist of some homegrown devices, third-party devices, and many different legacy devices, and hence, we cannot assume secure practices have been followed already, so we should make sure that secure practices are followed rigorously before launching an IoT solution. Securing an IIoT device can be broken down into three important aspects:

- IIoT device and IIoT device management
- IIoT device communication and privacy controls
- IIoT device placement in the network

In the upcoming sections, we will go into detail about these three key principles to make the device secure. We will look at key concepts that address security issues.

IIoT device and IIoT device management

Securing an IIoT device essentially consists of securing the device with hardened software components, secure management of the device for any software updates, and so on. The importance of hardening the devices in an IoT environment is self-explanatory, as vulnerabilities at the device level leave not only that device compromised, but can potentially lead to making the entire IoT network insecure. Hence, it's important that essential device-hardening techniques are deployed. Some of these include making sure that any unnecessary service (specifically remote access), applications, or software are removed from the device. Any unused accounts (including factory defaults) and legacy protocols and logins based on passwords should be removed from the device or replaced with custom ones.

The life cycle of IIoT devices typically begins with secure booting of the device. After booting, the device connects using the pre-provisioned certificate, either with the IIoT Gateway or the cloud, to complete its provisioning and setup. We have all seen this happening with Apple iPhones that require us to connect to an iCloud account before we can start using the phones—it is a similar case with IoT devices, whereby the IIoT device gets registered to the cloud service or the IIoT Gateway, in case the connectivity is blocked an common scenario in many different industries where security and privacy is an issue.

Provisioning processes should be automated and scalable mechanisms to generate an attestation identity for the device, usually a client certificate, with which the device registers with an authorized remote management service, such as an IIoT Gateway or a cloud service. Subsequent device updates use the same verified channel to harden software distribution to in-field devices over the air or over the web. Finally, continuously monitoring of the device using instrumentation the device runtime will help us monitor the device for performance.

IIoT device communication and privacy controls

Let's check the different IIoT device controls.

IIoT device communication and encryption

An IIoT device should always authenticate and authorize before starting communication with the gateway.

In addition, it is recommended that data processing at edge devices, and the exchange of data between devices, are covered by data encryption both at rest and in motion. However, with the variety of devices and connections available, standardization of protocols and processes becomes very challenging, not to mention the challenges of providing a complete key life cycle management solution.

Secure communication using TLS can be achieved by using a X.509 digital certificate and cryptographic key with life cycle capabilities, including public/private key generation (PKI), distribution, management, and revocation. The hardware specs for some IoT devices may limit or prevent their ability to utilize PKI. Digital certificates can be securely loaded onto IoT devices at the time of manufacture, and then activated or enabled by third-party PKI software suites; the certificates could also be installed post-manufacture.

IIoT device user privacy controls

In addition to authentication and security, we need to use an authorization policy for privacy protection for both data and user access, such that this is a key requirement for device-to-device and device-to-user connections. Privacy controls are a must for devices in the IoT world. The IoT devices are tied to the users of these devices, and hence, the user's information can be compromised through the devices. Privacy protection is recommended for the implementation on the IoT device as well.

IIoT device placement in the network

Given that the success of IIoT lies in the assimilation and leveraging of IT and **operational technology (OT)** data, it is important to take steps to make sure that security concerns for one do not impact the other. For example, the IT systems have been connected to the internet and have been secured through various solutions for a while; however, the OT devices are still in the process of being connected to the cloud, which makes them vulnerable to security threats. Moreover, these devices are well-ingrained into workflows, and therefore have contact with several pieces of plant equipment. One way to isolate these is to provide an on-demand secure network segment, separate from the one supporting traditional IT systems. That way, you quarantine the zone, and if the device is breached, the necessary steps to remediate it can be taken without any impact on any other systems on the network. The following is the ideal device placement inside the secure network of the company, with the device gateway deployed in the DMZ:

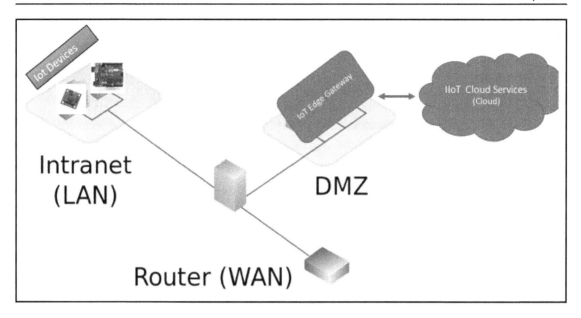

Ideal placement of IIoT devices and gateway

As we can see, the IIoT device is inside the company network and communicates with the IIoT Edge Gateway deployed in the DMZ. The IIOT Gateway communicates with the IIoT cloud services.

IIoT Gateway security principles

The IIoT Gateway acts as a bridge between devices, sensors, equipment, systems, and the cloud in providing reliable communication and compute resources. An IIoT Gateway typically provides computation and storage, as well as the ability to autonomously control IIoT devices based on data inputs from sensors. IIoT Gateways also help with aggregation, processing, and filtering of data for data pre-processing and processing, in some cases also running algorithms and generating alerts. The IIoT Gateway also helps securely transmit data from the edge to the cloud.

An IIoT Gateway is crucial for addressing the security concerns of the IIoT application. We can utilize pre-ensured hardware building blocks, such as the **trusted platform module (TPM)** and **trusted execution environment (TEE)**, to secure the whole communication chain, including the connectivity of legacy devices, data storage on a gateway, and secure data transmission, as well as the fast deployment of data on the cloud to perform intelligent analytics.

TPM

The TPM is often built into a system to provide hardware-based security. It is a combination of hardware and software to protect credentials when they are in an unencrypted form. TPM is based on a trusted execution environment (**hardware root of trust**) that provides secure storage of credentials and protected execution of cryptographic operations. It is isolated from the main CPU and implemented either as a discrete chip, a security coprocessor, or in firmware:

- The microprocessor scans the firmware and validates the key. If the key is valid, then the processor begins executing the firmware, but if not, the processor halts.
- The TPM is used to store platform measurements that help ensure that the platform remains trustworthy. It contains a set of registers that comprise of RTM measurements for launch modules of the boot software.
- The computing platform must have **a root of trust for measurement (RTM)** that is implicitly trusted to provide an accurate validation of the **boot code modules**. The TPM provides the **root of trust for reporting** and **a root of trust storage** for the RTMs. The TPM stores a set of known good measurements of boot components that are securely generated and stored.

> **Hardware root of trust/chain of trust**: This is a fundamental part of secured computing. The secure boot process is utilized to implement a chain of trust.
>
> Bootstrapping is a secure system or device that involves a chain of steps, where each step relies on the accuracy and security of the previous one. At the end of the chain, you assume or verify the correctness of the last step—this step becomes the **Root of Trust (RoT)**. The RoT is provided by hardware services, including cryptographic support, secure key storage, secure signature storage, and secure access to trusted functions. This allows the creation of a **trusted module** forming the basis, or root, upon which other components within the system can be validated. The chain of trust begins with the bootloader. From this bootloader, the OS is validated, and from the OS, the applications are validated, creating a chain of trusted elements.

TEE

The TEE is an insulated and secure area of the main processor, providing security functionality for application integrity and confidentiality. The TEE differentiates between security functionality and operational functionality. *How does it work?*—It mainly consists of three parts:

- Trusted OS
- Internal micro-kernel
- APIs

It is used for security checks which is parallel to standard OS. Common security functions include isolated execution of security operations, the integrity of code loaded and data stored, and the confidentiality of data stored in the TEE. It protects data both at rest and in use within the TEE. It also provides higher performance and access to a large amount of memory:

- Isolated execution
- Secure storage
- Device identification
- Device authentication
- Platform integrity

All of these security properties can be achieved using the measured boot, secured boot, and attestation, as outlined here:

- **Secured boot**: This is a security standard verified by trusted OEMs that ensures the authenticity and integrity of a device's boot. When the first boot happens, only the validated code from the device OEM is allowed to run to verify and validate the authenticity of software present in the gateway. This prevents attackers from replacing the firmware with versions created to perform malicious operations. It provides the APIs required for code signing, code validation, and secure firmware updates.
- **Measured boot**: Measured boot is generally used for integrity protection. As anti-malware software has become better at detecting runtime malware, attackers are also becoming better at creating rootkits that can hide from detection. Detecting malware that starts early in the boot cycle is a challenge. At this time, measured boot measures each block, from firmware up through the boot start drivers, and stores those measurements on the hardware, then making a log that can be tested remotely to verify the boot state of the client.

- **Attestation**: In a cloud computing scenario, attestation is an essential and interesting parameter, often rooted in using a trusted hardware component to build a trusted system. It is basically used in the process of validating integrity, in terms of software and information, for securing embedded systems. Attestation uses cryptographic identity techniques that confirm the identity and authentication credentials of remote devices, without revealing the devices and their own identities.

IIoT Gateway network security

Typically, a multitude of devices are connected to the IIoT Gateway and to the cloud as part of an IIoT solution. What makes network security a bigger challenge for IoT systems is the wide range of communication protocols, device protocols, and capabilities. While all the traditional security solutions, such as antivirus, malware, firewalls, and intrusion detection, need to be implemented at the endpoints, the focus is also on making these more efficient, given the large and complex network that they need to support, which may also potentially scale exponentially.

IIoT Gateway authentication

The major difference between traditional systems and IoT systems in the context of authentication is that, in the case of IoT, for the majority of the cases the authentication is for devices with no human interaction (machine to machine) and possibly for a single device with multiple users. How do we implement advanced measures, such as two-factor authentication, digital certificates, and biometrics? In such cases, these will be key in providing the required level of authentication.

In addition to a securely booting gateway, we need to secure the IIoT Gateway using secure authentication, which typically uses two-way SSL to securely connect IIoT cloud services, as shown here:

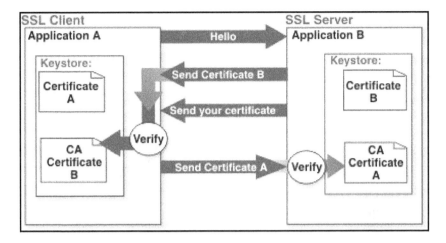

Illustration of the two-way SSL validation

IIoT cloud security architecture and design

IIoT cloud security is very important to the functioning of the IIoT application. Some of the common guidelines are shown in the following table for reference:

Password security	Recommendations
Insecure data storage	Store only what is absolutely required. Never use public storage areas, for example, SD cards. Leverage secure containers and platform-provided file encryption APIs, and do not grant files world readable or world writeable permissions.
Weak server-side controls	Understand the additional risks that mobile applications can introduce into existing architectures. Use the wealth of knowledge already available, for example, OWASP Web Top 10, Cloud Top 10, cheat sheets, and development guides.
Insufficient transport layer protection	Ensure that all sensitive data leaving the device is encrypted. This includes data over carrier networks, Wi-Fi, and so on.
Client-side injection	Sanitize or escape untrusted data before rendering or executing it. Use prepared statements for database calls (concatenation is a bad practice) and minimize the sensitive native capabilities tied to hybrid web functionality.
Poor authorization and authentication	Contextual information can enhance the authentication process, but only as a part of a multifactor authentication. Never use a device ID or subscriber ID as a sole authenticator. Authenticate all API calls to paid resources.
Improper session handling	Do not use a device identifier as a session token. Make users reauthenticate every so often and ensure that tokens can be revoked quickly in the event of a stolen or lost device.

Password security	Recommendations
Security decisions using distrusted inputs	Check caller's permissions at input boundaries. Prompt the user for additional authorization before allowing the consummation of paid resources. When permission checks cannot be performed, ensure additional steps are required to launch sensitive actions.
Side channel data leakage	Understand what third-party libraries in your application are doing with the user data. Never log credentials, PII, or other sensitive data to system logs. Remove sensitive data before screenshots are taken. Before releasing apps, debug them to observe the files created, written to, or modified in any way. Test your application across as many platform versions as possible.
Broken cryptography	Encoding, obfuscation, and serialization are not considered encryption.Prevention tips: Do not store the key with the encrypted data; use what your platform already provides. Do not develop in-house cryptography.
Sensitive information disclosure	Do not store the private API keys in the client. Keep proprietary and sensitive business logic on the server. Never hard-code the password.

IIoT API security

IoT implementations will have many API offerings to manage data movement between devices, backend systems, and apps. It is critical that these APIs are secure enough to provide the right level of access to the relevant developers and users of these APIs, otherwise these APIs can become a backdoor entry for hackers. Proper authentication and authorization of data movement through these APIs, as well as management of these APIs, is very critical and should be addressed comprehensively.

IIoT access control

As we know, the biggest threat to any network is the insider threat. When managing several devices on a network, it is necessary that identity access management for devices be implemented with certain best practices in mind. For example, scalability for the solution is very critical, and therefore, automatic load balancing should be part of the **Access Control Service (ACS)** for IIoT in order to provide robustness.

Similarly, denial of service detection should be an integral part of the solution, and so should adaptive authentication. Also, insider threats make IoT solutions in general susceptible to violations of privacy and personal data. So, features such as self-management for participating in communications and sharing data need to be an integral part of the IAM solutions for IoT. This also means a more centralized governance model for defining policies based on geography, IP addresses, and so on. The governance model should be executed across multiple channels and collection points.

IIoT identity store

In traditional systems, the identity of the user connecting to a service or application needs to be defined and stored in order to ensure proper authentication and access control. However, in IoT systems, the identity of things needs to be defined and managed. This has to be augmented with defining and managing the relationships between the connected devices, as this is the essence of IoT. This not only adds value from a security perspective, but it also enhances user experience (by ensuring proper usage of assets) and effective asset management that leads to inventory-based cost savings, as well as proper servicing of those assets.

IIoT security analytics

Given that the possible security risks are high and complex, advanced analytics for security data being collected is also very important. This will not only help with effective real-time monitoring, but also help with predicting and preventing attacks from happening. The need is for the identification of IoT-specific attacks with the use of advanced analytics and machine learning on the big data being collected. The nature of attacks will transform over the course of time, hence, AI-based solutions in this space are required.

IIoT application deployment

Adoption of **Continuous Integration/Continuous Deployment (CI/CD)** is very important for the successful deployment of an IIoT solution. Essentially, the idea is to use a Git repository to check the code regularly and implement automation for the testing unit, integration and regression tests. Deployment can also be automated using automated scripts. A sample CI/CD pipeline is shown here:

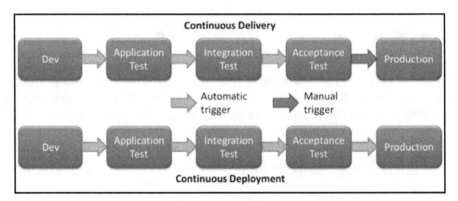

A sample of the CI/CD pipeline

- Use Jenkins to automate the build/deploy pipeline
- Use Git to check in code to the repository
- Use a good unit testing framework such as JUnit to do unit testing
- Use a good integration testing tool such as RestAsure to do API testing
- Use Selenium to do UI simulation testing
- Deployment scripts should be written using Terraform or Ansible

IIoT applications at scale

Understanding how to scale IIoT applications is very important. The system should be able to effortlessly process growing workloads, as measured by **transaction per second** (**TPS**), amount of data stored, or number of concurrent users/requests. The IIoT architecture and design guidelines we have discussed, about using microservices and gateways are inherently built to scale.

Let's look at a typical process for scaling IIoT applications:

1. Capacity planning
2. Test for load/performance
3. Measure and identify bottlenecks
4. Scale individual components

The basic idea is to do proper capacity planning as a first step, considering the business needs (for example, quality of service) and data growth for each of the components. These components can include various services, data stores, and so on. Once we come to planning the general capacity for production, it is a good idea to do load testing and analyze the load testing results to identify bottlenecks. We need to measure the various key parameters, such as response times of API calls, and the scalability of each of the components, by increasing the load. Finally, also consider future growth, such as data growth or new users being added, when coming up with a scalable solution.

Capacity planning

IIoT applications are very data and computation-intensive, and we need to plan carefully considering the business needs and anticipated growth. It is usually recommended to plan at least six months ahead. Also, it is very important to understand the quality of service that each of the components that will determine the capacity need. For example, a database may need a certain amount of disk space and computation requirements, and identifying this requires us to understand the quality of service and the expected request time that this component has to provide. Business requirements will drive the sizing requirements; for example, a projection of how many devices will be onboarded to the system in the first six months will help us in sizing the data stores, such as timeseries, and so on. In addition, the computation requirements will typically be driven by our own internal load testing or **service-level agreements** (**SLAs**), which will tell us how many servers or cores to run, and whether or not to use SSDs or HDDs.

Testing for load/performance

Once a basic understanding of the required component infrastructure is identified, usually, a deployment diagram is created and used as a mechanism to document the various capacity requirements of the different components in the applications. An example deployment diagram is shown here:

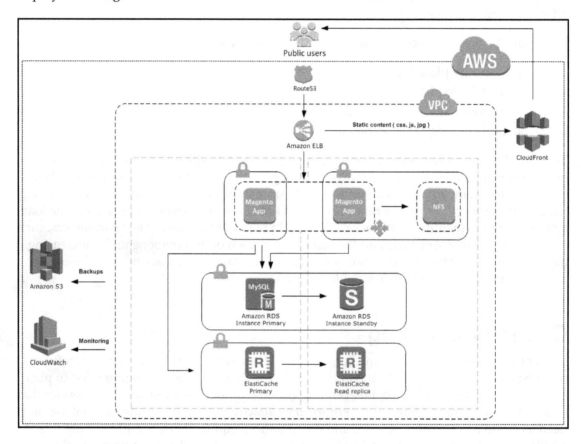

A sample deployment diagram

A load test usually happens using a scaled-down version of the production deployment footprint to determine a system's performance under real-life load conditions. There are a number of tools that we can use to simulate load. It gets complicated to simulate the needed data; database scripts and test scripts to simulate IIoT devices need to be written as part of the planning for load testing. To perform load testing, it is good to use tools such as JMeter or Load Runner, for which we will write these load testing scripts that simulate the common transactions. These tools also come with a reporting tool which gives details on the performance of the various components. In addition, it is good to use a monitoring tool to understand how various components react under load by looking at the statistics. The following is a sample JMeter report:

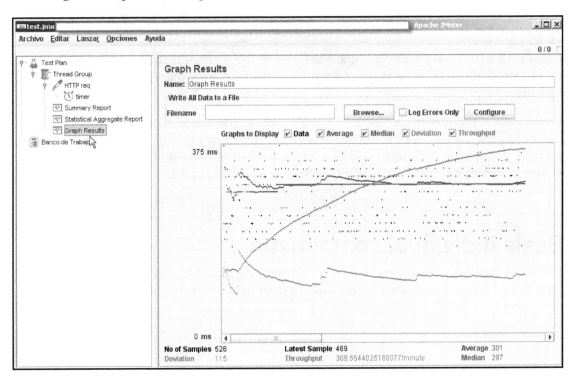

A sample JMeter test report

In addition to API testing, it is good to test the UI for load using Load Runner. With this, we can simulate a user interaction and measure the load time of the pages.

In the next section, we will look at how to measure and identify bottlenecks.

Measure and identify bottlenecks

There are a number of ways to instrument IIoT application components, including using a monitoring tool, such as **NewRelic** or **Prometheus**; by attaching a profiling tool, such as JProfiler; or using the profiling tools provided by the data stores while the load test in in progress to get all the metrics, such as CPU, memory, and other performance metrics.

Based on the load test results, it is good to focus on the services that have not met the SLAs, or, as a general rule of thumb—any UI requests that take more than 3 seconds need to be looked at.

Bottlenecks in the system can come in many forms. Key services, such as the service for authentication, for example, could get beaten and can cause cascading delays in other services. These need to be identified or we may run out of space in the database or file systems. Identifying bottlenecks will take time and careful analysis of the load testing results.

Scale individual components

It is recommended in IIoT design to use microservices, hence, it is inherently scalable. Let's look at the following scale cube framework to understand how to scale various components:

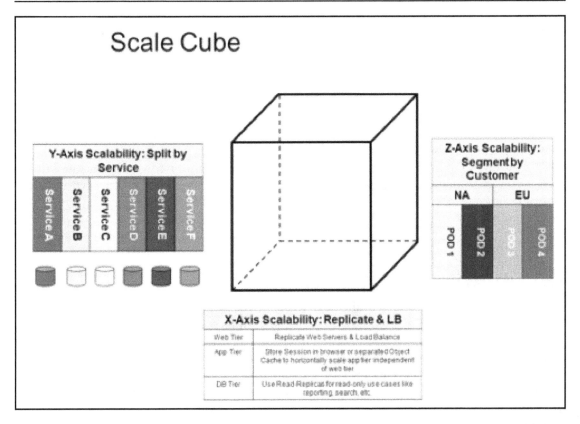

The scale cube framework

X-scaling or horizontal duplication

The idea here is to run the same instance of the software multiple times behind a load balancer for high throughput. With this, we can easily scale the API tier or web tier, but cannot do so for the database tier, which will become a bottleneck once it reaches an IoT scale, but can be used for small applications.

Y-axis scaling

This is our recommended approach for IIoT applications. In this case, we are splitting the applications into multiple microservices, each with its own data store. Each of these components can be scaled independently, but it makes the application complex to build, although it is a worthwhile investment for building a highly scalable application.

Z-axis scaling

Z-axis scaling is mainly used by database systems for sharing data, and only a subset is handled by each of the servers. Partitioning of the data is another example of Z-axis scaling.

Since the IIoT application is already decomposed into multiple smaller services, scaling these services independently, and depending on the load, essentially means adding more instances and load balancing the requests to flow to these instances seamlessly. It is also recommended to scale the data stores and event hubs appropriately. Data stores can also use a scale out solution, which essentially means adding another node to the cluster, but in some cases we may have to scale up, which means adding more power to the existing box by upgrading the CPU, memory, and so on. By choosing our architecture carefully, we will end up with a system that is easy to scale and performs much better.

Summary

In this chapter, we have looked at the how we can effectively secure the IIoT application and deploy it. We also discussed how to scale the various components and the best practices to use along the way. Security should be part of the software life cycle and should not be an afterthought. We provided a good framework to implement security as part of the entire software development life cycle. Scaling an application should also start with a good application architecture. We discussed how this can be achieved by adopting microservices built to scale, and in addition, we discussed how to build various components for scale using the scale cube. Finally, we looked at how to adopt good CI/CD practices to continuously deliver software to production.

In the next chapter, we will be looking at reliability, fault tolerance, and how to monitor IIoT applications.

8
Reliability, Fault Tolerance, and Monitoring IIoT Applications

In the previous chapter, we covered how IIoT applications can be deployed, secured, and scaled for large-scale industrial use cases. This chapter focuses on bulletproofing IIoT applications with a focus on building stable, reliable, and fault-tolerant IIoT applications that can be monitored on a 24/7 basis.

In this chapter, we will discuss the following key topics:

- How to build production-ready IIoT applications that are stable and reliable
- How to build performant IIoT applications on the edge and the cloud
- How to build fault-tolerant IIoT applications on the edge and the cloud
- How to monitor an IIoT application on the edge and the cloud

Complexity of an IIoT system

An IIoT system is a significantly complex ecosystem of diverse components that is in a state of continuous change, never static, and always evolving with various parts of the ecosystem prone to different types of stress and failures. A node on the edge will be added or removed every day, cloud connectivity will be lost, or new builds on the cloud will be deployed multiple times per day. In addition, old APIs could be swapped for newer and better ones at an astounding pace. Making the system reliable and fault-tolerant is paramount to the successful usage of the application. Before we dive into discussing the various aspects of this chapter, let's look at a typical architecture of the IIoT system for reference. A typical IIoT system consists of cloud services such as APIs, runtimes, a data store, messaging services, and edge gateways deployed on various sites or on devices which themselves need to be monitored and made reliable. The system is shown in the following diagram:

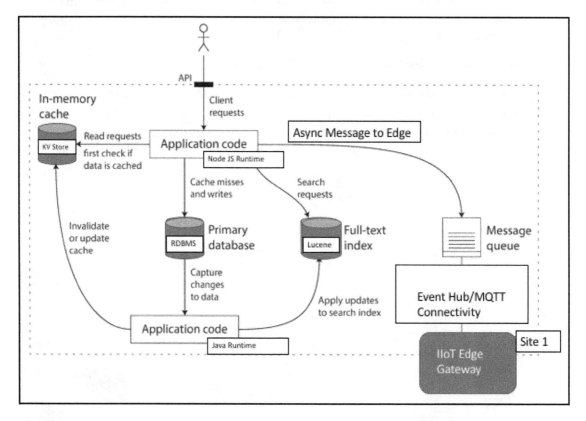

Typical IIoT application with cloud and edge components

IIoT applications are **data-intensive**, as opposed to compute-intensive, and heterogeneous with components on the cloud and the edge, which could be the customer site, and so on. The challenges in such a system are vast data diversity, network topology, the amount of data, connectivity, bandwidth constraints, and generally, there is more autonomy in these components.

An IIoT application is typically built from standard building blocks that provide commonly needed functionality. For example, IIoT applications have some of the following components:

- Edge gateways provide connectivity to the cloud and forward the data from sensors (gateways)
- Components that store telemetry data for sensors—(time series) data store
- Other data stores such as databases (RDBMS, and NoSQL), caches, key-value caches, and in memory
- APIs and services on the cloud that are built by the developers using *standard runtimes* such as Java, Node.js, and Go
- Messaging infrastructures such as Kafka, and RabbitMQ servers
- Analytics runtimes that periodically crunch a large amount of accumulated data (batch processing)
- Analytics runtimes that operate on real time or near real-time data (stream processing)

In this chapter, we will go over the details on how to achieve reliable, fault-tolerant, and maintainable IIoT systems.

Art of building reliable and resilient IIoT applications

We use the term reliability for a system that should continue to work correctly (performing the correct function at the desired level of performance) even in the face of adversity (hardware or software faults and even human error). A reliable system has some of the following characteristics:

- The application performs the function that the user expected
- The ability to self-configure to withstand changing environmental conditions

- Its performance is good enough for the required use case, under the expected load and data volume
- The system should be usable and maintainable in the long term
- Has application robustness in the face of uncertain information
- Has resistance to security problems such as preventing unauthorized access

In the following sections, we will discuss how to build and test for reliability on the cloud, at the edge gateway, and on the device.

Designing for reliability on the cloud

As we saw in Chapter 2, *IIoT Application Architecture and Design*, the cloud tier is one of the most important aspects of the IIoT application and it is paramount that the cloud component of the IIoT software is reliable and resilient for the application to function effectively. We discussed in Chapter 2, *IIoT Application Architecture and Design*, that for the cloud application, the choice of a good cloud platform such as AWS, Azure, or Predix is essential for successful IIoT application development. These **Platform as a Service (PaaS)** providers supply infrastructure components such as the databases, security components, messaging components, and various runtimes for different languages. The reliability of these infrastructure components should be addressed by the cloud/PaaS providers. Alternatively, if we assemble the platform using Docker, Kubernetes or Mesos, the reliability will be addressed by these infrastructures and are well documented and well known. Hence, the reliability concerns of developers are about the reliability of the application itself, which we will go over in depth. The following diagram shows these aspects where the infrastructure components are in the bottom layer and the application layer is in the microservices and IIoT application itself:

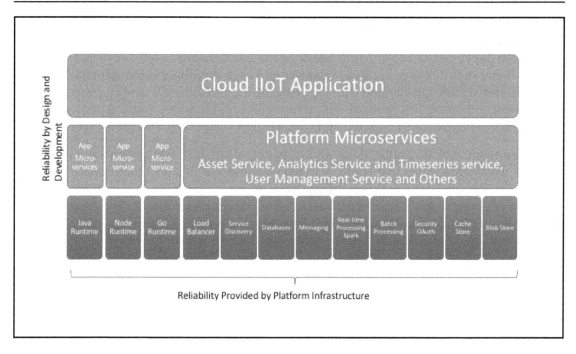

Infrastructure components at the bottom versus the application microservices at the top two layers

Building resilient applications is a concept that is decades old, with its roots in distributed computing, as described by L Peter Deutsch in 1994 when he was at Sun Microsystems, in *Fallacies of Distributed Computing* (`https://en.wikipedia.org/wiki/Fallacies_of_distributed_computing`), which has been augmented by a few others since then. The fallacies read as follows:

- The network is reliable
- Latency is zero
- Bandwidth is infinite
- The network is secure
- Topology doesn't change
- There is one administrator
- Transport cost is zero
- The network is homogeneous

For many years, traditional on-premises application developers and software engineers, due to the monolithic nature of the applications they built, mostly focused on the application development aspects and delegated the infrastructure aspects to separate teams of operational staff. These operational teams would keep their in-house production networks and servers healthy and running with sufficient bandwidth and resources. The deployment and scalability needs of typical monolithic applications running at moderate scale are fairly predictable, hence the application system was fairly straightforward.

With the advent of cloud applications, all that has changed. IIoT applications on the cloud typically use microservices that could be in the hundreds—and sometimes thousands—of small, interconnected software components, very often using different technology stacks. This type of polyglot environment with many, many components and APIs interacting in a system requires much more sophistication for it to remain up and running compared to a simple monolith. This is reflected in the following diagram where, to the left, is a typical monolithic application, and to the right is a typical microservice-based application which is composed of many different microservices:

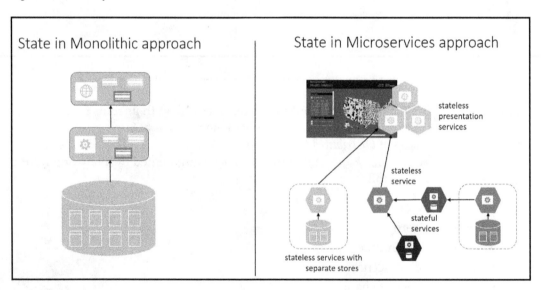

Monolithic application vs a micoservice-based application

Microservices developers need to handle all these fallacies and program defensively for any of these adverse scenarios. Some of the key areas developers need to focus on in a polyglot microservices environment are given here:

- Handling network latency
- Handling for bandwidth constraints and transport costs (gateway)

- Discoverability of the microservices to handle topology changes (Eureka)

Programming for network latency using the circuit breaker pattern

Network latency is a critical aspect of the IIoT application that needs to be handled to provide consistent SLAs by the cloud tier. A typical cloud service utilizes microservices design and hence, interacts with many different dependent services. A developer should use various strategies to isolate the microservice from any of the failures and latency arising due to transient faults, such as slow timeouts, network connections, or the resources being overexercised or the temporary unavailability of the dependent services. Developers should make sure to handle network faults and take appropriate corrective action to handle failures elegantly, so that the applications can carry on instead of going into an endless loop, retrying a service that is unavailable.

As an illustration, let's take an example of an **External API** that aggregates requests from many different internal services to serve its response to a mobile and web user interface. In this use case, due to network latency, any one of these three internal services may fail to return within the given time frame with a timeout or could throw an internal error. The developer of the **External API** should be able to gracefully handle any failures and send appropriate error codes to the frontend user interface for appropriate handling:

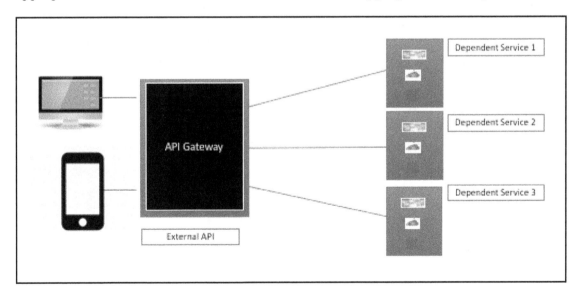

In addition, the service itself may not be performing and introduces latency due to various reasons, and this could lead to cascading failures in different parts of the application. Let's take the previous example; an **External API** service could implement a timeout and can handle the scenario, for instance, if any of the dependent services does not respond within a given time frame, the external service will return a timeout. But this error handling strategy has many drawbacks, such as dependent services will still be hammered with requests and these blocked requests will consume resources such as DB and network connections, server threads, and VM memory. Consequently, we will run out of these resources, thereby causing the failure of unrelated parts of the system that depend on these resources. An alternate solution is to let the request fail immediately and only attempt to execute the service if it can be serviced successfully. A viable option is to set a shorter timeout for the requests. This may remediate the problem partially but configuring this timeout is tricky. If it is too short, it may result in frequent failures that in turn will cause more retries, but a longer timeout will not solve the original problem of tying up system resources.

One of the techniques we will discuss in this section is the usage of the circuit breaker pattern to handle network latency and service failures. The circuit breaker pattern, at its core, prevents an application from continuously invoking a service that is already failing due to external or internal issues. As an illustration, in the previous example, let's assume **Dependent Service1** is down or not meetings its performance, the **External API** will not be continuously calling its **Dependent Service1**. In this example, once the **External API** knows one of the Dependent Services is down it continues without wasting any system resources and returns the response back to the caller. In parallel, the **External API** continuously probes the failed Dependent Service if it is working without any errors, before making the calls again. Essentially, using the circuit breaker pattern, the **External API** can detect any faults with its dependent services and not invoke it again till the issue with the service has been resolved.

The circuit breaker pattern differs from the retry pattern in that it does not keep retrying blindly but only invokes a service after it is deemed to be working properly. In a retry pattern implementation, the application keeps calling a service a configured number of times till it succeeds. In our example, an error from one of the dependent services can be handled by the **External API** service by calling the failed dependent service a configured number of times till it is successful. In contrast, the circuit breaker pattern prevents an **External API** from calling **Dependent Service1** once it has detected an error and waits for it to be resolved before invoking the services again.

In production applications, a combination of the circuit breaker and retry patterns are used by using the retry pattern to invoke an operation through a circuit breaker, as in, once it knows a dependent service is down, it may retry a few more times. If it fails again, it may call an alternative service or can potentially send default values to the clients. In addition, the retry logic should handle any exceptions returned and should gracefully exit, or call the alternate service if needed. We will go over in detail these scenarios using the following illustrations.

To illustrate the circuit breaker pattern, we are using a simple use case where we have an **External API** used by the user interface web and mobile applications. The **External API** is dependent on the multiple different cloud services, as shown in the following diagram.

In the following diagram, once the circuit breaker is triggered, the **External API** retries a few times before returning a failure message to the client. This is the basic error handling option and should be abandoned if we notice that the issue is not transient and should directly go to the error message, in order not to lock in client requests unnecessarily:

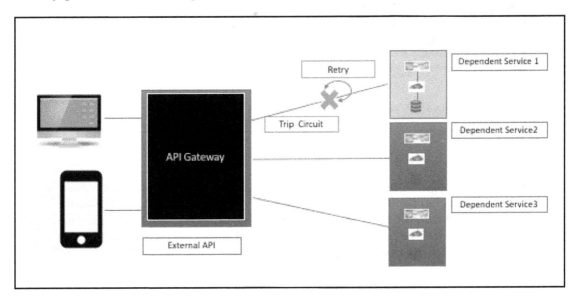

Retries in case of a failure of the dependent services

A better alternative is to detect the failures and then graciously exit with the default fallback message or payload that the client can use to service the requests. There are many advantages to this approach, for example, if we detect there is some error with the dependent service, we can respond quickly without making a call to the service and tying up the resources, and giving enough time for the failed service to recover. This approach is shown in the following diagram:

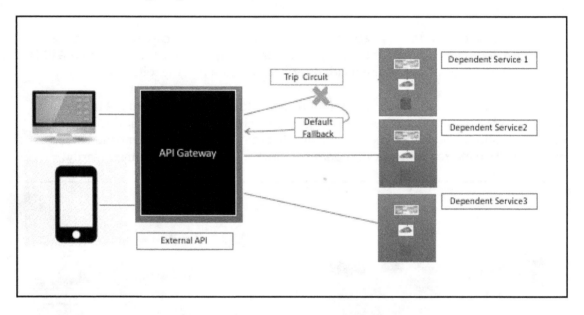

Fallback using default error messages or more typically default payload

An advanced alternative is to call the fallback service to handle the request call. This is typical in a multi-region configuration where if a service in one region, say the west, is down, we call fallback to the same services deployed in other regions, such as the east. One advantage of this is that the requests will get processed similar to the original service but this method could incur performance impacts. This method is shown in the following diagram:

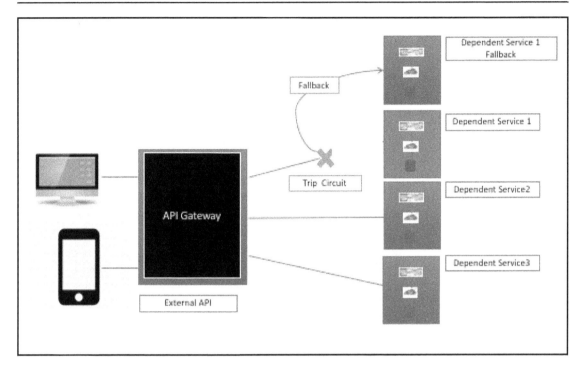

Fallback using the same service deployed in another region or data center

In the next section, we will go into the inner workings of the circuit breaker pattern and look at a sample implementation using a Netflix circuit breaker implementation that comes with Spring Cloud. The circuit breaker pattern essentially proxies the incoming HTTP requests or other method calls, since the circuit breaker can be used in multiple contexts. The circuit breaker keeps a count of recent failures that have occurred with the dependent service or method call, and utilizes this information to decide whether to allow the requests to continue or to return with an exception. The circuit breaker proxy implementation is typically a state machine that has defined states; open, half-open, or closed. Next, we will go over these various states and the state transition in detail by using a circuit breaker implementation in the HTTP client:

- **Open**: If the circuit is open, it means the dependent service is considered down and the requests to the dependent services are not made but returned immediately with an exception. The circuit breaker in this state assumes the dependent service is still perhaps down or unresponsive.

- **Closed**: This is the normal operation state where the dependent services are up and running hence, requests to the dependent services from the application go through to the target dependent service, that is, the HTTP client assumes the dependent service is operating perfectly and will call the dependent service and response returned. In this case, the circuit breaker keeps track of any recent failures and each failure will result in an increment to the circuit breaker count. And if the circuit breaker count exceeds the set threshold within the given time frame, the circuit is set to **open**. Once the circuit breaker reaches the open state, it resets the circuit count and the circuit timer. In addition, the circuit state is progressed into the **half-open** state.
- The circuit timer timeout is an important aspect in that it prevents requests from hammering a downed service, but enables it to recover from its unresponsive state by giving it enough breathing time to recover.
- **Half-open**: Assuming the dependent service is down for a while, we need some mechanism to test if the service is up and running. The half-open state is used to test and see whether the failed service is back up again by allowing only a subset of requests from the application to the destination service. Assuming these requests return without any errors, we can then assume perhaps the issues with the destination services have been resolved and the circuit breaker switches to the **closed** state, and in addition this resets the failure count. On the other hand, if the requests still fail, we can assume the issues are still plaguing the destination services; it remains in an **open** state and, will again be given the set timeout period before retry happens. The **half-open** state is primarily to check whether the dependent service is back to normal and, if it is still down, not to bombard it with too many requests. By carefully calibrating the requests to the dependent service, we can give it enough time to recover. On the other hand, if we allow all of the requests to reach the destination services, we may make the situation even worse. The following diagram gives us an insight into the workings of the circuit breaker:

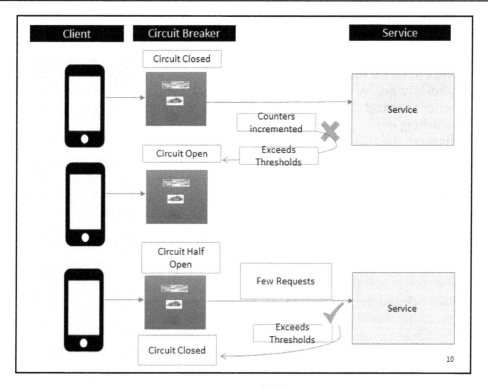

Initially, the circuit is closed but, as errors accumulate, the counter gets incremented and, once it exceeds the threshold, it is opened. During this time frame, the requests get returned immediately with an error and a few requests are sent to the service to test whether the service is working. Once a certain confidence is acquired, the circuit is closed again for the normal servicing of requests.

Issues and considerations

The circuit breaker pattern can be used in many different scenarios and it is very effective in systems where there are multiple dependent services that collectively form to get a higher level of service. Implementing a circuit breaker needs planning in the following areas:

- **Implementation**: Implementing the circuit breaker with a framework such as Spring Cloud is recommended since the implementation can be complex and should not add any additional latency to the requests. A few advantages include having common behavior across many different implementations and features such as logging, which can help with understanding the health of the application, and proper exception handling can be enabled uniformly.

- **Configuration and timeouts**: Configuring the circuit breaker with proper timeouts and fallbacks is essential to proper implementation. For example, if the circuit breaker timeout large configured open circuit state and the service errors out, even if the dependent service failure has been resolved and it is back up quickly, a proper timeout setting is essential. Similarly, with a small timeout period, a circuit could fluctuate and reduce the response times of applications by switching quickly between the open state to the half-open state, which will diminish the effectiveness of the circuit breaker.

- **Exception handling**: Applications, while utilizing the circuit breaker to invoke a service, must be able to handle exceptions and the default response payload that the circuit breaker returns, depending on the configuration. For example, an application could decide to throw the error back or invoke an alternative service.

- **Testing considerations**: Applications should be thoroughly tested for circuit open conditions before deployment to production testing. This can be tricky as, in this scenario, we need the service to be brought down and back again to be completely tested end to end.

- **Fallback and default response**: Configuring a proper fallback service to the circuit breaker is essential. For example, if the service is deployed to multiple availability zones or multiple data centers, fallback can be configured for the same service in an alternate data center or zone. Alternatively, if there are similar services, fallback could be pointed to that service. Another option is to send back a default response that can be handled by the client.

When to use this pattern

Typical usage of this pattern is to mitigate issues due to network latency and add resiliency to the microservice using the circuit breaker pattern is essential.

Example

We are going to use a very simple use case to illustrate the circuit breaker. In this use case, we are going to invoke an external service and use a very simple fallback for demonstration purposes. Imagine if the external service fails due to the network, or perhaps the system is very busy and cannot handle the load, and the client could be forced to wait for up to 60 seconds before an exception occurs. By sending more and more requests to an already exhausted service, resources such as memory, connections, and threads could be exhausted, preventing other clients from getting serviced, and this will bring down the overall SLA of the system.

Implementing the circuit breaker in the client could help to solve this problem and handle the service failure in a more appropriate way. Client requests still fail. By having the circuit breaker, they'll fail more quickly and will be handled gracefully using a default fallback. The following diagram shows the circuit breaker with an asset service and default fallback:

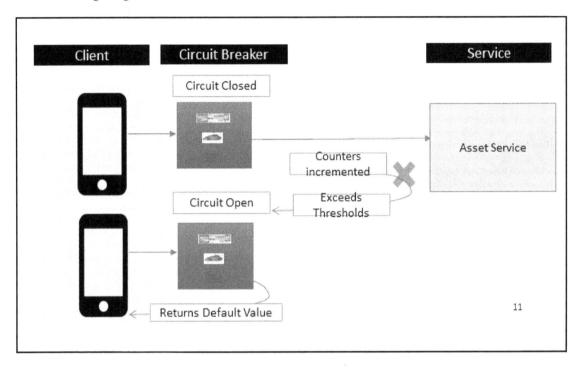

A circuit breaker with asset service and default fallback

The circuit breaker implementation is using a Netflix implementation called Hystrix. It is integrated nicely with Spring Cloud and can be used along with Spring Boot to implement a simple example. There is tons of documentation on Hystrix, Spring Cloud, and Spring Boot and so they will not be covered here. We will start off with the details of the gateway controller, which is a simple gateway with a RESTful endpoint, which exposes the /api endpoint and returns the value it gets by calling an asset service. It in turn delegates the work to GatewayManager.java:

```
GatewayController.java

/**

* Gateway for aggregating microservices for a client

*/
```

```
@RestController

@RequestMapping(value = "/api")

public class GatewayController {


@Autowired

private GatewayManager manager;


@RequestMapping(value = "/v1/customer-assets", method = GET)

public ResponseEntity<Map<String, List<AssetDto>>> getAssetsByCustomer() {

return manager.getAssetsByCustomer();

}


}
```

Details of the circuit breaker implementation is given here along with the fallback mechanism. Essentially, `GatewayManager` tries to call the Asset API and if the default timeout is reached, the circuit counter starts; if it exceeds the threshold, the fallback action gets called. We are using the default configuration of a Hystrix implementation as an example but these configurations need to be modified for the given scenarios:

```
@Component
public class GatewayManager {
    private static final Logger LOGGER =
LoggerFactory.getLogger(GatewayManager.class);

    @Autowired
    private RestTemplate restTemplate;
    @Value("${services.asset.url}")
    private String assetUrl;

    /**
     * Groups assets by customer
     *
     * @return
     */
    @HystrixCommand(fallbackMethod = "fallback")
```

```
    public ResponseEntity<Map<String, List<AssetDto>>>
getAssetsByCustomer() {
        ResponseEntity<Resources> responseEntity =
restTemplate.getForEntity(assetUrl + "/assets", Resources.class);
        Resources assets = responseEntity.getBody();
        Map<String, List<AssetDto>> response =
assets.getContent().stream().collect(Collectors.groupingBy(AssetDto::getOpe
rator));
        return okOrNotFound(response);
    }

    public ResponseEntity<Map<String, List<AssetDto>>> fallback(Throwable
t) {
        List<AssetDto> assetDtoList = Arrays.asList(new AssetDto(1L,
"Cached asset", "Test asset", "System", "System"));
        Map<String, List<AssetDto>> staticCache = Maps.newHashMap();
        staticCache.put("System", assetDtoList);
        LOGGER.warn("===================> Circit breaker:  Returning from
callback method. Reason {}", t.getMessage(), t);
        return okOrNotFound(staticCache);
    }

    @Bean
    public RestTemplate restTemplate() {
        ObjectMapper mapper = new ObjectMapper();
        mapper.configure(DeserializationFeature.FAIL_ON_UNKNOWN_PROPERTIES,
false);
        mapper.registerModule(new Jackson2HalModule());

        MappingJackson2HttpMessageConverter converter = new
MappingJackson2HttpMessageConverter();
converter.setSupportedMediaTypes(MediaType.parseMediaTypes("application/hal
+json"));
        converter.setObjectMapper(mapper);

        return new
RestTemplate(Collections.<HttpMessageConverter<?>>singletonList(converter))
;
    }

    /**
     * Return proper status code based on the response
     *
     * @param resourceMap
     * @param <K>
     * @param <V>
     * @return
     */
```

```
    private <K, V> ResponseEntity<Map<K, V>> okOrNotFound(Map<K, V>
resourceMap) {
        return resourceMap != null && !resourceMap.isEmpty() ?
ResponseEntity.ok(resourceMap) :
                new ResponseEntity<Map<K, V>>(HttpStatus.NOT_FOUND);
    }
}
```

The following code is executed if the circuit breaker is closed:

```
@HystrixCommand(fallbackMethod = "fallback")
    public ResponseEntity<Map<String, List<AssetDto>>>
getAssetsByCustomer() {
        ResponseEntity<Resources> responseEntity =
restTemplate.getForEntity(assetUrl + "/assets", Resources.class);
        Resources assets = responseEntity.getBody();
        Map<String, List<AssetDto>> response =
assets.getContent().stream().collect(Collectors.groupingBy(AssetDto::getOpe
rator));
        return okOrNotFound(response);
    }
```

If the circuit is tripped, it goes to the fallback option, which is essentially returning a basic default value so that the client can continue to process the requests:

```
public ResponseEntity<Map<String, List<AssetDto>>> fallback(Throwable t) {
        List<AssetDto> assetDtoList = Arrays.asList(new AssetDto(1L,
"Cached asset", "Test asset", "System", "System"));
        Map<String, List<AssetDto>> staticCache = Maps.newHashMap();
        staticCache.put("System", assetDtoList);
        LOGGER.warn("====================> Circit breaker:  Returning from
callback method. Reason {}", t.getMessage(), t);
        return okOrNotFound(staticCache);
    }
```

Handling for bandwidth constraints and transport costs using the API Gateway pattern

Another important challenge for IoT applications is the limited network bandwidth available between different components of the IoT application, such as between the IoT devices, constraints between the IoT edge and the cloud, or between the UI tier and the cloud tier. In this section, we will go over the API Gateway pattern. Although used primarily between the UI tier and the cloud tier, the concepts can be applied in other situations to resolve similar issues. Let's use an example to illustrate the concept. In the following diagram, we use a mobile application that calls three different services sequentially to the cloud to perform its application logic to illustrate the concept of the API Gateway:

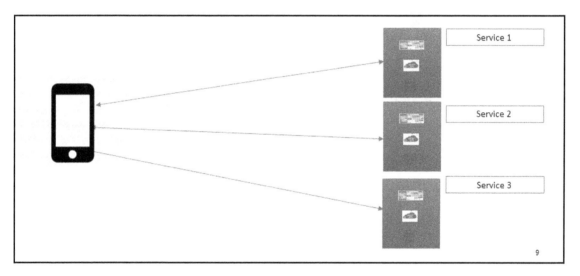

An example that uses excessive bandwidth

As we can see, there are many challenges with this design. The network calls make this application very chatty and the UI could be non-responsive during this time frame. The handling exception is another challenge and the payload from these APIs could be huge and needs to be processed correctly. In addition, the implementation of these APIs exposed over the cloud needs to be highly secure and should only expose the data that could be accessed by external applications. There are many ways to mitigate these issues. One of the best ways to implement this is use the API Gateway pattern as illustrated here:

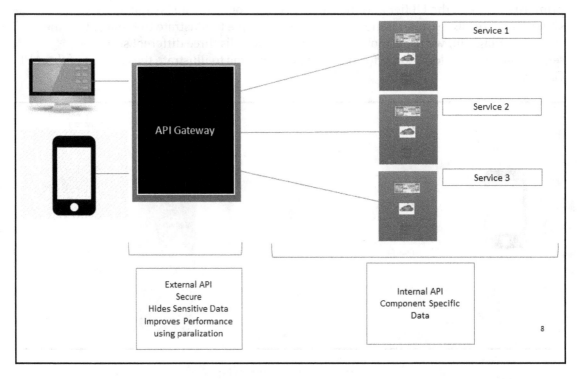

An API Gateway pattern

In this example, we have added an API Gateway that receives client requests, dispatches requests to the various services, and then aggregates the results and sends them back to the requesting client. This pattern can reduce the number of requests that the application makes to backend services and improve application performance over high-latency networks.

In the example, the mobile application sends a single request to the API Gateway. The API Gateway in turn sends requests to multiple different services such as **Service 1**, **Service 2**, and **Service 3**. It then processes each response back from these services, aggregates the results, and sends a consolidated response to the mobile app. The API Gateway can make these requests in parallel thereby reducing the total time taken for the request. The API Gateway also handles cross-cutting concerns such as certificate management, authentication, SSL termination, monitoring, protocol translation, or throttling, thereby taking over the complexity from the individual APIs.

A similar strategy can be used in IoT devices communicating with a cloud service, where the edge gateway can be used as an aggregator and can securely connect to the cloud, as opposed to enabling each individual IoT device to connect to the cloud individually, as shown here:

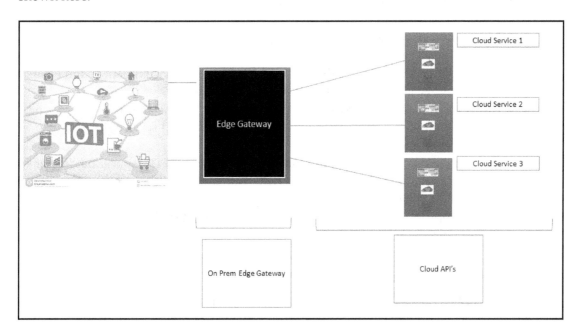

Example of how an API Gateway can be used as a proxy for IoT devices

We can use the edge gateway in conjunction with the API Gateway in the cloud, that way the interface from the edge is only one component in the cloud and it is the most common implementation in the field today.

Issues and considerations

The following are the issues and considerations we need to look into:

- Helps evolution of the different microservices without impacting the clients
- Utilizes the API Gateway to encapsulate orchestration of calls to different microservices such as service chaining, concurrent services
- Utilizes the API Gateway to improve performance of the APIs by using caching, concurrency
- We can distribute API development and remove development bottlenecks
- We can make sure the API Gateway is colocated near the backend services in order to reduce latency
- The gateway needs to be scaled appropriately to meet anticipated growth volumes
- Make sure you perform load testing against the gateway to test for cascading failures for services and appropriate error handling
- Design of the API Gateway should be able to handle service timeouts and errors and should be able to return partial results as applicable
- Utilizes a framework such as Spring Cloud, which has the ability to make async calls to services, as well as parallelize the calls to backend services to minimize the total response time
- Make sure your support excludes and includes in the HTTP request parameter so that the clients can select the needed fields rather than getting all the fields provided by the API
- Enable appropriate logging and tracing using correlation IDs to track each individual call for troubleshooting

When to use this pattern

Typical usage of this pattern is when the client would like to communicate with multiple backend services in a limited bandwidth environment such as a mobile app or IoT application.

A typical client may use networks with significant latency, such as cellular networks.

Example

The following example illustrates how to create a simple a gateway aggregation using Spring Cloud and RxJava implementations. As shown here, we have a /gateway, that exposes the /v1/shops API. This API gets the list of shops and their details by calling the asset service and finally, gets the details of the analytics by calling the analytics service. This implementation uses RxJava's Observable implemented by Netflix:

```java
@RestController
@RequestMapping(value = "/gateway")
public class ApiGatewayController {
    private static final Logger logger =
LoggerFactory.getLogger(ApiGatewayController.class);
    private static final ObjectMapper objectMapper = new ObjectMapper();

    private static Boolean isCloudDeployed = null;

    @Autowired
    HttpServletRequest request;

    @Autowired
    private ShopService shopService;
    @Autowired
    private AssetService assetService;
    @Autowired
    private AnalyticService analyticService;

    public static boolean isIsCloudDeployed() {
        return isCloudDeployed == null ? false : isCloudDeployed;
    }

  @RequestMapping(value = "/v1/shops", method = RequestMethod.GET)
    public DeferredResult<List<ShopResponse>> getAllShopDetails() {
        logger.info("*** inside getAllShopDetails()  ***");

        long startTime = System.currentTimeMillis();

        if (isCloudDeployed == null) {
            String requestUrl = request.getRequestURL().toString();
            isCloudDeployed =
!requestUrl.contains("http://localhost:8080");
            logger.info("*** requestUrl:" + requestUrl);
        }

        return toDeferredResults(getAllShopDetailedResponse(), startTime);
    }
```

```java
@SuppressWarnings("unchecked")
private Observable<List<ShopResponse>> getAllShopDetailedResponse() {
    logger.info("*** inside getAllShopDetailedResponse()  ***");

    return Observable.zip(
        shopService.getShops(),
        assetService.getAssets(),
        analyticService.getAnalytics(),
        (shops, assets, analytics) -> {
            List<ShopResponse> returnShopResponseList = new
ArrayList<ShopResponse>();

            for (Shop shop : shops) {
                ShopResponse shopResponse = new ShopResponse();
                shopResponse.setName(shop.getName());
                if (shop.getName() != null) {
                    shopResponse.setAssets((List<Asset>) assets);
                    shopResponse.setAnalytics((List<Analytic>)
analytics);
                }
                returnShopResponseList.add(shopResponse);
            }
            return returnShopResponseList;
        }
    );
}
```

The following code shows us how the request spawns out to invoke the services in parallel and the response gets consolidated, and finally it notifies the listener for it to construct the response. The parent thread is blocked until the final response gets sent:

```java
public DeferredResult<List<ShopResponse>>
toDeferredResults(Observable<List<ShopResponse>> detail, long startTime) {

    DeferredResult<List<ShopResponse>> result = new DeferredResult<>();

    detail.subscribe(new Observer<List<ShopResponse>>() {
        @Override
        public void onCompleted() {
            logger.info("*** inside OnCompleted ***");
            long endTime = System.currentTimeMillis();
            logger.info("==== GET tenant-Gateway::allShopDetails() took
[" + (endTime - startTime) + " ms]");
        }

        @Override
        public void onError(Throwable throwable) {
            logger.info("**inside OnError **");
```

```
                  throwable.printStackTrace();

                  List<ShopResponse> emptyShopResponseList = new
      ArrayList<ShopResponse>();
                  result.setResult(emptyShopResponseList);
              }

              @Override
              public void onNext(List<ShopResponse> shopResponseList) {
                  result.setResult(shopResponseList);
                  logger.info("***inside OnNext***");

                  try {
      logger.info("==========================================");
                      logger.info("\nFinal shops Response:\n" +
      Utils.object2JsonWithPrettyFormat(shopResponseList));
      logger.info("==========================================");
                  } catch (Exception e) {
                      e.printStackTrace();
                  }
              }
          });
          return result;
      }
  }
```

Enabling discoverability of the microservices to handle topology changes using Eureka

IoT devices and services typically need to call one another. In a typical system, services invoke one another through language-level methods or procedure calls and utilize configuration and so on. In a traditional distributed system deployment, services run at fixed, well known locations (hosts and ports) and so can easily call one another using HTTP/REST or some RPC mechanism. However, a modern IoT application service typically runs in a virtualized or containerized environment where the number of instances of a service and their locations changes dynamically.

In addition, a number of IoT devices get added dynamically and these devices need to discover the service. Having a centralized service and device registry is essential and these devices need to register themselves to the IoT system for them to be managed and monitored. The following diagram shows a typical IoT ecosystem with devices and services:

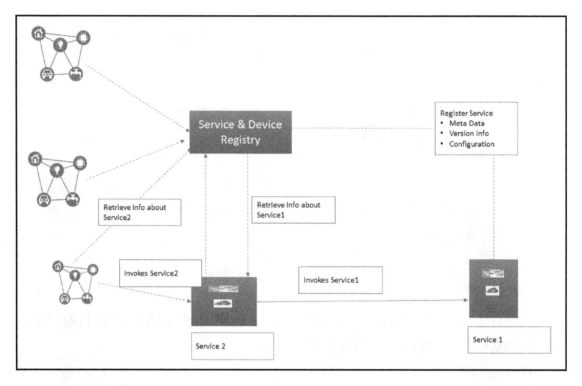

A typical IoT ecosystem with devices and services

This example illustrates a typical IoT ecosystem with a number of devices and services, all connected to each other. Essentially, the service or device registry is a database of services and devices, their instances and their locations—sometimes metadata and configurations are also stored. Service/device instances are registered to the service registry at startup time and are de-registered during shutdown. Clients of these services usually query the service registry to find the available instances of a service before invoking the services/devices. A service registry can also invoke a service instance's **Health Check API** (http:// microservices.io/patterns/observability/health-check-api.html) to check the availability of the device/services.

In the previous example, **Service 1** checks with the registry to find the location of **Service 2** before invoking the service. A similar scenario is also detailed where a device can look up the registry to find the location of **Service 1**.

Issues and considerations

The following are the issues and considerations we need to look into:

- It is good to have the service registry built into the infrastructure. If not, it is yet another infrastructure component that must be set up, configured, and managed.
- The service registry should be highly available since it is a very critical component, and clients typically cache the data so as not to be too tightly coupled with the service registry, but these configurations need to be refreshed periodically otherwise it will get stale.
- Service registration at startup is an essential task and the process varies between a device or a service and it should be part of the life cycle of the services. There are many different third-party tools available; a few popular ones are Eureka from Netflix, Zookeeper, or a console using a tool suitable for the given scenario is very important.
- The clients of the service registry should know the location(s) of the service registry instances. Each service registry instance must be deployed on fixed and well known IP addresses. Clients are configured to look up those IP addresses. For example, the Netflix Eureka (`https://github.com/Netflix/eureka/wiki/Configuring-Eureka-in-AWS-Cloud`) service instances are typically deployed using elastic IP Addresses. The available pool of elastic IP addresses is configured using either a properties file or via DNS. When a Eureka instance starts up it consults the configuration to determine which available elastic IP address to use. A Eureka client is also configured with the pool of elastic IP addresses.

When to use this pattern

Use this pattern when clients of a service or device use either **server-side discovery** (`http://microservices.io/patterns/client-side-discovery.html`) or **client-side discovery** (`http://microservices.io/patterns/server-side-discovery.html`) to determine the location of a service or device instance to which to send requests.

Example

The following example illustrates how to use Eureka to register your service and look up the service using the Eureka client:

```
import org.springframework.boot.SpringApplication;
import org.springframework.boot.autoconfigure.SpringBootApplication;
import org.springframework.cloud.netflix.eureka.server.EnableEurekaServer;

@SpringBootApplication
@EnableEurekaServer
public class Application {

  public static void main(String[] args) {
    SpringApplication.run(Application.class, args);
  }
}


application.yml file given below which looks up the eureka

server:
  port: ${PORT:8761}

eureka:
  client:
    registerWithEureka: false
    fetchRegistry: false
    server:
waitTimeInMsWhenSyncEmpty: 0
```

The art of building a fault-tolerant IIoT device and edge gateway

We will switch gears from the cloud tier and focus on Tier 1 and Tier 2, that is, the device and the gateway and how we can build reliability into these key components of the IIoT architecture.

Designing for reliability at the sensors and devices

The main pain point for the device is the ability to communicate reliably to the gateway or to the cloud and send the sensor data in a secure way. The reliability of communications can be attributed to the performance of a few critical components: a radio transceiver and communications microcontroller as part of the device. Wireless connectivity technologies utilized by consumer devices do not always satisfy the greater performance demands of industrial and healthcare systems. These systems give a higher priority to safety, accuracy, and time sensitivity, and hence demand a more reliable communication. Cellular systems may come close but they put a penalty on data throughput, battery, and cost requirements. Reliable communications are available in areas such as military but these prioritize reliability over everything else; IoT devices demand such a reliability but at a much lower cost.

Challenges in building reliable connectivity for devices in industrial environments

Let's look at the following challenges:

- **Industrial settings can cause missed packets**: The industrial environment poses many challenges that can negatively impact wireless communication. The steel construction and thick walls of factories create barriers for RF signals to the point where they cannot be properly received by the target device. The IoT gateway must be calibrated for signal sensitivity to properly receive the packets from the devices and sensors; a variation of as small as 2 dB change in sensitivity could be the difference between the successful or unsuccessful reception of a signal.

- **Crowded frequency bands can result in lost packets**: Connected devices will typically operate in the relevant ISM band for that region. ISM bands are license free and can be used for a wide range of applications requiring wireless connectivity; 2.4 GHz is standardized globally and is widely used by Wi-Fi and Bluetooth® devices. The challenge arises when multiple devices located in close proximity are sharing the same ISM band. Device transmission can interfere with nearby receiving devices; in most industrial settings many devices share the same ISM band. Another aspect to consider is the blocking specification, which is the ability of the devices to block certain frequencies to improve reception without sufficient blocking capability. Mobile devices and tablets operating nearby could cause a loss of communication in the system.

- **Environmental effects degrade performance**: Sensors and devices are built on processes that are prone to variations in performance, depending on the environment in which they're operating. Some variations include temperature changes, voltage supply reductions as batteries discharge, and silicon manufacturing variations across devices. These real-life events can cause changes in the operating stability of the device. Devices should be built to handle these variations.

Designing for reliable communication

One way to mitigate the communication issues and losses is by utilizing a proper communication protocol such as MQTT, which has built-in **Quality of Service** (**QoS**). MQTT is a lightweight protocol that uses the pub/sub pattern to connect interested parties with each other. It does this by decoupling the sender (publisher) with the receiver (subscriber). The publisher sends a message to a central topic which has multiple subscribers waiting to receive the message. The publishers and subscribers are autonomous, which means that they do not need to know the presence of each other.

MQTT may be a lightweight protocol, but it is used in some of the complex scenarios that demand reliable delivery of messages. Clients can configure different levels of QoS to ensure reliable message delivery. Since it is a part of the specification, MQTT brokers are expected to implement this feature.

Similar to other service-oriented environments, QoS in MQTT provides levels of agreement or contracts between the broker and clients. When both of them agree on a specific QoS level, it implicitly means that the broker honors the contract.

There are three levels of QoS in MQTT:

- **QoS 0**: At the most, one delivery; in this case, the message is delivered only once but it is not guaranteed
- **QoS 1**: At least one delivery will ensure the message is delivered at least once but it could be repeated
- **QoS 2**: Exactly one delivery, as the name says the message will be delivered exactly once but it is expensive

In addition to various QoS, MQTT also supports the ability to handle various error conditions and provides mechanisms such as keep-alive to check for heartbeats between client and servers, and can quickly identify connection issues and enable auto reconnect. In addition to reconnecting, MQTT brokers can persist messages during sessions and, hence, can even withstand crashes.

Designing for reliability at the gateway

As you recall, in our IoT architecture we have sensors in Tier 1, a gateway in Tier 2, and the cloud in Tier 3. Essentially, sensors at the edge gather the equipment parameters and stream the data through the edge gateway to the cloud system that stores data and analyzes the data, and eventually presents the data back to humans for taking actions, as shown in the following diagram. This architecture is very robust and scaleless but not reliable due to network latency and bandwidth constraints. In addition, the edge gateway has very little compute capability since its primary responsibility is to gather data and provide security and connectivity to sensors. Since logic and decision making are maintained at the cloud, it makes an IoT system dependent on the backend while adding latency to the decision making.

An alternate architecture called fog computing has emerged, which negates the disadvantage of the edge gateway and adds additional functionality, such as the ability to take decisions at the edge itself, closest to real time. This means adding storage and compute and storage resources at the edge:

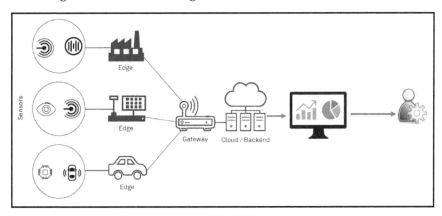

Typical IoT end-to-end system

Many analysts have predicted there will be close to 21 billion edge devices by 2020 and this will likely result in underlying networks transporting the data to run into bandwidth congestion. In such a network-constrained environment, depending on the cloud to take action results in lagging responses and failures, resulting in seriously jeopardizing operations of critical systems such as in power plants, utilities, aircraft operations, oil rigs, railways, and surveillance systems, which rely heavily on the IoT and cloud technologies.

Adopting a fog computing architecture solves these problems and fog computing essentially adds a layer of high-performance compute and storage services at the edge gateway. This results in many advantages such as the following:

- By utilizing the storage at the edge gateway, we can create data filters at the edge. These data filters store and process data closer to the devices, thereby reducing the volume of (real-time) data published to the cloud, hence reducing network congestion.
- Using the additional compute power, the edge gateway now has the power to run certain types of analytics nearer to the devices. Providing the ability to run analytics at the edge enables the edge gateway to take decisions without depending on cloud systems.

An example of a typical fog computing architecture is shown here:

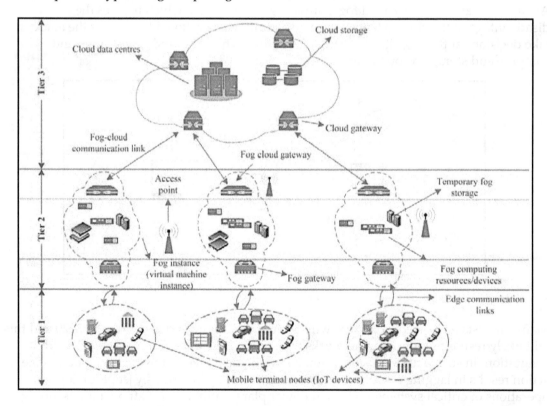

Typical fog computing architecture

Essentially, fog computing extends the cloud to be closer to the things that produce and act on IoT data. These devices, called fog nodes, can be deployed anywhere with a network connection: on a factory floor, on top of a power pole, alongside a railway track, in a vehicle, or on an oil rig. Any device with computing, storage, and network connectivity can be a fog node. Examples include industrial controllers, switches, routers, embedded servers, and video surveillance cameras. Fog nodes will store data and can process data by running predictive analytics such as forecasting analytics and anomaly detection analytics. The device can then respond to the outcome of these analytics. In addition to analytics, fog nodes can provide a control pane for managing the devices and provide additional workflows.

Monitoring IIoT applications (edge and cloud)

In this section, we will discuss monitoring various different components of IoT tiers such as the cloud tier, the gateway tier, and sensor tiers. We will go over the cloud microservices monitoring strategy subsequently over the general IoT monitoring approaches.

Monitoring IoT services on the cloud

Proper monitoring of IoT applications is very important and there are many benefits to implementing a very robust monitoring strategy such as the following:

- Monitoring provides a higher level of application and network security across the many different components of the IoT system
- Consistent monitoring and diagnosis/resolution of issues improves the ability to reach and maintain peak application performance
- Improved service availability due to more rapid reporting of issues, leading to faster resolution

As we discussed earlier, since the cloud tier typically uses microservices architecture, we are going to look at how we can use the health endpoint design pattern to monitor microservices. In a typical cloud application developed using microservices, there are many different factors such as network latency, the performance and availability of dependent services, availability of the underlying compute and storage systems, and the network bandwidth between them. The microservices can fail entirely or partially due to any of these factors. Therefore, we should monitor these microservices periodically to validate that the service is performing correctly to ensure the required level of availability or SLAs.

Monitoring microservices using health endpoints

Health monitoring is implemented by sending requests to a predefined microservices endpoint on a periodic basis. The microservices endpoint should in turn perform the necessary checks for its dependent resources such as storage, databases, dependent services, and other required resources for the successful running of the applications, and return an indication of its status. Usually the results of the health monitoring check are collected by a tool such as **New Relic** or **Prometheus** for persistent and further reports or alerting.

A health monitoring check typically combines two aspects:

- Health endpoint checks performed by the microservice in response to the request to the health monitoring endpoint
- Further analysis of the results by the a monitoring tool such as Prometheus, New Relic, or CloudWatch for reporting and actions

The response should clearly indicate the status of service and various dependent components it uses. The latency check is measured by the monitoring tool. The following diagram provides an overview of the pattern:

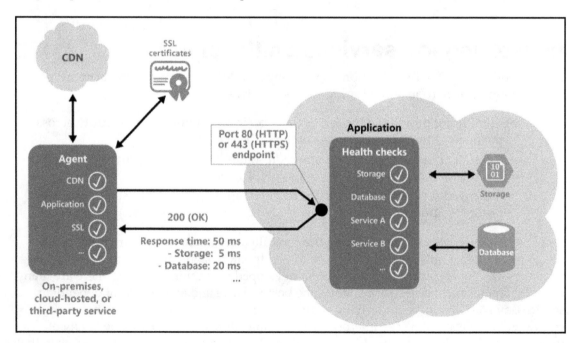

In this example, the microservice uses a database and a document storage such as Scality:

- Successful services return an HTTP response of 200 (OK) which indicates no issues. The monitoring system might also check for other response codes to give more comprehensive results.
- The monitoring tool should check for the content of the response to detect errors, even when a 200 (OK) status code is returned and usually it is embedded as part of the payload.
- We can use the health endpoint to measure the response time, which includes a combination of the network latency and the time that the application took to execute the request.
- In addition, we can use it to check dependent resources such as a DB and other microservices.
- Also, it can validate the expiration of SSL certificates.

Tests against this endpoint should be run periodically, run against all of the services used by the IoT application, stored in the common tools, and action taken if there are failures.

Example using Spring Actuator

Spring Actuator enables the monitoring of Spring Boot applications. It enables the gathering of various application metrics, database status, and traffic details.

The main benefit of this library is that we can get production grade tools without having to actually implement these features ourselves.

Actuator is mainly used to **expose operational information about the running application**—health, metrics, info, dump, env, and so on. It uses HTTP endpoints or JMX beans to enable us to interact with it.

You enable Actuator by adding the Maven dependency, and several endpoints are enabled out of the box, which can be extended or customized as needed:

```
<dependency>
    <groupId>org.springframework.boot</groupId>
    <artifactId>spring-boot-starter-actuator</artifactId>
</dependency>
```

Actuator comes with most endpoints disabled but two of the interesting endpoints are available by default: /health and /info. A sample output of a /health endpoint is given here:

```
Success
{
    "status" : "UP"
}

Failure
{
    "status" : "DOWN",
    "scalityCheck" : {
        "status" : "DOWN",
        "Error Code" : 1
    },
    "diskSpace" : {
        "status" : "UP",
        "free" : 209047318528,
        "threshold" : 10485760
    }
}
```

An example to add a custom indicator is given here:

```
@Component
public class IoTServiceHealthIndicator implements ReactiveHealthIndicator {

    @Override
    public Mono<Health> health() {
        return checkDownstreamServiceHealth().onErrorResume(
          ex -> Mono.just(new Health.Builder().down(ex).build())
        );
    }

    private Mono<Health> checkDownstreamServiceHealth() {
        // we could use WebClient to check health reactively
        return Mono.just(new Health.Builder().up().build());
    }
}
```

Monitoring IoT devices and gateway strategies

In addition to monitoring the microservices, we need to have a robust monitoring strategy for IoT devices and IoT gateways. Monitoring of these components can be further subdivided into device management, and provisioning vs performance monitoring of these devices. Usually, we have to use two different tool for the same or, in most cases, we may have to build a custom tools for both of these cases. In this chapter, we will look at a strategy for building both these tools.

IoT device management and provisioning strategies

IoT device management is all about fast device onboarding, organizing devices, and remote management of devices, to perform updates and control devices remotely. Investing in such a tool is essential to scale the application for many different tenants and help improve the SLAs and avoid downtime. There are a few out-of-the box solutions from the AWS IoT solution or Azure IoT, but due to the diversity of the devices and specific nature of the hardware it may not be possible to adopt an out-of-the-box solution. A typical architecture is given here:

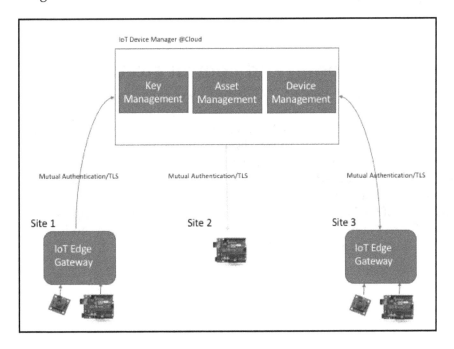

Typical architecture of the custom device management and provisioning solution

In this architecture, we can see key components:

- Key management, which generates a client certificate for each of the devices that needs to be part managed
- An asset manager, which manages the assets for the customers and helps with provisioning
- A device manager used for managing the devices such as controlling the devices to send updates

Device onboarding and discovery

Device onboarding is essential to scaling the IoT application to support hundreds of IoT devices. Usually, the mechanism is to ship devices or a gateway with a certificate and configurations so that, as part of the activation process, the devices register themselves with the cloud registry; for communication, they usually use the mutual TLS authentication. The certificate signing process involves creating a certification authority, self-signing the client certificate for each of the IoT devices, and installing the certificate on the IoT device. In addition, the cloud services should have the root certificate installed to validate the client certificate. The device registry should also handle any devices that gets removed. If so, the certificates should also be revoked.

IoT device monitoring and control strategy

Once the communication channel is established between the device and the cloud, as given in the previous section, we can use the same communication channel for various different purposes, such as monitoring of the devices, controlling the devices, and finally, updating or patching the device firmware/software. We can extend the preceding architecture to include a tool such as Prometheus, with which we can develop plugins to collect monitoring data that can be fed to a visualization tool such as Grafana to visualize various trends such as CPU, and network and data usage. Prometheus also comes with numerous client plugins out of the box to collect numerous client side data for application performance. Furthermore, we can also use the Prometheus alerting module to alert for any deviations for these metrics.

A typical IoT monitoring system with Prometheus and Grafana is shown here:

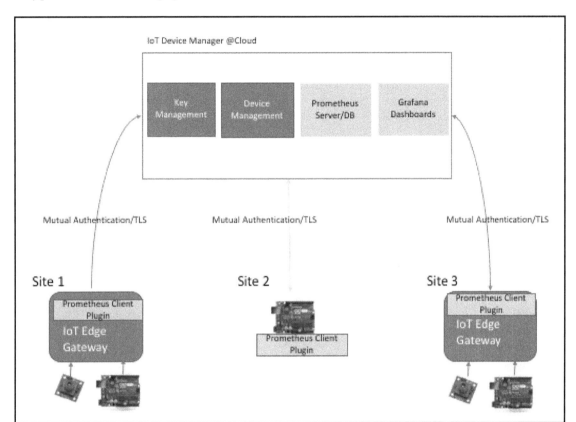

Typical IoT monitoring System with Prometheus and Grafana

Summary

In this chapter, we went though a detailed overview of how to build reliable IIoT applications at all of the three IoT application tiers using various design patterns. In addition, we looked at how to monitor the IoT system to successfully maintain the deployed system over the years to come.

Implementing IIoT Applications with Predix

9

In this chapter, you will learn in more detail about the components and capabilities of the Asset, Time Series, and Analytics Framework services from GE's Predix catalog. In particular, we will demonstrate how to create instances of the services, bind them with your apps, and configure client authentications. You will also learn how to use various HTTP requests in Postman to query and manage assets, and how to build and deploy apps to read and analyze time series data. Furthermore, we will provide detailed instructions on how to enable advanced visualization with components of GE's Predix UI Framework.

This chapter covers the following topics:

- Using the Asset service for asset modeling
- Creating an instance of the Asset service and binding it to your app
- Configuring client authentications for managing assets via the Asset service
- Adding assets to the Asset service
- Changing assets
- Viewing, deleting, and querying assets
- Additional capabilities of the Asset service
- Building an app to read time series data
- Creating an instance of the Time Series service
- Binding an instance of the Times Series service to your app
- Validating ingestions of time series data
- Components and capabilities of the Analytics Framework service
- Creating an instance of the Analytics Framework service and binding it to your app
- Building an analytical app to work with the Analytics Framework service

- Adding an analytical app to the Analytics Catalog of the Analytics Framework service
- Validating, testing, and deploying an analytical app
- Executing an analytical application
- Enabling data visualizations with GE's Predix UI Framework

Basics of asset modeling with the Asset service

This section overviews GE's Predix's Asset service, looking into how it can help to model assets. We will also provide two examples, illustrating how asset models describe objects in the JSON format.

The Asset service in detail

The Asset service by GE's Predix is designed to assist developers in creating, storing, and updating data for asset models, while enabling consumers to retrieve it.

An asset model consists of domain objects (for instance, classifications and assets) described in JSON. The objects are actually random sets of name-value pairs with a unique **Uniform Resource Identifier** (**URI**), indicating an appropriate asset instance stored in a graph database.

In the next subsection, we will provide an example of a classification object (Countries) to illustrate its JSON representation in an asset model.

An example of a classification object

The following figure is a graphical representation of a simple classification object consisting of two components:

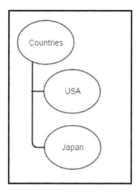

A hierarchy of the Countries classification object

In the JSON format, the `Countries` classification object will be represented this way:

```
[
    {
            "uri": "/countries",
            "name": "Countries",
            "obsolete": false,
            "attributes": {
            }
    },
    {
            "uri": "/countries/USA",
            "name": "USA",
            "parent": "/countries",
            "obsolete": false,
            "attributes": {
            }
    },
    {
            "uri": "/countries/Japan",
            "name": "Japan",
            "parent": "/countries",
            "obsolete": false,
            "attributes": {
            }
    }
]
```

 You can find this and more examples, as well as additional information about the Asset service in GE's Predix documentation: `https://docs.predix.io/en-US/content/service/data _management/asset/`.

Developing your first asset model with GE's Predix

In this section, we will demonstrate how to create an instance of the Asset service and authorize a **User Account and Authentication** (**UAA**) client, so it can use the service instance created.

Creating an instance of the Asset service

Assuming we already have an application deployed to GE's Predix and a UAA service instance running, our next step is to create an instance of the Asset service. To do this, follow these steps:

1. Sign in to `https://predix.io` and select the Asset service in GE's Predix catalog. To access the Asset service, go to `https://www.predix.io/catalog/services`.
2. Select a usage plan.
3. Select an organization, space, and UAA instance. Specify a name for the service instance created.
4. To complete the process, click **Create Service.**

Binding an Asset service instance to your application

Once you have created a service instance, you need to bind it to your application. To do that, follow these steps:

1. Create the `ui` folder:

   ```
   mkdir ui
   ```

2. Create the `index.html` file. It should be empty.

3. Create `manifest.yml` and paste the following code into it:

```
---
applications:
- name: ui
  memory: 64M
  buildpack: staticfile_buildpack
  random-route: true
```

4. Deploy the application base to the cloud, using the following command:

   cf push

5. Run this command from the console:

   cf bind-service ui asset-service-instance

   After running the command, you will get the console output shown in the following screenshot:

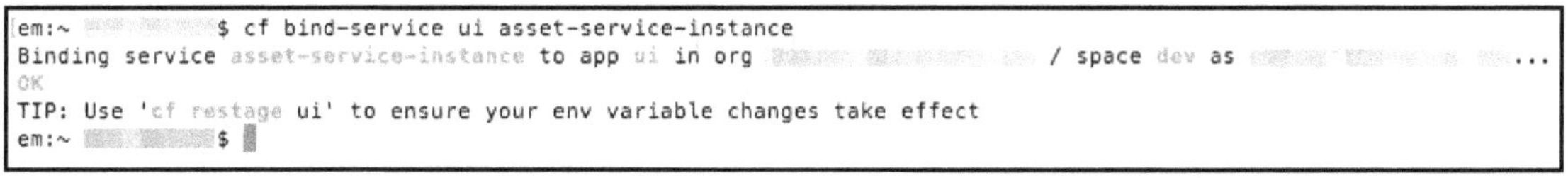

```
em:~            $ cf bind-service ui asset-service-instance
Binding service asset-service-instance to app ui in org                / space dev as                  ...
OK
TIP: Use 'cf restage ui' to ensure your env variable changes take effect
em:~         $
```

Console output after binding an Asset Service instance to an application

6. Run this command to get new environment variables:

   cf env ui

   The output will be as follows:

```
{
"VCAP_SERVICES": {
 "predix-asset": [
  {
    "credentials": {
    "instanceId": "2d86d5e7-5378-4f0b-b437-124bb75e5fd7",
    "zone": {
     "http-header-name": "Predix-Zone-Id",
     "http-header-value": "2d86d5e7-5378-4f0b-
b437-124bb75e5fd7",
      "oauth-scope": "predix-asset.zones.2d86d5e7-5378-4f0b-
b437-124bb75e5fd7.user"
      ...
  "predix-uaa": [
   {
```

```
    "credentials": {
     "uri":
    "https://e0fd8047-0a1d-4076-9143-fc4cbf60cd79.predix-uaa.run.aw
    s-usw02-pr.ice.predix.io",
     ...
```

We will need the environment variables (for instance, `instanceId`, `uri`, or `oauth-scope`) from the code in the subsequent sections of this chapter.

Enabling a UAA client to use the Asset service

To allow a UAA client to work with assets via the Asset service, proceed as follows:

1. Sign in to the UAA Dashboard, following this link: `https://uaa-dashboard.run.aws-usw02-pr.ice.predix.io/#/login`.

2. Create the `predix-asset.zones.<service_instance_guid>.user` group. In this example, the group will have the following name: `predix-asset.zones.2d86d5e7-5378-4f0b-b437-124bb75e5fd7.user`.

3. Assign the group to a client user. You can specify the `Scope` and `Authorities` parameters for the client manually, using the group name from item 2. Alternatively, you can select an **Asset service** instance from the **Authorized Services** list.

4. Get an authorization token for the client. You can do this on the **Client Info** page of the **UAA Dashboard** by clicking **Generate Token** or using the `uaac` tool:

Generating a token via the **UAA Dashboard**

The `uaac` tool is available at `https://github.com/cloudfoundry/cf-uaac`.

To install the `uaac` tool, proceed as follows:

1. Run the following command from console:
   `gem install cf-uaac`
2. Specify the target:
   `uaac target UAA_URI`
3. In this example, the target is as follows:
   `uaac target https://e0fd8047-0a1d-4076-9143-fc4cbf60cd79.predix-uaa.run.aws-usw02-pr.ice.predix.io`

5. To see the token, use the following command:

`uaac context`

The output of the command will be as follows:

```
[0]*[https://e0fd8047-0a1d-4076-9143-fc4cbf60cd79.predix-uaa.run.aws-usw02-pr.ice.predix.io]

[1]*[client]
    client_id: client
    access_token: LONG_TOKEN
    token_type: bearer
    expires_in: 43199
    scope: scim.me openid predix-
asset.zones.2d86d5e7-5378-4f0b-b437-124bb75e5fd7.user
    jti: 458f1783441f4429a6520811e49b44ea
```

Now, knowing the access token, you can start using the Asset service API to request asset data. In this example, we will query the Asset service for a list of assets using the following command:

```
curl -X GET https://predix-asset.run.aws-usw02-pr.ice.predix.io/v1/ -H
'authorization: Bearer LONG_TOKEN' -H 'content-type: application/json' -H
'predix-zone-id: 2d86d5e7-5378-4f0b-b437-124bb75e5fd7'
```

The command will have the output as: `[]`. In our case, the response is empty, since we have not added any assets to the Asset service yet. We are going to do that in the next section.

If you don't have a UAA instance, consult the following Predix documentation to create it: `https://docs.predix.io/en-US/content/service/security/user_account_and_authentication/`.

If you have no deployed application, follow the instructions in `Chapter 3`, *IIoT Edge Development*, of this book to build and deploy it.

Creating instances of assets

In this section, we will describe how to add an asset to the Asset service, as well as how to change, view, or delete it, using various HTTP requests in Postman. We will also look into how to query asset data with different GET parameters, as well as see an overview of the additional capabilities of the Asset service.

Adding an asset to the Asset service

To add an asset to the Asset service, we will need to create an HTTP request. For the task, we recommend using Postman (`https://www.getpostman.com`). This tool makes it easier to create complex HTTP requests, while enabling users to save the history of actions and share it with other people.

In this example, we will use the `Locomotives` asset.

To create an HTTP request in Postman, proceed as follows:

1. Click the drop-down button in the upper-left corner, select **POST**, and specify the following:
   `https://predix-asset.run.aws-usw02-pr.ice.predix.io/locomotives`.
2. On the **Headers** tab, specify the following:
   - **For Content-Type**: `application/json`
   - **For Authorization**: Bearer `LONG_TOKEN`
   - **For Predix-Zone-Id**: `2d86d5e7-5378-4f0b-b437-124bb75e5fd7`
3. Go to the **Body** tab and select the **raw** radio button.
4. Paste the following asset model data into the request body:

```
[
    {
        "uri": "/locomotives/1",
        "type": "Diesel-electric",
```

```
            "model": "ES44AC",
            "serial_no": "001",
            "emission_tier": "0+",
            "fleet": "/fleets/up-1",
            "manufacturer": "/manufacturers/GE",
            "engine": "/engines/v12-1",
            "installedOn": "01/12/2005",
            "dateIso": "2005-12-01T13:15:31Z",
            "hqLatLng": {
                "lat": 33.914605,
                "lng": -117.253374
            }
        },
        {

            "uri": "/locomotives/2",
            "type": "Diesel-electric",
            "model": "SD70ACe",
            "serial_no": "002",
            "emission_tier": "0+",
            "fleet": "/fleets/up-1",
            "manufacturer": "/manufacturers/electro-motive-diesel",
            "engine": "/engines/v16-2-1",
            "hqLatLng": {
                "lat": 47.655492,
                "lng": -117.427025
            }
        }
    ]
```

 You can find this and other samples of asset model data in GE's Predix documentation: https://docs.predix.io/en-US/content/service/data_management/asset/asset-model-sample-data.

Introducing changes to an asset

To introduce a change to an asset, we will need to use a **PUT** request. To create it in Postman, proceed as follows:

1. Change the hqLatLng parameter as indicated in the following screenshot.
2. Using the drop-down button in the upper-left corner, change the request type to **PUT**.

3. On the **Body** tab, paste the asset data from the previous example (item 4):

Creating a **PUT** request in Postman

If you have a lot of assets to change, you can use a **PATCH** request instead of the **PUT** one.

For a **PATCH** request, use the body content shown here:

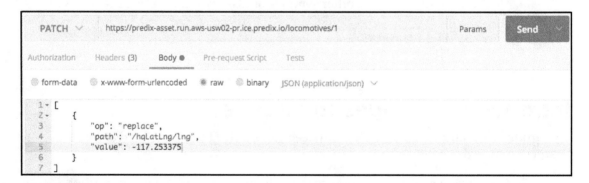

Creating a **PATCH** request in Postman

Viewing an asset

To view a created asset, use a **GET** request. In Postman, select **GET** from the request type drop-down list in the upper-left corner and paste this URL: `https://predix-asset.run.aws-usw02-pr.ice.predix.io/locomotives/1`. As a result, you will see this JSON syntax:

```
[
    {
        "uri": "/locomotives/1",
        "type": "Diesel-electric",
        "model": "ES44AC",
        "serial_no": "001",
        "emission_tier": "0+",
        "fleet": "/fleets/up-1",
        "manufacturer": "/manufacturers/GE",
        "engine": "/engines/v12-1",
        "installedOn": "01/12/2005",
        "dateIso": "2005-12-01T13:15:31Z",
        "hqLatLng": {
            "lat": 33.914605,
            "lng": -117.253375
        }
    }
]
```

Deleting an asset

To delete an asset, use a **DELETE** request. To run it via Postman, select **Delete** in the request type drop-down list, as shown in the following screenshot:

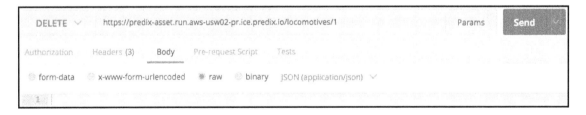

Running a DELETE request

Before deleting a request, make sure it will not impair the functioning of other services.

Additional capabilities of the Asset service

The Asset service features the following additional capabilities:

- The **Audit History** feature enables users to check the history of all the changes in the asset database. By default, it is disabled.
- Querying assets using a wide range of methods to filter results, including the special GEL language.
- Validating ingested data against a specified data validation schema in the JSON format.

 For more information, check out GE's Predix documentation: `https://docs.predix.io/en-US/content/service/data _management/asset/asset-service-overview`.

Adding Predix time series data to assets

In this section, we will describe how to build a Node.js application to simulate reading time series data from sensors connected to an asset (in this case, a Raspberry Pi hub). Furthermore, we will give instructions on how to create an instance of the Time Series service and enable the application to send data to it.

Building an app to read time series data

To build and deploy a Node.js app that simulates reading time series data from sensors, proceed as follows:

 Make sure to specify the correct data source in the asset attributes (in this example, devices: `/device/raspberry`).

1. Create the `assets` folder:

```
mkdir assets && cd assets
```

2. Create the `package.json` file and paste the following code into it:

```
{
  "name": "assets",
  "version": "1.0.0",
  "description": "",
  "main": "index.js",
  "scripts": {
    "start": "node index.js",
    "test": "echo \"Error: no test specified\" && exit 1"
  },
  "author": "",
  "license": "ISC",
  "dependencies": {
    "predix-uaa-client": "^1.2.2",
    "request": "^2.81.0",
    "websocket": "^1.0.24"
  }
}
```

3. Create the `index.js` file containing the following code. Make sure to specify the actual values for the `uaaUrl`, `clientId`, `clientSecret`, and `predix-zone-id` parameters:

```
var WebSocketClient = require('websocket').client;
var uaaUtil = require('predix-uaa-client');
var url = require('url');

var tsUrl = 'wss://gateway-predix-data-services.run.aws-usw02-
pr.ice.predix.io/v1/stream/messages';
var uaaUrl =
'https://e0fd8047-0a1d-4076-9143-fc4cbf60cd79.predix-uaa.run.aws-us
w02-pr.ice.predix.io/oauth/token';
var clientId = 'client name';
var clientSecret = 'client secret';
var min = 0;
var max = 100;
var interval = 1000;

/*
* Getting the UAA client token to be able work with the Time Series
service
*/
uaaUtil.getToken(uaaUrl, clientId, clientSecret).then(function
(token) {
 var headers = {
    Authorization: 'Bearer ' + token.access_token,
    'predix-zone-id': '6f6882ff-3a3b-45b2-b20b-b537e652471d',
```

```
        'Origin': 'http://localhost'
};
console.log('headers: ', headers);

var requestOptions = {agent: false};

var client = new WebSocketClient();

client.on('connectFailed', function (error) {
  console.log('connection error: ', error);
});

client.on('connect', function (connection) {
  /*
  * Debug output
  */
  console.log('connected to: ', tsUrl);
  connection.on('error', function (error) {
    console.log('connection error: ', error);
  });
  connection.on('close', function () {
    console.log('connection closed');
  });
  connection.on('message', function (message) {
    if (message.type === 'utf8') {
      console.log('response: ', message.utf8Data);
    }
  });

  /*
  * Scheduling data ingestion
  */
  setInterval(function () {
    /*
    * Generating a random value
    */
    var variable1 = Math.floor(max - Math.random() * (max - min));

    /*
    * Preparing a data object
    */
    var data = JSON.stringify({
      messageId: Date.now(),
      body: [
        {
          name: 'sensor1:variable1',
          datapoints: [
            [Date.now(), variable1, 3]
```

```
      ],
      attributes: {
        devices: '/device/raspberry'
      }
    }
  ]
});

/*
 * Sending data
 */
console.log('sending: ', data);
connection.sendUTF(data);
}, interval);
});

/*
 * Initializing a WebSocket connection with the Time Series service
 */
client.connect(tsUrl, null, 'http://localhost', headers,
requestOptions);
}).catch(function (err) {
console.error('failed to get token', err);
});
```

4. Create `manifest.yml` and paste the following code into it:

```
applications:
-
 name: assets
 memory: 128M
 no-route: true
 health-check-type: process
```

5. To deploy the app, run the following command:

```
cf push
```

Creating an instance of the Time Series service

To create an instance of the Time Series service, follow these steps:

1. Subscribe to a plan of your choice.
2. Go to GE's **Predix catalogue** and select the **Time Series** service tile.

Free plans allow for up to 100,000 data points and two concurrent connections per month.

Alternatively, you can subscribe to a plan using a CLI. To do that, run the following command:

```
cf create-service predix-timeseries Free timeseries-service-
instance -c '{"trustedIssuerIds":
["https://e0fd8047-0a1d-4076-9143-fc4cbf60cd79.predix-uaa.run.a
ws-usw02-pr.ice.predix.io/oauth/token"]}'
```

The value of the `issuerId` parameter is the URL of your UAA instance.

3. Bind the service instance created to your Node.js application:

```
cf bind-service assets timeseries-service-instance
```

4. Restart the application to refresh the environment variables:

```
cf restage assets
cf env assets
```

5. Check the response to make sure you have `predix-timeseries` in it:

```
{
"VCAP_SERVICES": {
 "predix-timeseries": [
  {
   "credentials": {
    "ingest": {
    "uri": "wss://gateway-predix-data-services.run.aws-usw02-
pr.ice.predix.io/v1/stream/messages",
    "zone-http-header-name": "Predix-Zone-Id",
    "zone-http-header-value": "6f6882ff-3a3b-45b2-b20b-
b537e652471d",
    "zone-token-scopes": [
     "timeseries.zones.6f6882ff-3a3b-45b2-b20b-b537e652471d.user",
     "timeseries.zones.6f6882ff-3a3b-45b2-b20b-
b537e652471d.ingest"
    ]
    },
    "query": {
    "uri":
"https://time-series-store-predix.run.aws-usw02-pr.ice.predix.io/v1
/datapoints",
    "zone-http-header-name": "Predix-Zone-Id",
```

```
    "zone-http-header-value": "6f6882ff-3a3b-45b2-b20b-
b537e652471d",
    "zone-token-scopes": [
    "timeseries.zones.6f6882ff-3a3b-45b2-b20b-b537e652471d.user",
    "timeseries.zones.6f6882ff-3a3b-45b2-b20b-b537e652471d.query"
 ...
```

Enabling an app to send data to the Time Series service

To enable the application to send data to the instance of the Time Series service created, follow these instructions:

1. Sign in to the **UAA Dashboard** and create groups (`https://uaa-dashboard.run.aws-usw02-pr.ice.predix.io`). Alternatively, you can do this via the CLI by running the following commands:

```
uaac target
https://e0fd8047-0a1d-4076-9143-fc4cbf60cd79.predix-uaa.run.aws-usw
02-pr.ice.predix.io
uaac token client get admin
uaac group add "timeseries.zones.6f6882ff-3a3b-45b2-b20b-
b537e652471d.user"
uaac group add "timeseries.zones.6f6882ff-3a3b-45b2-b20b-
b537e652471d.ingest"
uaac group add "timeseries.zones.6f6882ff-3a3b-45b2-b20b-
b537e652471d.query"
```

2. Add the required new values to the **Authorities** and **Scope** field on the **Client Edit** page of the **UAA Dashboard**. In this example, we should add the following values:

```
timeseries.zones.6f6882ff-3a3b-45b2-b20b-b537e652471d.user
timeseries.zones.6f6882ff-3a3b-45b2-b20b-b537e652471d.ingest
timeseries.zones.6f6882ff-3a3b-45b2-b20b-b537e652471d.query
```

Alternatively, you can run the following command via the CLI:

```
uaac client update -i
```

3. Follow the instructions displayed to add the required authorities and
   scope. When the application is up and running, it will be sending time series data
   to the Time Series service instance every second, as shown here:

```
sending:  {"messageId":1501664966991,"body":[{"name":"sensor1:variable1","datapoints":[[1501664966991,86]],
"attributes":{"devices":"/device/raspberry"}}]}
response:  {"statusCode":202,"messageId":1501664966991}
```

Console output with data sent by a running time series app

Validating data ingestion

To check whether the sensor data from an application was ingested correctly, we can query
it. In this example, we will query an average time series value for an hour.

To do this, you need to create a POST request in Postman and link it to the following
URL: `https://time-series-store-predix.run.aws-usw02-pr.ice.predix.io/v1/datapoints`.

The headers in the request should be as follows:

```
Content-Type: application/json
Authorization: Bearer LONG_TOKEN
Predix-Zone-Id: 6f6882ff-3a3b-45b2-b20b-b537e652471d
```

In the body, we need to specify the start and end time, a sensor name, an aggregation
function, and a filter with a device name, as shown here:

```
{
    "start": 1501664960967,
    "end": 1501664973018,
    "tags": [
        {
            "name": ["sensor1:variable1"],
            "limit": 1000,
            "aggregations": [
              {
                "type": "avg",
                "interval": "1h"
              }
            ],
            "filters": {
                "attributes": {
                    "devices": "/device/raspberry"
                }
            }
```

```
            }
        ]
    }
```

The query will return an average value per hour:

```
{
    "tags": [
        {
            "name": "sensor1:variable1",
            "results": [
                {
                    "groups": [
                        {
                            "name": "type",
                            "type": "number"
                        }
                    ],
                    "filters": {
                        "attributes": {
                            "devices": [
                                "/device/raspberry"
                            ]
                        }
                    },
                    "values": [
                        [
                            1501664960967,
                            58.23076923076923,
                            3
                        ]
                    ],
                    "attributes": {
                        "devices": [
                            "/device/raspberry"
                        ]
                    }
                }
            ],
            "stats": {
                "rawCount": 13
            }
        }
    ]
}
```

To get a complete list of the supported aggregation functions that can be used for queries, check out GE's Predix documentation: `https://docs.predix.io/en-US/content/service/data_management/time_series/using-the-time-series-service`.

Deploying your first GE Predix analytics

In this section, we will overview the features of the Analytics Framework service from GE's Predix catalog. We will describe how to create an instance of the service, as well as how to build and deploy an application to analyze time series data and get statistics.

The Analytics Framework service

The Analytics Framework offers a set of advanced features for developing and using analytics in a range of industrial and business applications. These features include the following:

- **Scheduler**: Ensures the execution of jobs (for instance, individual analytics and orchestrations) at preset time intervals. Moreover, it allows for viewing the history of scheduled executions.
- **Runtime Orchestration**: Makes it possible to configure and execute a group of analytical functions as a single set. In addition, it ensures validation and monitoring of the execution process.
- **Analytics Catalog**: Enables developers to access and share reusable analytics, facilitating its management and deployment to production.

For more information about the Analytics Framework service, read the Predix documentation: `https://docs.predix.io/en-US/content/service/analytics_services/analytics_framework/`.

For examples of the code for building an analytical app, go to `https://github.com/PredixDev/predix-analytics-sample`.

All of the code we will use in the subsequent subsections to build and deploy an app working with GE's Predix Analytics Framework can be found in the following GitHub repository: `https://github.com/Altoros/iot-book/tree/master/aggregator`.

To enable analytics for time series data as described in subsequent subsections, you will need a ready-to-use GE Predix account, a running application that reads time series data, and a console. In addition, you will have to install Python (`https://www.python.org/downloads/`) and Postman (`https://www.getpostman.com/`).

Creating an instance of the Analytics Framework service

To create an instance of the Analytics Framework service, follow this sequence of actions:

1. Sign in to your GE Predix account and go to the **Analytics Framework** tile.
2. Select a plan and click **Subscribe**.
3. Fill in the fields on the **New Service Instance** page displayed. The ones that are marked with an asterisk (*) are mandatory

When filling in the fields on the **New Service Instance** page, make sure to follow these recommendations:

Field	Recommendation
UI domain prefix	In this field, you should specify the unique identifier of the domain for URI of the user interface (UI). For example, if the domain prefix is `my-prefix`, the full URI is `https://my-prefix.predix-analytics-ui.<predix_base_uri>`.
UI client ID	In this field, you should enter a non-admin client ID to be used for authentication. When needed, you can create a new UAA client for the UI, using the **UAA Dashboard**.
UI client secret	In this field, you should specify the password that will be used for authentication of the non-admin UAA client.

4. Click **Create Service** to finish the creation process.

Alternatively, you can create an instance of the service using the CLI.

Binding an instance of the Analytics Framework service to your application

After a new service instance is created, we need to bind it to the `asset` application we built earlier in the section, *Building an app to read time series data.*

To do this, run the following commands from the console:

```
cf bind-service assets predix-analytics-framework-service-instance
cf restage assets
cf env assets
```

In the response shown here, you will see the important environment variables (for instance, `execution_uri`, `zone_oauth_scope`) we will need in the subsequent subsection:

```
{
  "VCAP_SERVICES": {
    "predix-analytics-framework": [
      {
        "credentials": {
          "catalog_uri":
"https://predix-analytics-catalog-release.run.aws-usw02-pr.ice.predix.io",
          "execution_uri":
"https://predix-analytics-execution-release.run.aws-usw02-pr.ice.predix.io"
,
          "zone-http-header-name": "Predix-Zone-Id",
          "zone-http-header-value": "09009e2e-d2f2-4ffa-b77c-2d78a814fc3a",
          "zone-oauth-scope": "analytics.zones.09009e2e-d2f2-4ffa-
b77c-2d78a814fc3a.user"
  . . .
```

To be able to work with the Analytics Framework service, we will also need to configure the authentication rules. To do that, follow these instructions:

1. Go to the GE Predix Console
   (`https://uaa-dashboard.run.aws-usw02-pr.ice.predix.io/#/clients`).
2. Find the UAA instance that manages your instance of the Analytics Framework service.
3. Sign in to the **UAA Dashboard** and go to the **Client Management** tab.
4. Select an existing client or add a new one by clicking **Add a new client**.
5. Make sure the **Authorized Grant Types** specified on the **Client Management** tab have the following values: `client_credentials`, `password`, `authorization_code`, and `refresh_token`.

6. Add a new redirect URI to the client, `<your_analytics_ui_url>/callback`. The value for `<your_analytics_ui_url>` can be copied from the environment variables in the preceding console output:

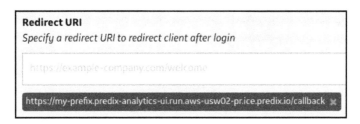

Adding a redirect URI to a client

7. Switch to the **Services View** page. In the list on the left side of the tab, select the `predix-analytics-framework-service-instance` name:

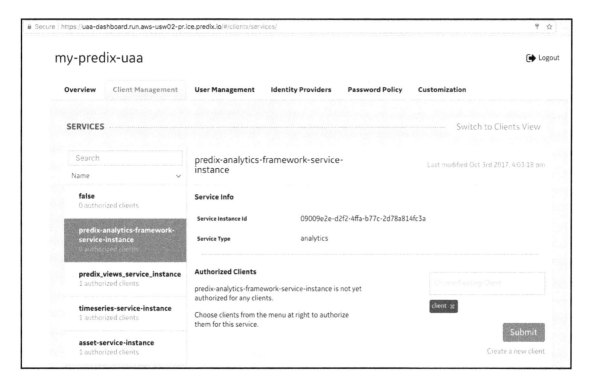

Adding a client to a service instance

8. Create a new group with the `analytics.zones.<service_instance_guid>.user` name and assign it to the user of the selected client. The `<service_instance_guid>` parameter in the group name stands for the Predix zone ID—an environment variable from the preceding console output. In our case, it is `analytics.zones.09009e2e-d2f2-4ffa-b77c-2d78a814fc3a.user`.

Now, you can sign in to the Analytics Framework UI using your user credentials.

Alternatively, you can configure a client using the UAA CLI.

The URI for signing in is available in the environment variables from the console output. In our case, it is `https://my-prefix.predix-analytics-ui.run.aws-usw02-pr.ice.predix.io/analytics`.

When you sign in to Analytics Framework for the first time, you should also authorize permissions. To do that, you need to click the **Authorize** button:

Authorizing permissions for the Analytics Framework service

Building an analytical application to work with Analytics Framework

Currently, the Analytics Framework service supports Java, MATLAB, and Python. For our example, we will use Python, because it fits our purposes.

The code of the application we are building should contain a special function that will be called by Analytics Framework. This function will accept the input data for analysis. In our case, it is the following time series data: `{"timeseries":` `[[1501664960967,12,3],[1501664961973,48,3]]}`.

In our analytical application, we will sum up the input time series data. Consequently, the expected output is `{"result": 60}`.

To build an application for analyzing time series data, proceed as follows:

1. Create the `aggregator` folder. To do this, run the following command:

   ```
   mkdir aggregator
   ```

2. Create the `config.json` file and paste the following code into it:

   ```
   {
     "entry-method": "analytic.aggregator.sum",
     "non-conda-libs": [
       "boto"
     ],
     "conda-libs": [
       "numpy",
       "scipy"
     ]
   }
   ```

   The file describes the path to the entry method named `sum`.

3. Create the `analytic` folder and the `file __init__.py` file inside it, then insert the following code into it:

   ```
   from aggregator import aggregator
   ```

4. Now, we are ready to proceed to writing the logic of our analytical app. Inside the `analytic` folder, create the `aggregator.py` file, which should contain the following code:

```
import json


class aggregator:
    def __init__(self):
        print "Create aggregator"

    def sum(self, data):
        sum = 0
        timeseries = json.loads(data).get("timeseries")
        for item in timeseries:
            sum += item[1]
        return {"result": sum}
```

With this file, we sum up the values in each time series entry and obtain a final result.

You can change the application logic and check how it works in the Python interpreter (console). To do this, proceed as follows:

1. Go to the `aggregator` folder, specifying the following path in the console:

   cd /path/to/aggregator

2. Run a Python interpreter with this command:

   python

3. Import the `aggregator` module as indicated here:

   from analytic import aggregator

4. Initialize the following class:

   ```
   a = aggregator()
   ```

5. Execute the sum function, running the following command:

   **a.sum('{"timeseries":
   [[1501664960967,12,3],[1501664961973,48,3]]}')**

Creating tests for an analytical application

Tests are required to make sure the application we have built works correctly. To enable testing, you need to create the `testbench` sub-folder with the `testAggregator.py` file in the `aggregator` folder. The `testAggregator.py` file should contain the following code:

```
from analytic import aggregator

if __name__ == "__main__":
    a = aggregator()
    assert a.sum('{"timeseries":
[[1501664960967,12,3],[1501664961973,48,3]]}') == {"result": 60}
```

Adding the analytical app to the Analytics Catalog

To enable the app to work with the Analytics Framework service, we need to add it to the **Analytics Catalog**. To do that, follow these steps:

1. Open the web interface of the Analytics Framework service. For our purposes, use the URL from the environment variables (see the console output in the *Binding an instance of the Analytics Framework service to your application* section). In our case, the URL is `https://my-prefix.predix-analytics-ui.run.aws-usw02-pr.ice.predix.io/analytics`:

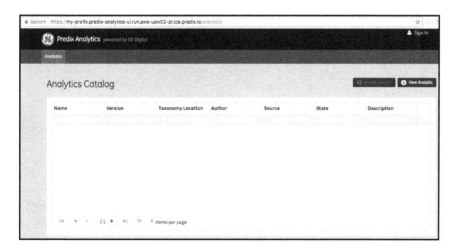

The Analytics Catalog page

2. Click the **New Analytic** button and fill in the form as shown in the following screenshot:

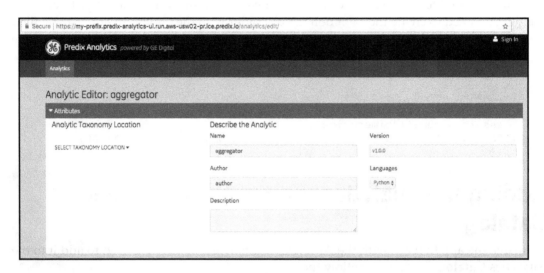

Adding a new analytical app to the Analytics Catalog

3. Zip the content of the `aggregator` folder into an archive and attach it, using the **Select a file to attach** button.

4. Check the **Executable** checkbox and press **Save**. The source code will be uploaded to the Predix cloud:

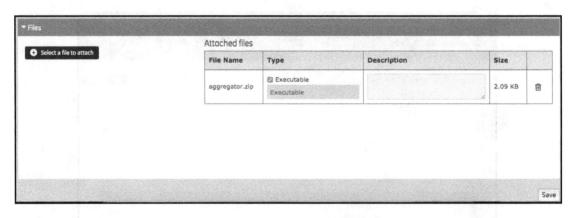

Uploading an archive to GE's Predix cloud

ceivedSegment

Validating, testing, and deploying an analytical app

Clicking the **Save** button to save the archive with the executables will also open a window where you can validate, test, and deploy your analytical app. To validate your analytical application works correctly, proceed as follows:

1. On the **Validate and Test** tab, paste the following content into the **Analytic Input** field:

   ```
   {"timeseries": [[1501664960967,12,3],[1501664961973,48,3]]}
   ```

2. Click **Submit**. It will take some time before the new application gets deployed to the Predix cloud. To check the validation status, use the **Refresh** button:

Validating analytics

Once the analytics are deployed, you can test this on the **Test** tab. All you need is to paste a number of time series values into the **Analytic Input** field and check it provides the expected result:

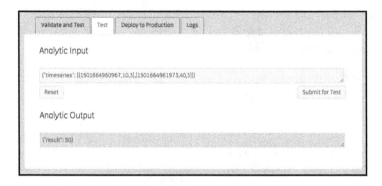

Testing the analytics

For example, if we use the following input: `{"timeseries":` `[[1501664960967,10,3],[1501664961973,40,3]]}`, the output will be `{"result":` `50}`.

After you have tested the analytical app, you are ready to deploy it to production. To do that, go to the **Deploy to Production** tab and fill in the fields as shown in the following screenshot:

Deploying analytics to production

To find the cause of incorrect behavior if it occurs, you can check the logs on the **Logs** tab.

Alternatively, you can perform all the operations via the REST API. For
more information, read the Predix documentation: `https://www.predix.`
`io/services/service.html?id=2114`.

Executing the analytical application

To execute the deployed analytics, you can use the REST API or
configure appropriate scheduling jobs. However, before execution, we need to get a valid
token for the Analytics Framework service. To get it, proceed as follows:

1. Open Postman, create a **POST** request, and link it to the following URL: `https:/`
   `/e0fd8047-0a1d-4076-9143-fc4cbf60cd79.predix-uaa.run.aws-usw02-pr.ice.`
   `predix.io/oauth/token`. The URL specified for the **POST** request is the address
   of the UAA service. The address can be found in the environment variables (see
   the console output in the *Binding an instance of the Analytics Framework service to
   your application* subsection).

2. Select `x-www-form-urlencoded` as the data type for the body of the **POST**
   request and specify the required values for the keys, as indicated here:

   ```
   client_id:client
   client_secret:secret
   grant_type:client_credentials
   response_type:token
   ```

   The `client` is the name of the client selected for the Analytics Framework service
   in the **UAA** dashboard (see the **Binding an instance of the Analytics Framework
   service to your application** subsection). The `secret` is the client's password.

3. Configure the headers as indicated here:

   ```
   Content-Type: application/x-www-form-urlencoded
   Accept: application/json
   ```

The request body should contain the values shown in the following screenshot:

Creating a **POST** request to get a token

The **POST** request will return a valid token that will enable us to use the Analytics Framework service.

Now, we are ready to execute the analytics. For this purpose, you need to create another **POST** request, following this sequence of actions:

1. Next to the request type, specify the following
   URL: `https://predix-analytics-catalog-release.run.aws-usw02-pr.ice.predix.io/api/v1/catalog/analytics/2c5f51a3-b97a-4cab-84e4-e68c2ffd01df/execution`.

2. Select the **raw** radio button to indicate the body type and paste the following content into the body of the created request:

```
{
    "timeseries": [
        [1501664960967,32,3],
        [1501664961973,43,3]
    ]
}
```

3. Configure the headers as indicated here:

```
Content-Type: application/json
Authorization: Bearer LONG_TOKEN
Predix-Zone-Id: 09009e2e-d2f2-4ffa-b77c-2d78a814fc3a
```

In this example, `LONG_TOKEN` is the token returned in response to the previous **POST** request. The `09009e2e-d2f2-4ffa-b77c-2d78a814fc3a` parameter is the Predix zone ID from the environment variables (see the console output in the *Binding an instance of the Analytics Framework service to your application* subsection).

4. Click **Send** to submit the request. In the response to the request, you should see the result of the executed analytical operation. In this example, it is `{"result": 75}`:

Creating a **POST** request to execute analytics

Advanced visualization using GE's Predix web components

This section overviews GE's Predix web components, which can facilitate building a user interface for visualizing data from a time series app. We will demonstrate how to develop an app to work with the components and how to create an instance of the Views service to store, add, and relocate them. In addition, we will provide instructions on running REST queries to add and manage elements of a user interface.

Predix Design System

To understand the current status of the statistics from a time series app, we need a convenient and easy-to-understand UI. For this purpose, GE's Predix Design System (available at `https://www.predix-ui.com`) includes a catalog of components that can speed up building a UI. All of the components are mobile-compatible and feature cross-browser support.

For our UI, we will also use GE's Predix Views service, which allows for adding and relocating interface elements by simply running REST queries.

Building a web application

To be able to work with GE's Predix web components, we need to build a web application.

To speed up creating an application, you can copy the source code from this GitHub repository: `https://github.com/Altoros/iot-book/tree/master/ui`.

You can skip the first four items in the following sequence if you have already created a `ui` application as described in the *Developing your first asset model with GE's Predix* section.

To build the required web app, follow these steps:

1. Create the `ui` folder:

   ```
   mkdir ui
   ```

2. Create the `index.html` file. It should be empty.
3. Create `manifest.yml` and paste the following code into it:

   ```
   ---
   applications:
   - name: ui
     memory: 64M
     buildpack: staticfile_buildpack
     random-route: true
   ```

4. Deploy the application base to the cloud, using the following command:

   ```
   cf push
   ```

    Pay attention to the `urls: ui-bleeding-blue.run.aws-usw02-pr.ice.predix.io` line. It contains the URL of the deployed web application.

Creating an instance of the Views service

To create an instance of the Views service, proceed as follows:

1. Sign in to your GE Predix account and open GE's Predix catalog, using this link: `http://predix.io/catalog/services`.
2. Select the **Views** service.
3. Select a **plan** and click **Subscribe.**
4. Fill in the form and click **Create Service.**
5. Bind the service instance to the previously deployed web app:

   ```
   cf bind-service ui predix-views-service-instance
   ```

6. To get the endpoint URL of the Views service, run this command:

   ```
   cf env ui
   ```

The command will return the following response in JSON:

```
{
  "VCAP_SERVICES": {
    "predix-views": [
      {
        "credentials": {
          "instanceId": "b3e07566-273f-4d1e-85ce-a5d4b2632a27",
          "uri": "https://predix-views.run.aws-usw02-pr.ice.predix.io"
  ...
```

 Pay attention to the `predix-views` credentials. We will need them later for running REST queries to add and manage interface elements.

7. Navigate to the **UAA Dashboard** (`https://uaa-dashboard.run.aws-usw02-pr.ice.predix.io/#/dashboard`). Open the **User Management** tab.
8. Create the following groups and assign them to the user:
    - `views.zones.<views-zoneId>.user`
    - `views.zones.<views-zoneId>.admin`
    - `views.admin.user`
    - `views.power.user`

 `<views-zoneId>` is the instance ID we got in the `predix-views` credentials. In our case, it is `b3e07566-273f-4d1e-85ce-a5d4b2632a27`.

9. Update the `OAuth2` client by creating the following scopes and authorities on the **Client Management** tab:

Client scope value	Description
`views.zones.<views-zoneId>.user`	Grants the user the right to access to the instance of the Views service with the corresponding ID (`<views-zoneId>`).
`views.zones.<views-zoneId>.admin`	Grants the admin the right to access to the instance of the Views service with the corresponding ID (`<views-zoneId>`|).
`views.admin.user`	Allows CRUD operations with UI elements (cards and decks) via the Views service APIs.

`views.power.user`	The user has the same permissions as for the `views.admin.user` role, except for the right to delete UI elements (cards and decks) via the Views service APIs.

 For more details, read this documentation: `https://docs.predix.io/en-US/content/service/app_services/views/get-started-with-views-service#task_y1l_vms_2s`.

Adding and managing UI elements with the Views service

The Views service is designed to store and manage visual data used by a web application, including the following elements of GE's Predix UI framework:

- **Components**: UI widgets for adding features and accessing services.
- **Cards**: UI areas consisting of a single object (for instance, a button) or a set of logically connected objects (for instance, a button and a field) (`https://docs.predix.io/SD00300694#concept_nc4_5vg_qv`).
- **Decks**: UI elements that control a number of associated cards in a simple layout.
  - **Views**: Allow for combining cards, decks, and components into visualizations to be displayed in a web application:

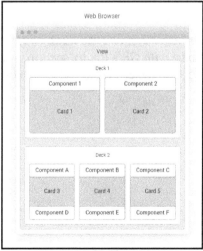

An overview of the **Views** service

The Views service makes it possible to save information about the state and layout of the **card** and **deck** instances, as well as the relationships between them and a database. Subsequently, the **deck** and **card** instances can be reproduced from the database and rendered as a view in a browser. This allows for flexibility in creating data visualizations, depending on actual user needs at a given moment.

Creating a card

We will create a card that will show us the latest value from one of our devices posting data to the Time Series service.

To create a card, you should run a **POST** query via POSTMAN. The **POST** query should be linked to the following URL: `https://predix-views.run.aws-usw02-pr.ice.predix.io/api/cards`. Its headers should be as shown here:

```
Content-Type:application/json
Authorization:Bearer LONG_TOKEN
Predix-Zone-Id:b3e07566-273f-4d1e-85ce-a5d4b2632a27
```

The body of the query should contain the following:

```
[{
    "title": "Current value",
    "slug": "device-card",
    "attributes": {
        "name": "sensor1:variable1",
        "device": "/device/raspberry"
    }
}]
```

To get the `LONG_TOKEN` for authorization, use the `uaac` context command described in the *Developing your first asset model with GE's Predix* section. Alternatively, you can run a **POST** request to the UAA service as described in the *Deploying your first GE's Predix analytics* section:

Output after running a **POST** query to create a card

Creating a deck

If you want to group a number of cards together, you can create a deck. To do this, you need to run a **POST** query and link it to the following URL: `https://predix-views.run. aws-usw02-pr.ice.predix.io/api/decks`. For this **POST** query, you can use the same headers as we used to create a card. The body, however, should be as follows:

```
{
  "title": "Deck Title",
  "cardOrder": [],
  "id": "deck-1"
}
```

The output after running a **POST** query to create a deck is as follows:

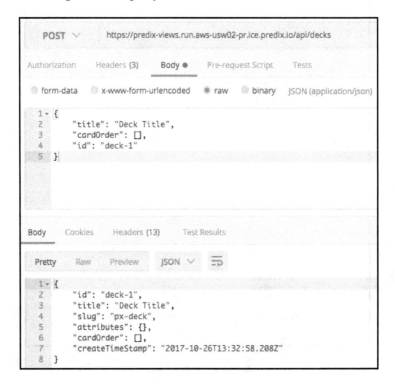

Linking a card to a deck

To associate a card with a deck, you need to run a **POST** query and link it to the following URL: `https://predix-views.run.aws-usw02-pr.ice.predix.io/api/decks/deck-1/cards/add`.

The headers of the query should be the same as we used to create a card. The body of the query should contain the IDs of the cards you want to associate with the deck, arranging them in any order you choose:

```
["HJmzRLJR-"]
```

To get a list of the cards assigned to a deck, run a **GET** query and link it to the following URL: `https://predix-views.run.aws-usw02-pr.ice.predix.io/api/decks/deck-1/cards`.

Again, the headers for the **GET** query will be the same as we used in the previous example:

```
1 ▾ [
2 ▾     {
3           "id": "HJmzRLJR-",
4           "tenantId": "b3e07566-273f-4d1e-85ce-a5d4b2632a27",
5           "title": "Current value",
6           "slug": "device-card",
7 ▾         "attributes": {
8               "name": "sensor1:variable1",
9               "device": "/device/raspberry"
10          },
11          "createTimeStamp": "2017-10-26T13:07:23.014Z"
12      }
13 ]
```

Output of the **GET** request with a list of cards assigned to a deck

For more details, go to `https://docs.predix.io/en-US/content/service/app_services/views/get-started-with-the-views-service-database`.

Displaying a multicard deck

Now, we will demonstrate how to visualize a deck created with multiple cards. To do this, follow this sequence of steps:

1. Update the `index.html` file and paste the following code into it:

```
<!DOCTYPE html>
<html ng-app="">
<head>
  <title>UI</title>
  <meta name="viewport" content="width=device-width, initial-scale=1.0">
  <script src="bower_components/jquery/dist/jquery.js"></script>
  <script src="bower_components/angular/angular.js"></script>
  <script src="predix-uaa-client.js"></script>

  <link rel="import" href="bower_components/px-card/px-card.html"/>

  <link rel="import" href="device-card.html"/>
</head>
<body>

</body>
</html>
```

2. Create the `device-card.html` file, which should contain the following code:

```html
<dom-module id="device-card">
  <template>
    <style>
      :host {
        display: block;
        padding: 5px;
        width: 200px;
        border: 1px solid black;
        border-radius: 5px;
        box-shadow: 10px 10px 50px 0px rgba(0,0,0,0.75);
      }
    </style>

    <div>device: {{device}}</div>
    <div>name: {{name}}</div>
    <div>timestamp: {{timestamp}}</div>
    <div>value: {{value}}</div>
  </template>
  <script>
    Polymer({
      is: 'device-card',
      properties: {
        device: {type: String, observer: '_deviceChanged'},
        name: {type: String, observer: '_nameChanged'}
      },
      _deviceChanged: function (newValue, oldValue) {
        if (this.device && this.name) this.loadData();
      },
      _nameChanged: function (newValue, oldValue) {
        if (this.device && this.name) this.loadData();
      },
      loadData: function () {
fetch('https://time-series-store-predix.run.aws-usw02-pr.ice.predix
.io/v1/datapoints', {
          method: 'POST',
          body: JSON.stringify({
            start: 0,
            tags: [{
              name: this.name,
              limit: 1,
              filters: {
                attributes: {
                  devices: this.device
                }
              }
            }]
```

```
      }),
      headers: new Headers({
        'Content-Type': 'application/json',
        Authorization: `Bearer ${ACCESS_TOKEN}`,
        'Predix-Zone-Id': TIMESERIES_ID
      })
    }).then((r) => r.json()).then((response) => {
      const values = response.tags[0].results[0].values;
      this.set('value', values[0][1]);
      this.set('timestamp', values[0][0]);
    });
  }
});
</script>
</dom-module>
```

3. Create the `bower.json` file and insert this code into it:

```
{
  "name": "ui",
  "dependencies": {
    "px-card": "^2.0.0",
    "jquery": "^3.3.1",
    "angular": "1.4.3"
  }
}
```

4. Install `bower`:

   npm install -g bower

5. Install its dependencies:

   bower install

6. To be able to load data from GE's Predix services, we need to get a token and service IDs. For this purpose, you should create the `predix-uaa-client.js` file and specify the corresponding ID and token values, as shown here:

```
const UAA_ID = 'e0fd8047-0a1d-4076-9143-fc4cbf60cd79';
const VIEWS_ID = 'b3e07566-273f-4d1e-85ce-a5d4b2632a27';
const TIMESERIES_ID = '6f6882ff-3a3b-45b2-b20b-b537e652471d';
const CLIENT_ID = 'PUT_CLIENT_ID';
const CLIENT_SECRET = 'PUT_CLIENT_SECRET';
let ACCESS_TOKEN;

const data = {
  client_id: CLIENT_ID,
```

```
        client_secret: CLIENT_SECRET,
        grant_type: 'client_credentials',
        response_type: 'token'
};
const body = Object.entries(data).map(pair =>
pair.map(encodeURIComponent).join('=')).join('&');

const addCard = (card) => {
    const el = document.createElement(card.slug);
    el.setAttribute('id', 'card-' + card.id);
    el.setAttribute('title', card.title);
    el.setAttribute('context', '{{context}}');
    if (card.attributes && typeof card.attributes === 'object') {
        for (const attr in card.attributes) {
            if (typeof card.attributes[attr] !== 'object') {
                el.setAttribute(attr, card.attributes[attr]);
            }
            else {
                el.setAttribute(attr,
JSON.stringify(card.attributes[attr]));
            }
        }
    }
    Polymer.dom(document.body).appendChild(el);
};

$(document).ready(() => {
fetch(`https://${UAA_ID}.predix-uaa.run.aws-usw02-pr.ice.predix.io/
oauth/token`, {
    method: 'POST',
    body: body,
    headers: new Headers({
        'Content-Type': 'application/x-www-form-urlencoded',
        Accept: 'application/json'
    })
}).then((r) => r.json()).then((context) => {
    ACCESS_TOKEN = context.access_token;

    const $http = angular.element('body').injector().get('$http');
    $http.defaults.headers.common['Predix-Zone-Id'] = VIEWS_ID;
    $http.defaults.headers.common['Authorization'] = `Bearer
${ACCESS_TOKEN}`;

    const deck = 'deck-1';

$http.get('https://predix-views.run.aws-usw02-pr.ice.predix.io/api/
decks/' + deck +
'?filter[include][cards]&filter[order]=cards').success((data,
```

```
status, headers, config) => {
    data.cards.forEach(addCard);
  }).error((data, status, headers, config) => {
    console.error('Failed to load cards for deck ' + deck);
  });
});
});
```

Make sure that the client specified in this file has only user access rights (`views.zones.<views-zoneId>.user`). This is important because the client credentials will be visible in the source code of the web page, and someone could use them to modify or destroy your data.

7. Redeploy the application:

   cf push

8. To open the deployed application, insert the `https://ui-bleeding-blue.run.aws-usw02-pr.ice.predix.io` link into a browser line:

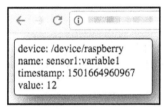

UI of the deployed application

 For more information, go to `https://docs.predix.io/en-US/content/service/app_services/views/example-display-a-multicard-deck`.

Adding more UI components to the created web application

In this example, we will add the px-gauge component of GE's Predix Design System. To accomplish this task, proceed as follows:

1. Install the px-gauge dependency:

   ```
   bower install -S px-gauge
   ```

2. Add the px-gauge dependency to the index.html file:

   ```
   <link rel="import" href="bower_components/px-gauge/px-gauge.html"/>
   ```

3. Replace the basic text value in the device-card.html file with the following code:

   ```
   <px-gauge value="{{value}}"></px-gauge>
   ```

4. Redeploy the application:

   ```
   cf push
   ```

5. To open the deployed application, insert the https://ui-bleeding-blue.run. aws-usw02-pr.ice.predix.io link into a browser line:

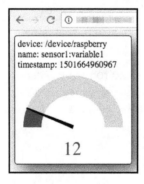

UI of the deployed web app with the px-gauge component

For more UI components, explore the following GE Predix catalog: https://www.predix-ui.com.

Summary

This chapter provided an overview of the Asset, Time Series, and Analytics Framework services from GE's Predix catalog. We demonstrated how to create instances of the services, bind them to your apps, and configure client authentications. Then, we showed how you could create various HTTP requests in Postman to query and manage assets. This chapter also contained instructions on building and deploying apps to read and analyze time series data. In addition, we outlined how to enable advanced visualization with the components of GE's Predix UI Framework.

The next chapter will focus on the best practices for IIoT applications. In particular, we will look into things to consider when choosing a language to build your microservices. Furthermore, we will discuss how to enable the discovery of microservices using Hystrix, Zookeeper, and so on, and how to integrate IoT applications with an enterprise system and other cloud providers (for instance, Salesforce).

10
Best Practices for IIoT Applications

In the previous chapter, we discussed how to build an IIoT application using Predix services. This chapter takes it further and looks at various different best practices to successfully build a multitenant, maintainable, reliable IIoT application. We will look at the following areas in this section:

- Best practices for API development
- The power of the polyglot programming choice
- Eventual consistency for higher performance
- Strategies to handle multiple versions of the application at scale
- The advantages of using established trust between microservices
- UX strategy for application adoption
- Tracing and logging end to end

Best practices for API development

We will start with discussing API development best practices because the API is the cornerstone for good microservices-based architecture, which in turn forms the basis of the IoT cloud tier. APIs in a microservices context are always RESTful interfaces. RESTful APIs use constructs of HTTP at their core and JSON as their payload for request and response. We will look at a few key aspects of developing an awesome API. We can develop RESTful APIs using frameworks such as Spring Boot, Node—Express, or Python—Flask.

The API endpoint should be descriptive

The endpoint of the API should be self-descriptive and should use HTTP methods such as GET, PUT, POST, and DELETE to perform the operations. In addition, the API should leverage the HTTP codes such as 200, 4xx, to describe operations or faults. Let's use an example for illustration. In this example, we will design an API that gets the list of IIoT devices and does operations such as adding a new device, updating the device details, and deleting a device:

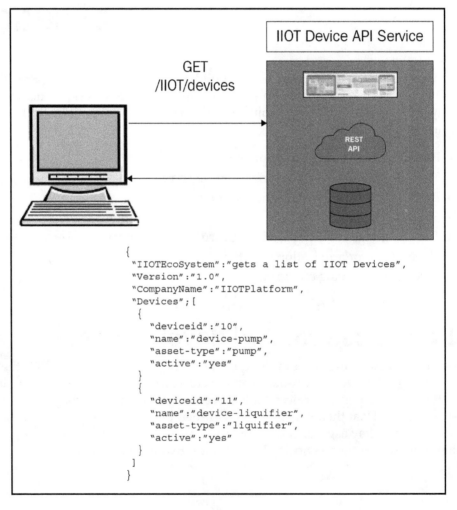

An example API endpoint

Getting the list of devices

We use the verb devices to get the list of IIoT devices and hence the endpoint should be /iiot/devices and the response should be as in the following example. It should use the HTTP GET method to get the list of devices, as can be seen in the following example:

```
HTTP GET--> /iiot/devices
```

The HTTP response is given as follows:

```
{
    "IIoTEcoSystem": "gets a list of IIoT Devices",
    "Version": "1.0",
    "CompanyName": "IIoTPlatform",
    "Devices": [
    {
        "deviceId": "10",
        "name": "device-pump",
        "assetType": "pump",
        "active": "yes"
    },
    {
        "deviceId": "11",
        "name": "device-liquifier",
        "assetType": "liquifier",
        "active": "yes"
    }
    ]
}
```

Attributes should be self-descriptive for ease of use and, in this example, we are using the JSON outputs. For consistency, it is advisable to use the same case for attributes or field name conversion.

If the list is big, it is good to support pagination of the response such that we only show a subset of results.

If we use pagination as in the following example, we can also request certain pages with size attributes by passing the page and size attributes, and the service should be able to handle it appropriately.

In the following example, we are requesting one page of devices with size 10 and including only a few attributes:

```
/iiot/devices?page=1&per_page=10&include=metadata
```

HTTP response is given as follows:

```
{
  "IIoTEcoSystem": "gets a list of IIoT Devices",
  "Version": "1.0",
  "CompanyName": "IIoTPlatform",
  "Devices": [
    {
        "deviceId": "10",
        "name": "device-pump",
        "assetType": "pump",
        "active": "yes"
    },
    {
        "deviceId": "11",
        "name": "device-liquifier",
        "assetType": "liquifier",
        "active": "yes"
    }
  ]
  pageNumber=5,
  pageSize=10,
  totalSize=510
}
```

Adding a new device

Adding the device should be by using the same /iiot/devices/ endpoint but, by using the HTTP POST method, we can add a new device to the list of devices, and, if it is successfully created, it should return an HTTP 201 Created status code. This can be seen in the following example:

```
HTTP POST --> /iiot/devices
{
        "name": "device-pump2",
        "assetType": "pump",
        "active": "yes"
}
```

HTTP response will be as follows:

```
201 Created
```

In this case, the payload does not have the device-ID since it will be autogenerated by the service itself.

Once the device is added, we can actually get the details of the device using a nested URL with the ID by accessing the `url/iiot/devices/11`. It should return the device details only for that device.

The following example shows how we are getting details of a device with the ID `11`:

```
HTTP GET --> /iiot/devices/11
{
     "deviceId": "11",
     "name": "device-liquifier",
     "assetType": "liquifier",
     "active": "yes"
}
```

If the device ID is not present the response should return with an HTTP status code of 404 Not Found.

Updating the attributes of an existing device

To update all device attributes, we use the HTTP `PUT` method and, if it is successful, the response should be HTTP 200 OK. In the following example, we will update the attribute of the existing device with ID `11`. If the device ID is not present it should create a new device. If the intent is to only update certain attributes, we use the HTTP `PATCH` operations and it should update the attribute specified. If the given attribute has issued an error response, we should use the HTTP status code 4xx ranges, such as error code 400 for a bad request.

In the following example, we will update details of the device with ID `11`:

```
HTTP PUT --> /iiot/devices/11
    {
         "name": "device-liquifier1",
         "assetType": "liquifier1",
         "active": "false"
    }
```

HTTP response will be as follows:

200 OK

If we choose to only update a certain attribute, we can use the HTTP `PATCH`, as follows:

```
HTTP PATCH --> /iiot/devices/11
```

The response for the PATCH operation is given in the following example:

```
{
    "name": "device-liquifier111",
}
```

HTTP response will be as follows:

200 OK

Deleting a device

If we want to delete a device, essentially we use HTTP DELETE to delete that instance of the device. The response we should get is HTTP 204 No Content, which says that the request has been processed but does not have any content to return.

In the following example, we are deleting a device with the ID 11:

```
HTTP DELETE --> /iiot/devices/11
```

HTTP response will be as follows:

204 No Content

The message HTTP 500 Internal Server Error is returned if there is anything wrong with the request. It can be returned for any of the HTTP requests which represent an internal error in the server; these could include any issues, such as an error with servicing the requests.

Sorting, filtering, searching, and versioning

In addition to the CRUD operation, we need to handle various other regular operations, such as searching for certain device names. In addition, we can get the list of devices and sorting them into ascending or descending the results. Filtering is another interesting feature we can utilize to filter the responses, so that, by using includes, we can get only the fields we are interested in. Finally, we can have the endpoint support searching capability so that we can request certain types of devices with a name or asset of certain types.

Sorting of devices by name

Sorting is essentially a request for a sorted list of items, for example, a list of devices sorted by name. By default, it is sorted in ascending order by the field name given but, if prefixed by – it is sorted in descending order. This can be seen in the following example:

```
HTTP GET--> /iiot/devices?sort=name
```

Sorted HTTP response is given as follows:

```
{
    "IIoTEcoSystem": "gets a list of IIoT Devices",
    "Version": "1.0",
    "CompanyName": "IIoTPlatform",
    "Devices": [
    {
        "deviceId": "11",
        "name": "device-A",
        "assetType": "liquifier",
        "active": "yes"
    },
    {
        "deviceId": "10",
        "name": "device-B",
        "assetType": "pump",
        "active": "yes"
    },
    ]
}
```

Filtering attributes of the device

Filtering is, essentially, requesting only a certain set of fields. You can use either `includes` or `excludes` to request only the list with the attributes of interest. `includes` only includes the requested attributes whereas `excludes` removes the attributes passed. An example for includes is given in the following code:

```
HTTP GET--> /iiot/devices?includes=name
```

Sorted HTTP response is given as follows:

```
{
    "IIoTEcoSystem": "gets a list of IIoT Devices",
    "Version": "1.0",
    "CompanyName": "IIoTPlatform",
```

```
    "Devices": [
    {
        "name": "device-A"
    },
    {
        "name": "device-B",
    },
    ]
}
```

Searching given an input

Searching essentially enables the API user to search for certain types of items in a list. In the following example, the search for devices with certain asset types will only return those devices. We can use regular query parameters to add more search constraints:

```
HTTP GET--> /iiot/devices?assetType=pump
```

HTTP response is given as follows:

```
{
    "IIoTEcoSystem": "gets a list of IIoT Devices",
    "Version": "1.0",
    "CompanyName": "IIoTPlatform",
    "Devices": [
    {
        "deviceId": "10",
        "name": "device-B",
        "assetType": "pump",
        "active": "yes"
    }
    ]
}
```

Let's have a look at one more constraint:

```
HTTP GET--> /iiot/devices?assetType=pump
```

HTTP response is given as follows:

```
{
    "IIoTEcoSystem": "gets a list of IIoT Devices",
    "Version": "1.0",
    "CompanyName": "IIoTPlatform",
    "Devices": [
      {
          "deviceId": "10",
          "name": "device-B",
          "assetType": "pump",
          "active": "yes"
      }
      ]
}
```

Versioning and documentation

As the adoption of APIs increases, we need to do versioning in order to support future changes. Because many users may not be in a position to upgrade at the same time, we have to use minor and major versions to handle changes. It is good to start using versions from the initial releases, as can be seen in the following examples:

- **Minor versions**: `v1.1/iiot/devices`
- **Major versions**: `v2.0/iiot/devices`

Documentation for the API is critical, and using a tool such as Swagger or API Docs is useful. No matter which tools you use, make sure you provide examples using Postman, which is very useful.

The power of polyglot programming

IoT development is, by nature, polyglot, which means it is using different programming languages, frameworks, and so on, for developing IoT applications. It is essential to appreciate the power of polyglot programming and use it wisely to get the maximum mileage. In this section, we will go over some of the benefits and traps of leveraging polyglot programming to improve IoT development.

Using Java programming for microservices development is advisable due to the plethora of tools available for Java, in addition to frameworks such as Spring Boot. Java has good support for many databases, and security tools such as OAuth integration. In addition, Java has many IDEs, built tools, code coverage tools, and so on, and this make it the winner for microservices development. Java stands out as a clear winner for API/microservices development. In addition to Java, I also recommend looking at Node.js and GoLang for certain specific tasks. Use Node.js if you would like to prototype faster, but there are some weaknesses to Node.js in its variety of tool support, and readability is a challenge as well. GoLang can be considered if you would like to develop heavily concurrent programming. It is also easy to learn, but its lack of tools is an area of concern.

In the development of machine-learning/analytics, the choice is very clear, with Python leading the way. It is widely used and has numerous tools and third-party libraries for various machine learning algorithms.

For development of the web tier, it is good to use Angular.js or React.js, both of which are powerful frameworks. For mobile apps, SWIFT and Java for Android are the languages of choice.

In addition to choosing the languages, it is wise to standardize on code coverage tools and Sonar for code security.

Eventual consistency for higher performance

In this section, we will argue why eventual consistency design is an important consideration for the higher performance of IoT applications. Eventual consistency is a specific form of weak consistency; the system guarantees that if no new updates are made to the object, eventually all accesses will return the last updated value. This mechanism is very effective in the highly distributed world of IoT applications. The maximum size of the inconsistency window can be determined based on factors such as communication delays, the load on the system, and the number of replicas involved in the replication scheme. **Domain Name System** (**DNS**) implements this system; in this case, updates to a name are distributed according to a configured pattern and in combination with time-controlled caches; eventually, all clients will see the update.

Let's go over this concept using a simple use case, as follows:

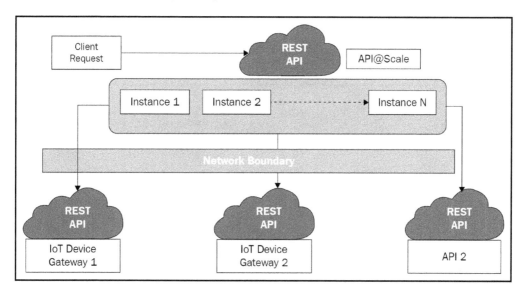

An example IoT application with a Cloud API @Scale and with dependent API 2

In this example IoT application, we have a cloud microservices API which depends on three other REST APIs to compute its response to the client request. These dependent APIs are distributed over the network both in the cloud and other data centers. As we have seen before, the latency of these calls will be pretty high due to the network. In addition, it has all the pitfalls of network fallacies such as reliability, faults, and so on, and it cannot put client requests on pause while it waits for the dependent APIs to come back. This approach is not dependable as it has the following flaws:

- Latency for the response is high due to the network
- Dependent services may have not performed well, thereby jeopardizing the SLAs of the highly scaled APIs
- Unnecessary load on the dependent APIs, forcing the dependent APIs to proportionately scale to meet the SLA
- A long wait time for client requests

To solve the problem due to latency and the network, we can use the eventual consistency mechanism by reading the data from the local or distributed cache. This gets refreshed on a periodic basic by making a direct request to the dependent API service using a background thread, thereby avoiding the network round trip. In the following illustration, we can see the first-level cache in action:

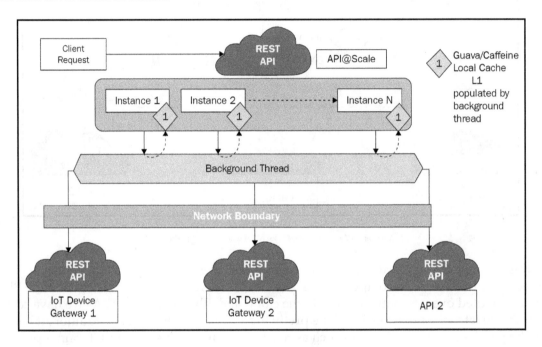

To eliminate the network round trip we introduce the local cache such as Guava

In the previous example, we used the local Guava cache, which replicates the remote data in memory and has an expiry time in minutes. This cache gets refreshed by a background thread, which accesses the remote APIs concurrently and keeps the data up to date. In each of these instances, this frees up the services from the need to wait for the remote calls to return on time and hence the request could be processed. This scenario is applicable if we do a read-only lookup of remote dependent APIs. Some of the advantages are in the following list:

- It eliminates the wait time for dependent APIs to return
- There is a faster response time and adherence to SLA
- It eliminates the need for unnecessary calls to the remote APIs, since the calls are decoupled

Although adding a local cache eliminates some of the challenges, this still has some disadvantages, such as managing the local cache in multiple application instances. However, because the local cache may expire at various different intervals, it is still inefficient. We can make the system robust by adding another level of L2 cache, which is distributed, such as Redis, which can hold the data across instances. This mechanism will eliminate even further calls to the remote system, as can be seen in the following example:

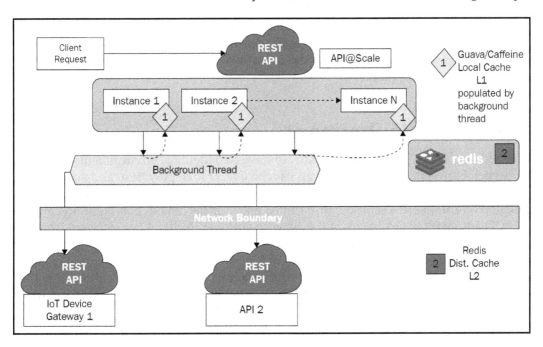

Adding L2 distributed cache, which further decouples application instances

As described in the previous illustration, we have added Redis as an L2 cache and the system is programmed to look up a local cache. If this is not present, it will look at the Redis cache and only subsequently call the remote APIs. Once the cache gets populated, the requests are served by the local or Redis caches, and it gets refreshed by a background thread which periodically populates with newer datasets. This effectively creates a back pressure for the remote dependent APIs and improves the performance of the API @scale.

Strategies to handle multiple versions of the @scale application

Typically, to manage applications at scale, we need to make sure we can seamlessly update, deploy, and run multiple versions of the applications in parallel for testing and certification before releasing the application for production use. Automation using CI/CD is mandatory for creating a continuous deployment pipeline. There are certain challenges, such as when to cut over to the newer version, and DB upgrades are still a challenge that need to be overcome. In this section, we will cover the concepts of Blue-Green deployment and best practices of database migration.

Blue-Green deployment

The idea behind Blue-Green deployment is to have two identical environments that we can easily switch between. In this way we can use the CI/CD to deploy, test, and successfully open up the new environment for production use and subsequently make the current production environment a standby, or it can be used for the next deployment. Even with full CI/CD automation, challenges still exist with cut-over itself; taking software from the final stage of testing to live production has to be done in the minimum time frame without any service downtime or with very minimal downtime. Blue-Green deployment enables a smooth cut-off by having two identical production environments. At any given time frame, one of the environments, say Blue, is live. During the deployment of new software, we can update the Green environment with new software, update the database, test, verify, and perform the final stage of testing in the Green environment. Once the Green environment is validated, we can use the router to switch incoming requests to go to the Green environment—the Blue one is now in standby mode. An example of this can be seen in the following diagram:

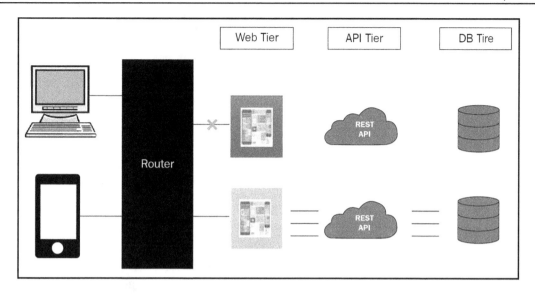

Deployment in action using two identical production-like environments

For it to be effective, the Blue-Green environment should be identical in all aspects, with respect to software and hardware. Once deployment is done, we can successfully cut off or roll back the deployment as needed, without impacting the production system. There are different strategies for Blue-Green deployment. One option is to use the same database but have web and API tiers running on different hardware. This has some limitations as it only adds new columns to the table rather than having its own database. Also, sometimes the DB could be a bottleneck if we were to do indexing and so on, hence a separate DB is recommended. This DB can be a replica of the primary DB. In the next section, we will go over how to handle DB updates seamlessly.

DB migration best practices

DB schema changes should be versioned and automated using tools such as Liquibase or flywheel. However, even if we have done the automation, updates have to be planned very carefully, especially if the data is huge, in the TB range:

- Use tools such as Liquibase or Flywheel to version, and for automation of DB changes
- Use the Blue-Green strategy to update the standby DB before going live:
    - This helps with applying indexing which can take a long time and will impact any incoming traffic

- It helps with complex schema changes by isolating the migration to the replicated DB
- We will still need a downtime to do catch-up to the primary db before going live
- It is mostly manually done using the help of a DBA, it is difficult to automate these types of DB migration

The advantages of using established trust between microservices

Since microservices at the IoT scale can generate a huge amount of load, it is essential we use best practices to handle security. As we have seen in the chapter on security, we typically use OAuth to handle authentication and authorization between the services, and in typical use cases the user gets authenticated using a UAA, which generates a JWT token for subsequent calls to the services. But this JWT token needs to be validated by each of the microservices. This can generate lots of traffic to the UAA service. Alternatively, we can use a Client Credential Grant, as will be detailed in this section, to establish trust between the microservices.

The **Client Credentials Grant** (defined in RFC 6749, section 4.4) allows an application to request an access token using its Client ID and Client Secret. It is used for non-interactive applications (a CLI, a daemon, or a service running on your backend) where the token is issued to the application itself, instead of to an end user.

In order to be able to perform the Client Credentials Grant, the application needs to have the Client Credentials Grant Type enabled. Machine to Machine Applications and Regular Web Applications have it enabled by default.

Client Credentials Grant flow

The following illustration shows the typical flow of the client credentials authentication flow:

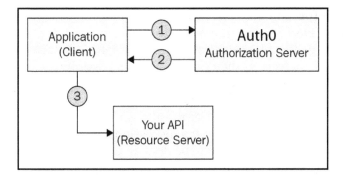

Sequence of interaction to initiate the client credentials

Steps for performing the client credentials are detailed as follows:

1. The application authenticates with Auth0 using its client ID and client secret
2. Auth0 validates this information and returns an access token
3. The application can use the access token to call the API on behalf of itself

Once the service is granted the token, it does not need to be authenticated again until the token has expired. This improves performance because the expensive authentication gets bypassed.

UX strategy for application adoption

Having a good UI design is critical for any application or software solution. A good UI design not only helps drive adoption through ease of use but is also critical for stickiness through aesthetics and visual appeal. The aesthetics aspect is more critical for consumer applications and solutions as most of the personas using the IIoT applications are operators, and service engineers and other industrial applications consume the data through APIs and SDKs. The UI design for Industrial IoT should be effective and error-free as the performance and availability requirements for IIoT solutions are high. Given these high-level goals, we make the following recommendations for UX design best practices:

- **A user-centric and persona-based approach**: A typical IIoT solution will be used by scientists for analytics, operators for monitoring, service technicians for diagnostics, and so on. Each of these personae has a unique need that they are trying to satisfy from the IIoT solution. They have different visualization needs that need to be satisfied by the solution. Consequently, special care needs to be paid to defining the UI requirements for each persona.

- **Scalable information architecture**: The flexible and customized UI design will provide the ease of use, but it needs to be backed by a scalable architecture. This means that, as the adoption grows, the expectation of the users from the IIoT solution will increase as they can see various possibilities where the solution can help them. This means more real-time and batch data are to be collected, ingested, stored and analyzed. If the information architecture is not scalable, the performance degradation will show on dashboards and reports which will degrade user experience. Thus the discussions on UX design and scalable information architecture need to be done in parallel.

- **A consistent style**: Given that IIoT applications cannot be built using solutions from a single vendor, there will always be integrated solutions across the various layers in the stack. It is evident that this will create a disjointed look and feel for the entire solution, which will be detrimental to the overall user experience. Consequently, special attention needs to be paid to achieving consistency across the stack. This may mean customizing the UI for each solution utilized in the stack, or at least using a single overall frame for each UI page.

- **Extensible (interfaces and data points)**: It should be assumed that the solution will be extended through its life cycle to include more and more interfaces and data points to satisfy various use cases. Thus having reusable components will be critical in providing an extensible architecture and consistent scalability for the solution. The solution should not limit the possibility to explore further due to lack of extensibility as the applications for IIoT are expected to grow exponentially.

- **Seamless Integration (of third-party solutions)**: These integrations are not limited to software as a significant part of IIoT is hardware. Providing for seamless (or non-disruptive) integration helps with user experience as well. This requires us to look beyond the basic platform modules and think of all the other integrations possible, or what may be required as utilization increases.

In order to achieve the preceding best practices, we recommend the adoption of tools and techniques available that will help drive consistency and easy adoption of these best practices across the organization. One such tool is Yeoman.

Recommended technology for overall consistency: Yeoman helps start new projects, defining the best practices and tools to stay productive. They also provide a generator ecosystem that consist the building blocks of the Yeoman ecosystem. They're the plugins run by `yo` to create files for end users. The generators come after a Yeoman workflow. This workflow is a robust and assertive client-side stack, consisting tools and frameworks that helps the developers build beautiful web applications quickly, which will be consistent and adhere to the organization's standard guidelines. It will take care of everything which is required to create a project ready for development. The developer doesn't have to worry about the required resources or plugins to set up to make the web application run. They will not have to waste time at all doing manual setup.

The Yeoman workflow comprises three types of tools for improving the productivity and satisfaction when building a web app: the scaffolding tool (`yo`), the package manager (like Bower and NPM) and the build tool (Grunt, Gulp, and so on) as shown in the following chart:

Scaffolding tool	Package Manager	Build Tool
`yo` scaffolds new application with all of the default screens, designs, and configurations. It also takes care appealing in relevant build tasks and package managers required to build and run the application.	This is used for dependency management, so that you no longer have to manually download and manage your scripts. Bower and NPM are two popular options.	The build system is used to build, preview and test your project. Grunt and Gulp are two popular options.

All three of these tools are developed and maintained separately, but work well together as part of Yeoman workflow. The process to install and use the tool can be referenced on the website: `http://yeoman.io/`. Let's look at the recommended technologies for the frontend and backend:

- **Recommended technologies for the frontend**: The following technologies are recommended for building an effective and scalable frontend:
  - **Framework**: Angular5 is the recommended framework; it provides the application framework for defining services, components, and dependency injections. It also provides the mechanism for iterative compilation, local development serving, and distribution building.
  - **DOM Middleware**: D3 provides the DOM for specific components and each D3 view will be contained in an angular component, which provides the DOM, and data will come from an injected angular service. Not all components have to be D3 though.
  - **Development language**: TypeScript.
  - **Module management**: NPM enterprise.

- **Recommended technologies for the backend:** The following technologies are recommended for building the scalable backend required to support the frontend:
  - Java 8, NodeJS, TypeScript, Golang
  - Server framework—Jetty
  - DI—Guice
  - Modules—Maven

Tracing and logging end to end

In IIoT applications, things could go wrong in any of the components. Consequently, it is very important to be able to identify the root cause of the problem quickly so that we can bring the system back up quickly and avoid prolonged downtime. Having robust logging and tracing, along with a monitoring solution, can help resolve system issues quickly.

In a typical IIoT application, there are application logs and device/platform logs, as can be seen in the following diagram:

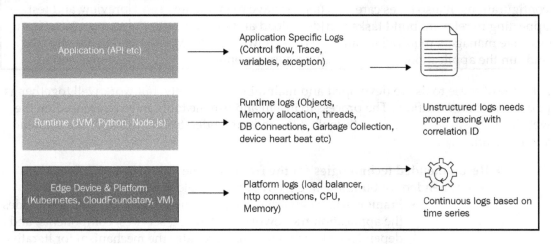

Logs from different IIoT components

The different logs in a typical IIoT application are as follows:

- Application logs usually logged by application, should have a correlating ID
- Runtime logs from VMs, such as JVM, Node.js, Python and so on
- Platform and device logs

Application logs

IIoT application logs are typically unstructured and usually contain control flows, exceptions, and variables with different trace levels. These logs are usually stored in a file with a given trace format, for example in Java using Log4j. Logging application logs is a common practice and tracing of application logs is essential for identification of the same request or session across different microservices and devices.

Tracing of application logs

Let's take an example of a request from an IIoT device that goes through multiple services, as seen in the following diagram:

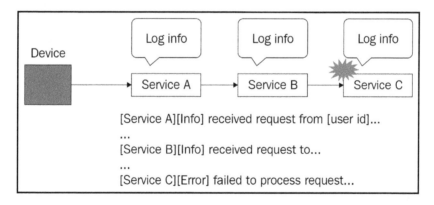

Requests from the device go to multiple services

Each service logs the name of the service logs, but this is not enough information to trace the log back to the request, so it is ideal to generate a correlation ID and pass it between the services using HTTP headers. Each service should look up the HTTP header and log it as part of the log format in such a way that we can then trace the request all the way to the end of the session. This is illustrated in the following diagram:

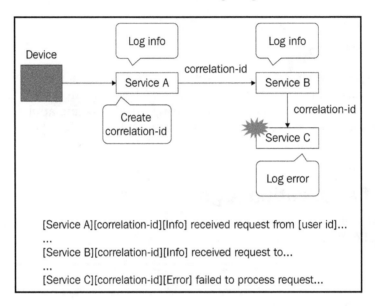

Logs with correlation ID for easily tracing a request between services

By adding a correlation ID, it is easy to trace the request as it flows between different components and services.

Runtime logs

Runtime logs are typically gathered by an agent interacting with the JVM, Node.js, or Python instrumentation APIs. These VMs provide a treasure trove of information regarding runtime systems. Metrics such as objects, memory allocation, threads in use, and DB connections can all be collected on a periodic basis and sent to a centralized system for monitoring.

In addition to the runtimes, these could also have the device heartbeats to know the status of the devices, and whether it is in working conditions or not can also be collected.

Platform logs

Platform logs provide details on resources such as VMs, Dockers, containers, their network, CPU, memory usage, and whether it is functional or not. Usually the same agent that collects details on the runtime can also collect information regarding the platforms, and it is also sent to an centralized service for analysis and alerting.

Logging architecture guidelines

As a common guideline for logging, using tools such as Prometheus or Grafana is recommended, as can be seen in the following diagram:

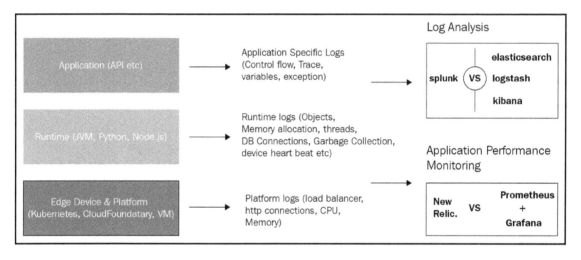

Logging architecture that uses open source and vendor tools

In the previous architecture example, we are using two distinct toolsets for different purposes for application log analysis which are typically unstructured and in a filesystem. We have used Splunk or **ELK** (**Elasticsearch**, **Logstash**, **Kibana**) for gathering log files from various different services using a Logstash tool, and then used Kibana for visualizing the logs. For the search we are using Elasticsearch, so given a good tracing with correlation ID, we can easily find our logs of interest by doing a search in the Kibana or Splunk tools.

For application performance monitoring we have used an agent based toolset either from a third party vendor, such as NewRelic/AppDynamics. Alternatively we can use an open source tool, such as a combination of Grafana and Prometheus. Prometheus is a timeseries DB which also provides collectors for various OS and runtimes, and it also has alerting capabilities to send out alerts to admins and other stakeholders. Grafana can be used to visualize various dashboard and reports. An example APM report is shown in the following diagram:

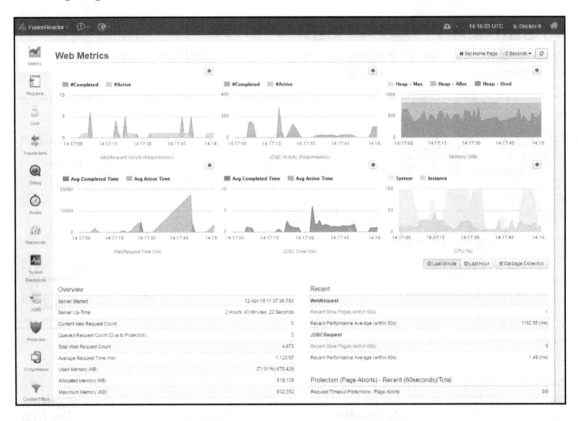

Dashboard from NewRelic APM tool

Summary

In this section, we covered some of the key best practices to follow while developing IIoT applications.

In the next chapter, we will cover the future of IIoT.

11
Future Direction of the IIoT

All of the chapters in this book have covered the technical building blocks for developers to build IoT applications, especially for industrial domains. In this final chapter, we will look at the potential directions in which the industry will get pulled by the various forces of business and technological evolution. The goal is to paint a picture of the near future and help the reader prepare in terms of technology to support the solution holistically.

In this chapter, you will learn about the following topics:

- Emerging use cases for the IIoT
- IoT industry standards and their evolution
- IoT security challenges and opportunities
- Blockchain for the IoT and security
- Machine learning and the IoT
- The IIoT landscape and market direction

Introduction

As we have discussed in this book, the IIoT covers all aspects of data capture and processing. A complete IIoT product is a comprehensive end-to-end solution that should cover data capture, ingestion, storage, search, analytics, and visualization. As we touched upon in previous chapters, most of these areas have a number of products on the market that can satisfy most requirements. Hence, building a good IIoT solution is about choosing the right technology stack and creating the right interfaces to achieve non-functional requirements such as scalability and high performance. As the technology stack evolves, so will solutions to address key gaps that we see today as blocking the progress of the IIoT. Some of this will be driven by the needs and issues that we will see in deployments (such as security) and some of these will be driven by rapid evolution in related areas such as machine learning and blockchain that will open new doors for the IoT. It's important to keep an eye on these evolution and go deeper into the potential issues, as they will plague the growth of this area. We will deep dive in these areas in the sections of this chapter.

Emerging use cases

We list here some of the emerging use cases that we see as growing in the near future, so it may be prudent for IIoT developers to take note and plan on supporting these in different ways:

- Remote monitoring and diagnostics (RM&D) 2.0: These are use cases that have been enabled today and have already shown returns for industries. However, application today to this domain has provided incremental improvements and essentially is seen as an improved way of monitoring remote systems. The emerging use cases in this area will be focused on showing exponential improvements beyond just better data handling of more data being generated through advanced sensors. An example could be the leverage of voice-based services in these solutions, which will be a significant improvement from the to help the service agent.

- Advanced analytics on the edge: Many verticals, such as manufacturing, require high availability (five 9s) for which they need significant analytics to be done on the edge. Others will be forced to do that in order to cut costs that come from managing the data ingestion pipeline and latency. The nature of the problem is such that you cannot leverage a data pipeline to migrate the data to the cloud from the private datacenters. Edge IoT devices need to act locally based on data they generate, as well as take advantage of the cloud for security, scalability, configuration, deployment, and management. We expect a significant investment in edge computing and a rise in adoption rates.

- Large infrastructure plays: There has been a lot of media coverage of smart cities and several use cases enabled already by cities and infrastructure providers. As these enabled use cases show measurable returns, we should see more demand by this group and, given the population pressures that growing cities all over the world are seeing, its natural that they will be looking to consume more of these kinds of products and solutions. Cities need to automate, remotely manage, and collect data through visitor kiosks, surveillance systems, bike rental stations, rental cars, and so on. The growth will be such that there will be large number of industrial internet applications developed compared to others in the near future

- Real-time learning systems: The data collected from sensors of all kinds (environmental, human, and so on) is telling a story that needs to be processed by systems in a way to learn and adapt. Only then will the true value of the IoT be revealed, otherwise it is limited in scope to advanced monitoring. With the increase in availability of infrastructure to support advanced learning systems (for example, DeepLearning using TensorFlow models running on GBU compute), we will see an exponential increase in learning systems. The integration of these learning systems with the IoT stack will be a focus area and will lead to use cases such as the smart thermostat that learns the behavior and pattern of temperature of an industrial factory floor and controls the optimal tempreature .

- Frameworks for supporting evolving solution stacks: The major challenge for the IIoT (and for the IoT in general) is that there are a lot of moving parts, since so many of its components are changing rapidly in the entire stack. The IoT adds the additional complexity of scale and security that will lead to the advent of new technologies to address these challenges. It will require adoption of new paradigms (such as Blockchain) to solve some of these challenges. In the following sections, we will highlight some relevant details that pertain to these focus areas.

There are non-technical issues that need to be addressed as well. For example, an IIoT application can track a remote device from the data it receives from the sensor on the device. However, upgrading the software on the device or the sensor itself may require handling licensing, serviceability, cost, and remote upgrade security issues. Hence, the solutions will have to be looked at holistically. It also requires industry-wide standards to be established. There has been a lot of work in this area and we will present the current landscape for standards and how it will evolve in the near future.

IoT industry standards and their evolution

In order for the IoT to succeed, the basic requirement is that devices are able to communicate with each other seamlessly. This is a challenge, given the different types of devices and the number of industries in which the IoT will be leveraged. Given a highly distributed value chain and a number of proprietary device implementations makes it hard to interconnect them. One single standard that covers every device and industry would be an ideal state, however, it's evident that is not practical.

The result is predictable—a development of standards across verticals and application domains. This is what is happening in the industry today, leading to fragmentation, serving the different needs and satisfying the different operating conditions of various devices. How do we achieve consistency among these standards and promote reuse of technologies? One solution is to have a standard of standards, such as oneM2M that aims at becoming the unifying standard for most of these fragmented initiatives. The objective of oneM2M is to avoid competing standards, duplication, and conflicts stemming from alliances and consortia tackling similar or overlapping issues. It is involved in concerted reports to bring in interoperability among architectural layers across IoT applications, spanning different industry verticals.

The oneM2M standardization is helping this dire challenge of fragmentation in realizing the vision of the IoT and it stands out as the interoperability enabler for the entire M2M and IoT ecosystem.

The following highlights some of the existing standards bodies and their focus areas:

Consortium/Alliance	Focus area and charter
Industrial Internet Consortium	The Industrial Internet Consortium is the world's leading organization transforming business and society by accelerating the Industrial Internet of Things (IIoT).
AllSeen Alliance	The AllSeen Alliance is a cross-industry consortium dedicated to enabling the interoperability of billions of devices, services, and apps that comprise the IoT.
Open Mobile Alliance	Open Mobile Alliance (OMA) specifications support billions of new and existing terminals across a variety of wireless networks, supporting machine-to-machine device communications for the IoT.
3rd-Generation Partnership Project	The 3rd-Generation Partnership Project (3GPP) unites telecommunications standard development organizations to standardize cellular telecommunications network technologies, including radio access, the core transport network, and service capabilities. Specifically to the IoT, they released the NB-IOT specification.
Institute of Electrical and Electronics Engineers	The mission of the Institute of Electrical and Electronics Engineers (IEEE) IoT initiative is to serve as the gathering place for the global technical community working on the IoT.

International Telecommunication Union	The purpose of the International Telecommunication Union (ITU) Global Standards for the IoT is to provide a visible single location for information on and development of IoT standards, these being the detailed standards necessary for IoT deployment and to give service providers the means to cover the wide range of services expected from the IoT.
IPSO Alliance	IPSO is an alliance that promotes and supports smart objects, and manages an IPSO Smart Object Registry. The objective is to develop, establish, and create the industry leadership of an "IPSO platform" that includes the definition and support of Smart Objects with an emphasis on object interoperability on protocol and data layers and of identity and privacy technologies.
Internet Engineering Task Force	The **Internet Engineering Task Force (IETF)** originally focused on running IP over IEEE 802.15.4 radios and has since then evolved into a much larger project, covering IPv6 adaptation layer (6LoWPAN), and **Constrained RESTful Environments (CoRE)** to allow the integration of constrained devices with the internet at the service level.
OIC/OCF	Unified as OCF in Feb 2016, it's an entity whose goal will be to help unify IoT standards so that companies and developers can create IoT solutions and devices that work seamlessly together.
oneM2M	oneM2M is the global standards initiative that was formed in 2012 and consists of eight of the world's preeminent **Standards Development Organizations (SDO)** namely ETSI (Europe), ARIB (Japan), ATIS (U.S.A), TIA (U.S.A), CCSA (China), TSDSI (India), TTA (Korea) and TTC (Japan). These SDO Partners collaborate with six industry consortia (Broadband Forum, Continua Alliance, GlobalPlatform, HGI, Next Generation M2M Consortium, and OMA) and have over 220 member organizations to produce and maintain globally applicable, access-independent technical specifications for a common M2M/IoT Service Layer.

IIoT security challenges and opportunities

As data collection increases and scaling is required, the focus will be on challenges in the area of governance, specifically security, as we expect that to be the area where a lot of challenges will appear. The proliferation of new technologies in this domain will add to the complexity and the emergence of novel solutions. We will also cover the overall IIoT landscape and players and how we expect the market to move in the next three to five years.

There are several incidents in the recent past that highlight the growing concerns around security in the IoT domain. Just to provide hard data, we will list some of the popular ones that have been widely published in the media, such as Mirai Botnet of Things; connected toymaker CloudPets hack; 8,000 Telnet credentials of IoT devices were exposed on the internet; the public release of the working code to hack Huawei routers used by the Satori botnet; a firmware update broke Lockstate-connected smart locks for several customers.

The reasons why we picked security as the area that will be the focus for research and new opportunities are touched upon here. As we have discussed in this book, IIoT solutions comprise of multiple technologies that are hooked together, and securing an IIoT solution requires securing each and every piece as the entire solution will be as secure as its weakest link. As the number of devices increases exponentially, security solutions have to be scalable and highly available. How do we enable a solution that cost effectively scales to millions of end points in a way that end point availability does not get affected? Also, the data generated by IIoT solutions requires handling big data (large and varied datasets), and securing the datasets in a cost effective manner without compromising performance will be required. The IIoT edge devices that capture data from machines are primarily in remote locations and are limited in resources (CPU, memory, and storage), so the security solutions have to be extremely resource efficient. Add to this the fact that many of these devises will be in a mobile and dynamic environment and avoid service delay (by degrading service time or causing service degradation). Security solutions will have to satisfy the basic **Authorization**, **Authentication** and **Audit** (**AAA**) protocols and provide for integrity, confidentiality, non-repudiation, and forward as well as backward secrecy.

As discussed previously, IoT solutions have three domains (sensor domain, fog domain, and cloud domain) that interact with each other and each of them needs to be protected properly. In the following tables, we identify potential attacks in each domain and possible ways to avoid those attacks. We expect that several solutions will emerge in the near future to address these. The first table lists the various security breaches, why these are likely to happen, and possible steps to contain them, based on which new solutions will emerge in the near future:

Security breach	Reason	Defense measures
Blocked sensors	Shared communication channels between the sensors makes them vulnerable to potential jamming attacks	Physical techniques such as directional antennas, frequency hopping, or spectrum spread can be used for defense
Power outage	Battery lifetime is limited, especially for low-power edge devices and sensors	Deploy techniques to limit rates for each access and detect and avoid loops

Data flow pipeline redirection	Due to limited transmission capability, a third-party device can pretend to be the shortest path and direct all sensor data through it	In order to counter these attacks, IoT solutions need to have increased transmission ranges and the ability to analyze routing information from multiple objects
Authentication of sensors by fog devices and trust verification for fog devices can be compromised	Fog devices are on the edge and can be provided by several small third-party vendors as opposed to cloud devices	Requires formal ranking and rating of providers using reputation systems and using these ratings in implementations
Virtual machine migrations may lead to potential threats	VM migration between fog devices is done on the open internet and so is susceptible to attacks	Encryption of VMs being migrated and increased authentication measures for VM migration messages among fog devices
Denial of service attacks	Lower computing capacity of fog devices	Deployment of low-power consumption (DOS) avoiding techniques
Container security threats	Sharing the same OS for all fog objects that leverage containers	More focused solutions on container security will be required in the near future
Privacy violations	The fog devices will know the locations of the sensors and can track it over time	Advanced techniques such as obfuscation need to be deployed to prevent privacy violations due to location sensing
Data leakage across VMs	Shared hardware components across VMs such as cache leading to confidentiality breaches	Need to deploy solutions that provide for hard isolation or mechanisms to flush the caches or deploy techniques for limiting cache switch rates and so on
VM migration breaches	Improper software bug handling and migration without authentication	Proper authentication and encryption techniques to be applied for migrations
Theft of service	Malicious VMs utilizing more resources than those assigned due to periodic sampling	Mechanisms for fine grained and random sampling using high precision clocks
VM escape attacks	Hypervisor software bugs	Isolation layer between hypervisor and hardware

In addition to these specific concerns for each security layer, these are the following areas that will be the focus for IoT solutions in the future:

- Collaborative defense
- Lightweight cryptography
- Lightweight network security protocols
- Digital forensics

Blockchain for the IoT

The fact that the IoT will enable connections at a very large scale means that a centralized security model will fail to address all of the concerns that we have outlined.
The **decentralized model** of Blockchain technology-based solutions will be a perfect fit to address these concerns and make the IoT system resilient by eliminating single points of failure.

IoT systems cannot be sustained by a solution that leverages third-party brokers. It needs trust-less peer-to-peer communication with guaranteed service delivery. This is enabled by Blockchain technology as *no third-party intervention* is required for guaranteed service peer-to-peer service delivery.

Apart from security solutions, private Blockchain infrastructure can be used between enterprises to enable businesses to access and supply IoT data without the need for centrally managing it. Each business partner would be able to verify each transaction, ensuring accountability and avoiding disputes. The IOTA organization is trying to do similar implementations at a global scale as a decentralized data marketplace. General connectivity is another area of interest that has come up recently for Blockchain. Startups such as Filament (long-range wireless networks to connect machinery and industrial infrastructure to the network) and Helium (a FirstMark portfolio company) are just a few examples of such emerging applications.

Given below is a overview of the overview of Blockchain technology and how it is relevant to the Industrial Internet of things.

The goal of Blockchain technology is to record all transactions in a public ledger as that eliminates the need to maintain a single central validation system, thereby making it a truly open, independent, and self-managed network. In implementation, it is essentially a distributed database that needs to manage data records that will be growing continuously over a period of time. Nodes get added to the network and each one will get a copy of the chain and, when any node adds a transaction to the chain, it has to complete a validation from all of the nodes of the chain (there is no central node performing this task). Each successive block contains a hash, which is a unique fingerprint, of the previous block. This validation system is what makes the Blockchain system decentralized as, through this, every transaction is announced on the network and the history of that transaction is maintained on the open public ledger, which can be referenced at any time. It makes it more open and secure but, at the same time, it adds the complexity of validation (which is done through complex algorithms) and management of the ever growing ledger as the network grows.

Machine learning and the IoT

Most of the use cases for the IoT today are centered around predictive maintenance and better servicing of digital and physical assets. This requires connectivity of these assets through sensors and simple telemetry, along with threshold-based messaging and alerting. As the use cases become more complex and advanced, a higher level of precision and predictability is required from the data that is captured. An example would be the use of clustering algorithms to group devices and assets into healthy or defective, based on the data they are emitting. If the vibrations coming from windmills or power generators fall in a certain range along with other parameters, they can be classified as defective or requiring servicing. This is the application of data science to the IoT and it requires dynamic modeling to be supported, as the static models of traditional analytics will not scale.

In advanced use cases, it may further be required that the desired end state or goal is defined, yet dependency on the various parameters that affect that outcome is not predetermined. For such use cases, the application of learning algorithms such as neural networks is required as the system learns from the data the sensors are generating and modifies the model accordingly over time. Hence, future IoT systems will require that the advanced infrastructure to support learning algorithms be leveraged properly.

Machine learning involves two steps—building models and training them on datasets to ensure they reach a fair level of accuracy in predictions and then hosting them in production in order to offer these as services. As the adoption of data science and machine learning grows in enterprises, so will the demand to scale the infrastructure required to support it. In the open source world, Kubernetes with TensorFlow Serving provides this high performance system for machine learning models.

In the following screenshot, we depict our recommended architecture that will scale dynamically to support machine learning in IoT systems and the following paragraphs describe details for this recommended architecture:

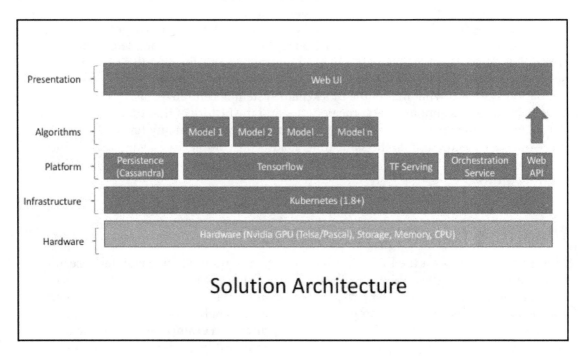

You can implement any machine learning model (say classification) with TensorFlow trained on a relevant dataset to be used by applications in production. Once the model is trained and exported, TensorFlow Serving uses the model to perform inferences—predictions based on new data presented by its clients. Inference can be very resource intensive. The server needs to execute the TensorFlow graph to process every classification request it receives. It should be able to support millions of parameters and run billions of floating point operations per inference. This is where GPU or TPU processors and containerization using Kubernetes helps.

Kubernetes provides the virtual cluster of pods where the load is distributed (it has an external load balancer). The cluster pods have TensorFlow Docker images of the server and trained machine learning models. Each model consists of the following set of files: model weights, assets, and the shape of the TensorFlow graphs. This packaging is helpful in providing the required scalability with the Kubernetes replication the controller can replicate based on the service demands.

Data analysis has made a significant contribution to the IoT; therefore, to apply a full potential of analysis to extract new insights from data, the IoT must overcome some major problems. The following is a description of the problem categorized into three different types and a brief on how machine learning (and data science in general) can help address these challenges.

IoT data types

Because data is the basis of extracting knowledge, it is vital to have high quality information. This condition can affect the accuracy of knowledge extraction in a direct manner. Since the IoT produces high volume, fast velocity, and varieties of data, preserving data quality is a hard and challenging task. Although many solutions have been and are being introduced to solve these problems, none of them can handle all aspects of data characteristics in an accurate manner because of the distributed nature of big data management solutions and real-time processing platforms. The abstraction of IoT data is low, that is, the data that comes from different resources in the IoT are mostly of raw data and not sufficient enough for analysis. A wide variety of solutions is proposed, while most of them need further improvements. For instance, semantic interpretation using a digital Asset Model or Digital Twin of the asset tend to enhance the abstraction of IoT data through digital representation of an Asset and its sensor tags with measurement units algorithms can be applied to predict insights at scale, while still work needs to be done to quantify the persistent rates etc

Future IoT applications

IoT applications have different categories according to their unique attributions and features. Certain issues should be proposed in running data analysis in IoT applications in an accurate manner. First, the privacy of the collected data is very critical, since the data collection process can include personal or critical business data, which is inevitable to solve the privacy issues. Second, according to the vast number of resources and simple designed hardware in the IoT, it is vital to consider security parameters such as network security, and data encryption. Otherwise, by ignoring the security in design and implementation, an infected network of IoT devices can cause a crisis. Machine learning can enable a number of such solutions for the IoT. A trend towards companies adopting fully built SaaS application such as Asset Performance Motoring from GE to monitor the industrial asset is foreseeable similar to CRM from Salesforce gaining wide adoption in the Customer Relations Management space

IoT data analytics algorithms

According to smart data characteristics, analytics algorithms should be able to handle big data, that is, the IoT needs algorithms that can analyze the data that comes from a variety of sources in real time. Many attempts are made to address this issue. For example, deep learning algorithms, an evolved form of neural networks, can reach a high accuracy rate if they have enough data and time. Deep learning algorithms can be easily influenced smart noisy data; furthermore, neural network-based algorithms lack interpretation, that is, data scientists cannot understand the reasons for the model results. In the same manner, semi-supervised algorithms, which model the small amount of labeled data with a large amount of unlabeled data, can assist IoT data analytics as well.

A use case highlighting these three problems

The IoT consists of a vast number of devices with varieties that are connected to each other and transmit huge amounts of data, for example, a smart city—one of the most important applications of the IoT provides different services in domains such as energy, mobility, and urban planning. These services can be enhanced and optimized by analyzing the smart data collected from these areas. In order to extract knowledge from collected data, many data analytics algorithms can be applied. Choosing a proper algorithm for a specific IoT and smart city application is an important issue. Here three facts should be considered in applying data analytics algorithms to smart data. The first fact is that different applications in the IoT and smart cities are characterized by the number of devices and types of the data that they generate; the second fact is that the generated data has specific features that should be realized. The third fact is that the taxonomy of the algorithms is another important point in applying data analysis to smart data.

The IIoT landscape and market direction

The advantage that consumer IoT businesses have is that they typically don't require long sales cycles, unlike any other consumer products or services. That is why we have seen several of these products and services succeed in the market. The industrial IoT is targeted at large enterprises, which typically have long sales cycles. That being said, there are advantages of being in the enterprise space. One big advantage is that large enterprises will adopt a product/service that fits into the existing business workflow and does not change the behaviors drastically in a short period of time. They offer ways of better extracting and analyzing data from machines, whether in manufacturing factories or oil fields, something large industrial conglomerates have done for many years. Therefore, clear RoI can be demonstrated by leveraging IT and OT data through their existing workflows and showing value addition through their advanced technologies. Also, once the sale is made, they can reap the continued returns, as these enterprises do not replace their technology directions easily and go for upgrades and longer term technology road map.

The industrial IoT – from horizontal platforms to vertical AI-powered solutions

The early years of the IIoT have been dominated by companies focusing on building platforms that will provide all of the plumbing work required to build IIoT applications. These platforms have been successful to some extent in providing core services but we are still in early days. There are technical problems that have not been solved yet such as connectivity in remote or hot environments. While the ultimate goal is to run AI on the data extracted from machines in the field, its still a challenge to get the data from these sources, as they are often without proper interfaces or don't support standard protocols.

Industry is still maturing as is evident by IT spending patterns. Large industrial companies are trying to figure out their overall strategy and direction and are investing in small amounts in new products from both small scale providers and established bigger vendors; not to mention their own internal efforts of building solutions on top of open source and small scale hardware (such as Raspberry Pi). Over the next couple of years, we will see some of these efforts give way to others and clear winners will emerge. However, patterns have started to emerge, such as horizontal plays, which may not work for every segment. Companies have realized that, instead of coming up with a solution for all verticals, it's best to focus on each vertical separately and focus on addressing the challenges for that domain. This will also be beneficial in the long run, given that AI applications will only be successful if they are able to address deep domain challenges for verticals, not just a plethora of tools that have the capability to run generic data science algorithms.

IoT connectivity – key infrastructure progress

The first step in the IoT has been connecting the devices to the cloud. There has been a lot of work done by carriers and providers on protocols to connect to the internet and we expect this field will also see interest and investment over the coming years. Here, we will provide an overview of the technologies that are available to use now and planned for future.

Connectivity type	Technologies	Use cases and future work
Short-range connectivity	Z-wave	Used primarily for home automation and within building connectivity. Some drawbacks such as power consumption and costs will be worked on in the coming years. IEEE standards such as 802.11ah and 802.11ax will be leveraged in these areas.
Wide-area connectivity	Sigfox, LoRA	Unlicensed **Low-Power WAN** (**LPWAN**) wireless technologies, designed specifically to interconnect low bandwidth, battery-powered devices with low bit rates over long ranges. These will be the primary focus over the next two years as evident by the large amounts of funding in these areas and alliances promoting their adoption.
Narrow band connectivity	NB-IoT, LTE Cat M1	Both NB-IoT and CatM1 technologies have gained popularity with major telecom operators. There will be work done in this area on optimizing the costs, as for large device collections this becomes cost prohibitive.
Long range	5G	Dramatically faster data transmission capabilities, which could lend themselves very well to the more intense IoT use cases, such as autonomous vehicles. But it may take until well into the next decade to get widespread deployment of 5G (at least in the US).

Cloud for the IoT

Over the past few years, some of the industrial giants have put in significant work in trying to come up with their own cloud offerings to keep their data in-house as well as build domain-specific expertise required to do successful IoT implementations. However, running and operating a cloud offering is not their core business and they are increasingly turning towards major cloud providers to supply them with these required functionalities. The cloud providers will continue to provide more focused offerings in the IIoT space but the enterprises will need to invest in creating wrappers and customized solutions on top of these offerings.

All three major cloud providers have a large set of IoT infrastructure offerings—some of the key infrastructure components at the time of writing this book are listed in the following table. These are fully managed infrastructure offerings for edge computing, connecting and managing fleets of IoT devices, time series databases to handle their data, and so on:

Microsoft	Amazon	Google
• IoT Central	• IoT One click	• IoT Cloud Core
• IoT Edge	• IoT Device Defender	• BigQuery
• Time Series Insights	• IoT Device Manager	• DataFlow

In addition to innovation in the IoT infrastructure from the big cloud providers , we have innovation in building specialized IIoT platforms from PTC, C3IoT, Uptake, GE Predix gaining adoption although these vendors are struggling to gain market share. There are also some success in this space as can be seen by the acquisition of Mule Soft by Salesforce. In addition to platform innovations the real future innovation is going to come from SaaS applications for IIoT or IoT such as APM from GE we can see the industry moving in this direction but will require a level of trust from vendors and customers.

Most startups are focused on solutions to send device data to the big public cloud providers.

We can safely say that these three clouds will prevail for managing all data to be processed on the cloud. For industries that need tighter security and more privacy (healthcare, aviation, and so on), edge computing may be the holy grail that will help them do all their analytics on edge devices instead of taking them to the cloud.

Edge computing for the IoT

The promise of edge computing is that most processing will be done on the edge and only data that really needs to be sent to the cloud will be transported. This requires low-powered devices having adequate processing power to run AI and advanced analytics on real-time data as its collected. These will be the focus of attention for a number of IIoT companies as only then will they be able to successfully leverage the power of the IoT. Dumb edge devices will need to be smarter handling most of the processing and filtering of data to be further transported to the cloud.

Startups such as Foghorn have been doing interesting work on edge computing and analytics. However, edge computing is now a mainstream offering by large enterprises. Examples include AWS launching Greengrass; Microsoft launching Azure IoT Edge; Dell investing large amounts in this space; and Edge X Founder, a major new open source project, backed by several 50 contributors including Dell.

Summary

So far, the journey for the IIoT, and the IoT in general, has been a mixed bag of some successes and many learning opportunities. However, major accomplishments in basic infrastructure have already been accomplished in areas such as cloud offerings for IoT-specific solutions, and carriers providing all ranges of wireless communications. This will certainly springboard IoT development and adoption in the coming years. Still, much work remains to be done in key areas such as addressing security and privacy issues on the cloud and high-performance computing and low-power consumption on the edge. These are the areas in which most of the work will be done and successful players will emerge over the next two years.

Other Books You May Enjoy

If you enjoyed this book, you may be interested in these other books by Packt:

Internet of Things for Architects
Perry Lea

ISBN: 978-1-78728-275-9

- Understand the role and scope of architecting a successful IoT deployment, from sensors to the cloud
- Scan the landscape of IoT technologies that span everything from sensors to the cloud and
- everything in between
- See the trade-offs in choices of protocols and communications in IoT deployments
- Build a repertoire of skills and the vernacular necessary to work in the IoT space
- Broaden your skills in multiple engineering domains necessary for the IoT architect

Mastering Internet of Things

Peter Waher

ISBN: 978-1-78839-748-3

- Create your own project, run and debug it
- Master different communication patterns using the MQTT, HTTP, CoAP, LWM2M and XMPP protocols
- Build trust-based as hoc networks for open, secure and interoperable communication
- Explore the IoT Service Platform
- Manage the entire product life cycle of devices
- Understand and set up the security and privacy features required for your system
- Master interoperability, and how it is solved in the realms of HTTP,CoAP, LWM2M and XMPP

Leave a review - let other readers know what you think

Please share your thoughts on this book with others by leaving a review on the site that you bought it from. If you purchased the book from Amazon, please leave us an honest review on this book's Amazon page. This is vital so that other potential readers can see and use your unbiased opinion to make purchasing decisions, we can understand what our customers think about our products, and our authors can see your feedback on the title that they have worked with Packt to create. It will only take a few minutes of your time, but is valuable to other potential customers, our authors, and Packt. Thank you!

Index